Signs of the Times

Signs of the Times

SECOND EDITION

Edgar H. Shroyer

Illustrations by Susan P. Shroyer

Gallaudet University Press

Washington, DC

Gallaudet University Press
Washington, DC 20002
http://gupress.gallaudet.edu

© 1982, 2011 by Gallaudet University.

Second edition 2011

Printed in the United States of America

16 15 14 13 12 11   1 2 3 4 5

Library of Congress Cataloging-in-Publication Data

Shroyer, Edgar H.
   Signs of the times / Edgar H. Shroyer ; illustrations by Susan P. Shroyer. — 2nd ed.
            p. cm.
   "Clerc Books."
   Includes index.
   ISBN-13: 978-1-56368-446-3 (pbk.)
   ISBN-10: 1-56368-446-2 (pbk.)
   1.   American Sign Language—Dictionaries.   2.   Sign language—Dictionaries.   I. Title.
   HV2475.S528 2010
   419'.70321—dc22
2010029227

Interior Design and Production: Publishers' Design and Production Services, Inc.

Cover Design: Jeffrey Shroyer

To Trish, Jeffrey, Erin, and granddaughter Taylor.
We love you all to the moon and back

Contents

Acknowledgments

Several individuals coaxed, prodded, and finally persuaded me to do a second edition of *Signs of the Times*. Since 28 years had passed since the publication of the first edition of the book, I realized it was time. The layout of this book is somewhat similar to the first *Signs of the Times*, but the similarity stops there. The emphasis of this new edition is American Sign Language (ASL), my first language as a child.

Many people served as sounding boards to my ideas during the development of the book. Several made excellent suggestions for the new edition, particularly in some of the student and class activities. It would be difficult to name each of these individuals, but I want each of them to know that I appreciate their contributions regardless of how large or small.

I wish to extend a very special thanks to my wife Susan, who in addition to illustrating the book, also served as my primary sounding board, proofreader, and critic. She undertook a task that neither of us thought would be as demanding as it was. This edition is a tribute to her dedication and skill as an illustrator.

I am pleased to acknowledge that this edition of *Signs of the Times* became a family production. I want to thank our daughters, Trish and Erin, who served as models for many of the sign illustrations, and our son, Jeffrey, who designed the book's cover. I greatly appreciate their time and willingness to participate in bringing this book to fruition.

Ivey Pittle Wallace, my editor of Gallaudet University Press, also deserves a huge thank-you for her encouragement from inception to the final product of this book. Throughout the entire process, she gave specific ideas on content, illustrations, and format for which I was very grateful. She did an excellent job of putting the text together and proofreading the final product.

History

American Sign Language is a relatively new name for the language American deaf people have used since the early nineteenth century. It began as a combination of French Sign Language and sign languages used by deaf people in the New England area. At one time, the largest concentration of deaf individuals in this country lived on the island of Martha's Vineyard, just off the coast of Massachusetts. The deaf population on the island was so large that signing was a normal part of everyone's daily life and activities (Groce 1985).

The first permanent school for the deaf in the United States opened in 1817 in Hartford, Connecticut. Thomas Hopkins Gallaudet, a hearing American, went to the Paris Institute for the Deaf to observe and learn teaching methods that he wished to employ at the school he was planning to open. There he met Laurent Clerc, a deaf teacher, and he convinced Clerc to come to the United States to teach at the new school, the Connecticut Asylum for the Education and Instruction of Deaf and Dumb Persons (now the American School for the Deaf). Clerc taught using French Sign Language; however, the students from Martha's Vineyard and other areas of New England were unwilling to give up many of their own signs. Thus, American Sign Language (ASL) developed. Even today, approximately 60 percent of ASL signs have French origins (Woodward 1978).

Teachers and graduates from the American School, deaf and hearing, established schools for deaf children in other states throughout the United States. The founders of these new schools brought many teaching techniques and signs from Hartford, providing somewhat of a standardization of signs across the United States. However, local communities and states still retain some of their own signs, accounting for what is called regional variation.

For the Instructor

Most American Sign language instructors are very creative, knowledgeable, and skilled individuals. This book is designed to expand and add to their repertoire of procedures and methods of teaching ASL. The Grammatical Aspects of ASL sections throughout the book provide an introduction to ASL grammar, but instructors will have to decide how much in-depth explanation is necessary for their students.

Signs of the Times is not intended to be a cookbook to delineate how lessons and activities should be presented. The activities provide interactive exercises to reinforce information that has been introduced, and instructors can opt to use them to minimize class preparation. Instructors may use one or more of the lesson activities, depending on class time, or they may develop their own games or drills. Instructors can pick and choose how to present the ASL material. They may decide to skip some of the lesson activities until they are ready to introduce material relevant to those activities. This flexibility enables instructors to use *Signs of the Times* to best meet the needs of specific classes.

The class activities for students at the end of each lesson reinforce instruction from the current lesson as well as the preceding lessons. Redundancy of material helps to ensure mastery of the information, thus encouraging and expanding the students' perception and correct usage of ASL. Group work is suggested for most of the lesson reviews.

Organization of the Text

Signs of the Times is divided into 44 lessons with approximately 30 signs in each lesson. One of several unique features of the book is the presentation of vocabulary. Using a *spiral* approach, each sign is repeated several times within a lesson and from lesson to lesson, building on the previously introduced signs. The practice sentence under each sign contains the new sign being illustrated as well as signs already introduced. Signing each sentence allows the students to practice cumulative vocabulary to enhance retention.

Signs

This book contains 1,300 signs representing concepts and ideas in ASL. The signs represent approximately 8,000 English *glosses* (English words that convey the same meaning as a sign). *Signs of the Times* does not include every known ASL sign—no sign language book can make that claim because ASL is a living language and it is always in flux. In addition, it would be difficult to catalog all ASL signs due to the many local and regional variations. Many of these sign variations are documented in *Signs Across America* (Shroyer and Shroyer, 1992). This book contains 17 different signs for *tomato*, 16 different signs for *strawberry*, 11 signs for *favorite*, 11 signs for *clock*, and so forth. *Signs of the Times* attempts to incorporate the most frequently used signs used in the United States; however, such a task is somewhat arbitrary given all the sign variations that exist. Instructors may introduce regional signs and may even give them precedence over the signs in this book. This will reinforce the students' awareness of sign variations.

The very last lesson, Lesson 44, shows 25 signs for countries around the world that are frequently in the news or often discussed.

Synonyms

Signs represent concepts; therefore, almost all signs have several English synonyms (two or more words that have the same meaning). For example, the synonyms for the sign meaning *allow* include *let* and *permit*. All of these words represent the same concept and are signed the same way. Conversely, an English word may have multiple meanings, and, therefore, different ASL signs are needed to convey the different meanings. For example, three different signs for *left* would be used in the following sentences: Take a left turn at the next light; We left the party at 11:00; I left my book at home. Sign language texts that teach the same sign for one English word, no matter the meaning, do not follow the conceptual premise of ASL. *Signs of the Times* presents a number of English synonyms for each sign in the book to help students build their understanding of sign concepts, choose signs based on context, and remain true to ASL principles.

Vocabulary

The signs in this book were selected from several lists of most frequently used words in the English language. Additional signs represent vocabulary used in Deaf culture. Names of some popular stores, words associated with technology, and some new signs are also included in the book. Many signs that were considered new twenty years ago are now commonly used by the Deaf community and are considered ASL signs.

Sentences under Signs

Two sentences appear under each new sign. The first sentence is written in English, and it provides the context or meaning of the sign. The second sentence is written in ASL grammar and, if necessary, may show the conceptual meaning of the sign; that is, which sign should be used to convey the accurate concept. These ASL sentences are presented in bold lowercase letters.

My father likes to <u>run</u> every day.　　　　Father <u>left</u> early yesterday

everyday father my <u>jog</u> like　　　　**yesterday early father <u>depart</u>**

Some ASL sentences have parentheses around vocabulary. The parentheses indicate that the word may or may not be signed. For example,

Put the gasoline near the house.

gasoline near house (you) put

Sometimes a sign should be repeated for emphasis or to show that the concept is plural. In these situations, plus (+) signs follow the gloss. For example, the ASL sentence **girl+ play++** means *The girls are playing.*

Vocabulary Review

The English vocabulary and all the glosses for each lesson are presented at the beginning of each lesson. This allows students to see all English synonyms or meanings included in the lesson, thus greatly expanding their expressive vocabularies. For example, students will realize that they know the sign for *permit* or *allow* as well as the English word *let*. Students then review these within the lesson and, finally, apply their new vocabulary at the end of the lesson in the practice sentences.

Mnemonics

Following the presentation of new vocabulary in each lesson is a page of Mind Ticklers—mnemonic hints to help students remember specific signs. Some of the mnemonics may seem a little strange, but many are based on events, associations, and/or characteristics. For example, during World War II, students at Gallaudet University donated blood for the war effort. After their donation they received a Coke to drink. Thus the association of the needle to draw blood and the Coke afterwards provides the mnemonic and the sign for Coca Cola. The sign for *baby* is associated with rocking a baby in one's arms, and the sign for *fishing* is characteristic of someone throwing out a fishing line with a fishing rod. An additional benefit of mnemonics is that they may help clarify the movement of a sign.

Practice Sentences

Following the mnemonic section are pairs of practice sentences written in English and their ASL grammatical equivalents. The practice sentences include glosses for signs introduced in previous lessons, providing students with a continuous review of signs they have already learned. The sentences also provide sign practice with conceptually correct signs. Very little fingerspelling is required while signing the practice sentences. The goal is to learn and depend on signs rather than fingerspelling, which has a specific purpose in ASL. Fingerspelling is most often used for brand names, people's names, words without signs, and technical vocabulary.

Class Activities and Student Activities

Class activities are provided after the practice sentences. These activities can be done in a number of ways. Generally, group work is recommended when reviewing the activities, but the instructor and students may come up with different ways to cover these activities. Student activities following the class activities give students an opportunity to review and reinforce the signs and the information relevant to each lesson. The student activities can be assigned as homework, gone over in class, done as group work in class, used as quizzes, or done on an individual basis.

Information about Deaf Culture and American Sign Language Grammar

The second edition of *Signs of the Times* contains brief cultural and related bits of information about the Deaf community. Each lesson offers a close look at Deaf people and the culture in which they live. The information is included to provide students with additional knowledge and discussion points for class.

Also new to this edition are brief introductions to ASL grammar that provide just enough information to arouse the curiosity of students. They can then apply what they have learned to their ability to form ASL sentences. Instructors should select the grammatical information for class discussions and elaborate on the grammatical features they deem appropriate.

Conceptual Sign/Word Appendix

The Conceptual Sign/Word Appendix provides an extensive list of examples to show which ASL sign to use for various English glosses. In English the meaning of a word is understood from the context of a sentence. Similarly, in ASL the meaning is conveyed by the sign selected. Words like *run*, *store*, *match*, and *throw* have multiple meanings, and language users must determine which meaning a speaker or signer intends to convey by analyzing the context of the sentence. ASL uses what are called *conceptual* signs to make the context or meaning of what is being conveyed very clear. The following English sentences demonstrate different meanings of the word *run*, and the ASL sentences next to them contain the signs used to communicate these meanings.

English	ASL
His nose is running.	NOW MAN NOSE-RUN
She is running for the Senate.	NOW WOMAN FOR SENATE COMPETE
He runs every day.	DAILY BOY JOG
She runs the store.	NOW WOMAN STORE MANAGE
He ran away from home yesterday.	YESTERDAY BOY HOME RUN-AWAY
The water is running in the sink.	NOW WATER SINK DRIP[1]

In order for students to choose the correct conceptual signs for the ASL sentences written in this text, the sentences use a gloss (the English equivalent of a sign) that does not have multiple meanings and that conveys the intended message. The following signs can be glossed as *leave*, but the glosses below the signs make their meaning clear.

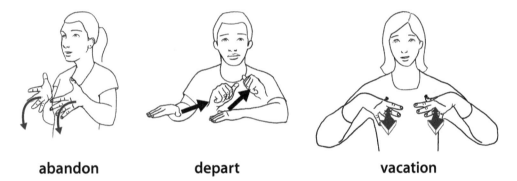

abandon **depart** **vacation**

When a word like *match* (used to set fire to something) has no other synonym to convey the desired concept without using another multiple meaning word (e.g., *light*), then the two words are linked together with a hyphen to illustrate the desired concept. Therefore, *match-light* represents one sign rather than two signs.

Agent Marker

The *agent marker* is added to a number of verbs to signify a person who performs the action of a verb (for example, teacher, artist, musician). Coincidentally, it is also the sign for *person*. This sign is often referred to as the *-er* sign, although it can also mean *-ent*, *-or*, *-ist*, or *-an*.

---

[1]In the text of this book, ASL glosses are presented in small capital letters.

teacher

musician

Making the Signs

The hand that moves the most while making a sign is called the *dominant* hand. Most people are right-handed, which is why the signs in this book are shown with the right hand as the dominant hand. When a sign is made with only one hand, the signer uses the dominant hand (see **my** in figure 1). When a sign is made with both hands but only one hand moves, the dominant hand generally moves while the other hand acts as a base (see **time** in figure 1).

Most signs have a beginning and ending position. In this text, only the hands appear in the first position. In the final position, the hands are attached to the signer's arms and the lines are slightly darker. If the hand touches a part of the body while making the sign, the contact point is shown as a thick black line or shadow (see **my** in figure 1). When both hands move, they often assume the same handshape (see **do**, **maybe**, and **big** in figure 1). If both hands begin at the same spatial level, they move in the same or opposite directions (see **do** and **hurt** in figure 1). When the hands begin on different spatial levels, they alternate making the same movement (see **maybe** in figure 1).

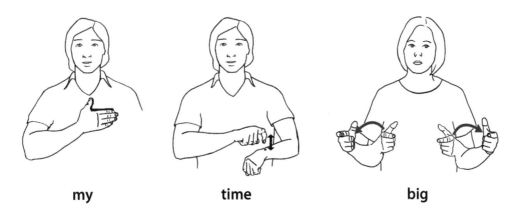

my   time   big

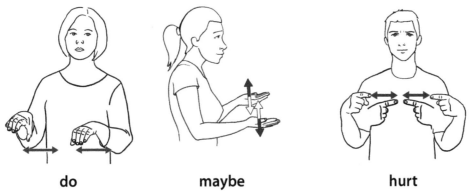

do   maybe   hurt

FIGURE 1. Examples of how the hands move when making signs.

UNDERSTANDING THE ARROWS

The arrows in the sign illustrations indicate how the hands move when making a sign. Arrows can be long or short, curved or straight, single or double-pointed. The following list details what each arrow means.

1. Movement in one direction with either one hand or both hands.

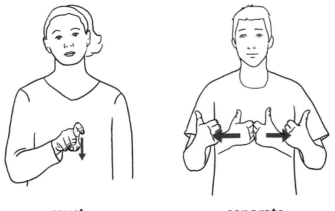

must   separate

2. Several movements in the same direction.

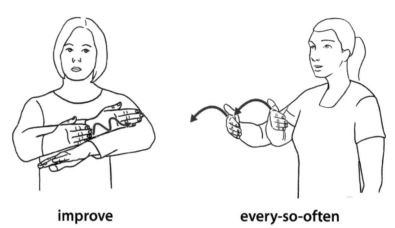

improve   **every-so-often**

3. Double or back-and-forth movements.

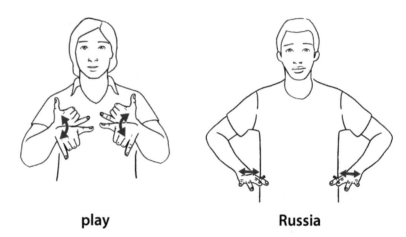

play   **Russia**

4. A single motion with change in direction or handshape.

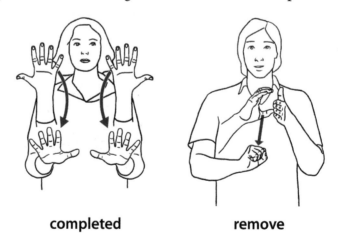

completed   **remove**

5. Multiple or repeated movements.

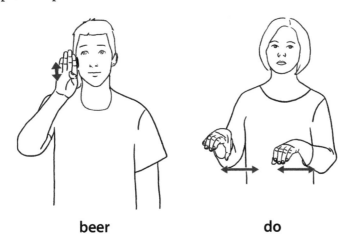

beer   **do**

6. A circular motion.

Monday   **sorry**

7. A circular motion moving forward or backward.

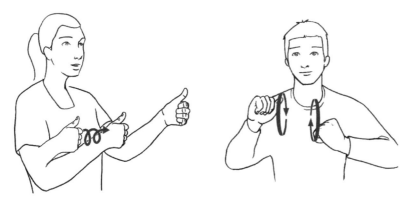

chase   **act**

8. A twisting motion.

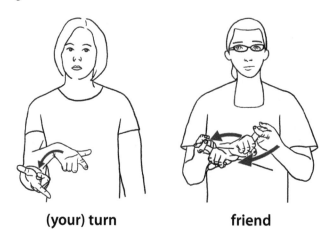

(your) turn   **friend**

9. A shaking or wiggling motion.

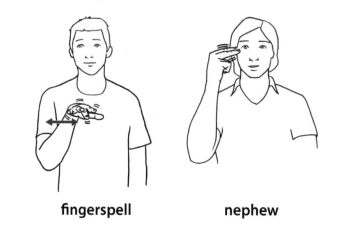

fingerspell   **nephew**

ASL Sentences

You may have already noticed in the example ASL sentences that verbs appear at the end of the sentence. This is true in most of the ASL sentences in this book. The purpose of this is twofold: it provides an excellent model for learning ASL, and it shows that verbs have considerable flexibility in ASL. For example, putting the verb at the end of an ASL sentence allows the signer to emphasize (a) direction, (b) movement toward a specific location, (c) reciprocal action, and (d) information about the location, size, and shape of an object.

DIRECTIONAL VERBS

Directional (or indicating) verbs change their movement and orientation to provide information about the subject and object of the sentence. For̄ example, HELP can move away from the signer toward the person being helped or it can move toward the signer to show that someone is helping the signer; and LOOK AT can face away or toward the signer, depending on who or what is doing the looking. In this way, the pronoun is incorporated in the sign.

look-at-me   **look-at-her**

Directional verbs also can show location. For example, to sign *the plane flew west*, the sign moves to the left; to sign *the plane flew east*, the sign moves to the right. To sign *come here*, the sign moves toward the signer.

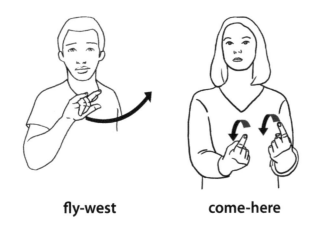

fly-west   **come-here**

RECIPROCAL ACTION

Some directional verbs are *reciprocal*, which means that each hand represents a person or thing. The hands face each other to show that the action is jointly performed by two people, two things, or two groups. To sign the sentence *The dog and cat looked at each other*, one hand represents the dog and the other hand represents the cat. The fingers of both hands face each other. To sign the sentence *The cars collided*, each hand represents a vehicle, and the hands move toward each other and bump into each other.

look-at-each-other

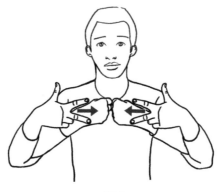

collide

INFORMATION ABOUT LOCATION

With some ASL verbs, the place where the sign is made reveals specific information. The sign meaning *hurt* or *ache* can be made at the forehead for *headache*, near the stomach for *stomachache*, near the arm for *my arm hurts*, etc. Similarly, changing the location of the sign WASH shows what part of the body is being washed.

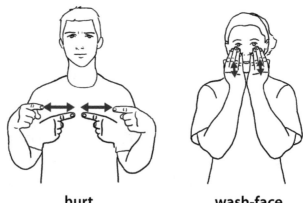

hurt   **wash-face**

INFORMATION ABOUT THE SIZE AND SHAPE OF AN OBJECT

Some verbs provide information about the size and shape of an object. To show that you are picking up a small object, like a penny, you hold it between two fingers to indicate the size. You can show the size of a stone by the manner in which you pick it up—with a small closed hand, a hand with the fingers wide apart, or with both hands. Similarly, the size and shape of a ball can be shown by forming a sphere with the hands and spreading the hands apart to show its size.

Visualize and do the following:

I am holding a penny. I picked up a large stone. I have a basketball.

FINGERSPELLING

Fingerspelling is used to represent words in a spoken language when there is no related sign. ASL has 26 different handshapes, each one corresponding to a letter in the English alphabet (see page xxix). Most proper names are fingerspelled, as are new terms in the language, such as *Blackberry* and *twitter*, until a sign is created. Over time some fingerspelled abbreviations have become signs in themselves; for example T-V (television), J-B (job), and A-C (air conditioning).

INITIALIZED SIGNS

Initialization occurs when the handshape of an ASL sign represents the first letter of the English word. Although there are differing opinions regarding the use of initialized signs in ASL, many deaf people use initialized signs to varying degrees. How much depends on the communication situation. For example, a deaf college student may prefer that an instructor use more initialized signs in order to better understand subject-specific vocabulary.

Many initialized signs have become a functional part of ASL, even in deaf families. My father was born deaf, had four deaf siblings and eight hearing siblings, and everyone in the family signed. Back then no one called signing *ASL*, but that is what they were using. All five of the deaf siblings went to the Ohio School for the Deaf in the 1920s and '30s. When Dad was in his early 70s, I videotaped him sharing some of his childhood experiences. I was really surprised when he used a D handshape at the side of his mouth to indicate *dining* room. Up to that time, I had never seen him use an initialized sign. On the other hand, my mother was the only deaf person in her family, and she learned to sign when she was a teenager. When she was older, she used specific initialed signs frequently and was eager to see new and regional signs, whereas my dad had little interest in either.

dining room

Initialized signs also are used to distinguish English concepts that have similar meanings. For example, the ASL sign for a "group of people gathered together" can be initialized to show the following English meanings: <u>a</u>ssociation, <u>c</u>lass, <u>f</u>amily, <u>g</u>roup, <u>o</u>rganization, <u>s</u>ociety, <u>t</u>eam, or <u>u</u>nion. Inside *Signs of the Times*, an asterisk (*) appears before glosses that can be initialized signs.

class

SIGNING SENTENCES

In English, the words in a sentence can sometimes be rearranged without changing the meaning of the sentence. The same is true of ASL, as the examples below show.

<u>English</u>	<u>ASL</u>
It rained almost all day yesterday.	RAIN ALMOST ALL-DAY YESTERDAY

Yesterday it rained almost all day.	YESTERDAY RAIN ALMOST ALL-DAY
Almost all day yesterday it rained.	RAIN YESTERDAY ALMOST ALL-DAY

In order to alleviate students' frustration when trying to sign ASL sentences, the practice sentences in this book follow a specific language pattern. The repetition of this pattern provides students with a sense of continuity and should serve as a springboard to feeling comfortable with the language. However, students need to remember that there is more than one way to express an idea.

The sentences follow a topic/comment format. This structure is like drawing a picture. First, you draw the most important thing/object, which is often the noun in the sentence (for example, a dog). Then, you add the relevant information about the object—its size, color, collar, tail, etc. Next, you create the environment by placing objects appropriately in the space, like in a painting (big trees, grass, house, and children). Time indicators can also be added (snow, leaves on the ground, sunshine, pumpkins, Christmas trees, and green grass). The following sentences illustrate the format.

English   The black dog is big.

	topic	comment
ASL	DOG	BLACK BIG

English   I see the big black dog.

	topic	comment	action
ASL	DOG	BIG BLACK	ME SEE

English   I saw the big black dog yesterday.

	time indicator	topic	comment	action
ASL	YESTERDAY	DOG	BIG BLACK	ME SEE

English   I didn't see the big black dog yesterday.

	time indicator	topic	comment	action	negation
ASL	YESTERDAY	DOG	BIG BLACK	ME SEE	NOT

English   Why didn't you see the big black dog yesterday?

	time indicator	topic	comment	action	negation	interrogative
ASL	YESTERDAY	DOG	BIG BLACK	YOU SEE	NOT	WHY?

Eye Contact and Signer Perspective

Deaf people maintain eye contact at all times while signing. Eye contact is so important in Deaf culture that it is considered impolite to look away during a conversation. This is not true in hearing culture, where speakers frequently break eye contact when in conversation. Therefore, hearing students need to know that it takes time and practice to maintain eye contact when signing. One way to reinforce this idea is to watch Deaf people when they sign to one another. Students also should observe how their instructor signs to the class.

Signers always face one another when having a conversation. For that reason, most of the signs in this book are shown facing straight out. In certain instances, some of the signers are shown at an angle or from a profile perspective to make the movement clear.

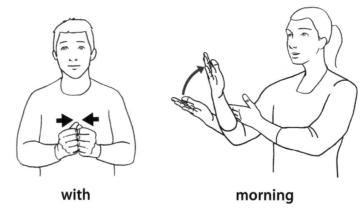

with   morning

Facial Expressions/Body Movements

As important as eye contact is, the use of facial expressions and body movement is even more important in the process of communicating with Deaf people. In addition to the basic components of a sign—the shape, orientation, position, and movement of the hands—ASL signers add subtle changes in facial expressions and head and body movements (called nonmanual signals) to convey meaning. When used in differing combinations, these nonmanual signals make possible a large number of linguistic expressions. For example, raising the eyebrows at the end of a sentence indicates the signer is asking a question that requires a yes or no answer. When a signer asks a question beginning with *wh-*, the eyebrows are lowered and the head tilts. Instructors should introduce nonmanual signals to students and reinforce their use in the classroom. Some of the lesson activities and the sections on grammatical aspects of ASL reinforce the use of nonmanual signals.

Final Notes

TO THE INSTRUCTOR

After reading the introduction and browsing through the student and class activities, I hope that the format of *Signs of the Times* appeals to you and will serve as a strong foundation for the daunting task of teaching American Sign Language. The lesson format of the original *Signs of the Times* helped make it a bestseller. I sincerely hope that this new version, with its focus on ASL, will also be a hit with ASL instructors and students alike. It is my intention that the various activities delineated in the book, as well as the introductions to ASL grammatical constructs, will be helpful to you and make planning easier. Once you become familiar with your students' learning styles, you should have an excellent handle on which sections of this book will work best in your classes. Good luck and happy teaching!

TO THE STUDENTS

By reading the introductory sections you have gained a very basic understanding of American Sign Language. There is no need for you to study and memorize the plethora of information thrown at you in this section. The information is provided as a reference and a resource as you progress through the lessons in *Signs of the Times* and tackle the student activities. The mind ticklers, practice sentences, and group activities will help you remember the new vocabulary in each lesson. Be sure to work with your instructor on nonmanual signals, which are a very important part of ASL. It is always best to have study groups or another student with whom to study. Try reviewing vocabulary and grammatical structures frequently as languages are best learned through many short reviews rather than a long session the night before class. You are to be applauded for your interest and the endeavor you are about to undertake.

In addition to learning American Sign Language, you are giving yourself a wonderful opportunity to learn and experience a unique and welcoming culture, the Deaf culture. In many ways Deaf culture is very similar to hearing culture, while in many ways it is unique. You may be quite surprised at the differences. Take the time to explore information regarding Deaf culture on the Internet and research opportunities to associate with deaf individuals within your community. Deaf people are excited when hearing individuals take an interest in their language and culture, and they are often happy to talk with you regardless of your communication skill level. The snapshots of cultural information throughout the lessons should lead to excellent class discussions while increasing your knowledge of Deaf culture. Best of luck to each of you and happy signing!

References

American Sign Language grammar. Wikipedia, the free encyclopedia. http://en.wikipedia.org/wiki/American_Sign_Language_grammar (accessed March 20, 2009).

American Sign Language: Grammar. www.lifeprint.com/asl101/pages-layout/grammar.htm (accessed March 20, 2009)

Groce, Nora. 1985. *Everyone here spoke sign language.* Cambridge, MA: Harvard University Press.

Humphries, Tom, and Carol Padden. 1992. *Learning American Sign Language.* Englewood Cliffs, NJ: Prentice Hall.

Liddell, Scott K. 2003. *Grammar, gestures, and meaning in American Sign Language.* Cambridge: Cambridge University Press.

Lucas, Ceil, Robert Bayley, and Clayton Valli. 2001. *Sociolinguistic variation in ASL.* Sociolinguistics in Deaf Communities, vol. 7. Washington, DC: Gallaudet University Press.

Padden, Carol, and Tom Humphries. 1988. *Deaf in America: Voices from a culture.* Cambridge, MA: Harvard University Press.

Padden, Carol, and Tom Humphries. 2005. *Inside deaf culture.* Cambridge, MA: Harvard University Press.

Shroyer, Edgar. H. 1998. *American Sign Language activities.* Greensboro, NC: Sugar Sign Press.

Shroyer, Edgar. H., and Susan P. Shroyer. 1984. *Signs across America: A look at regional differences in American Sign Language.* Washington, DC: Gallaudet University Press.

Terp Topics: Interpreter topics rendered faithfully. July 17, 2008. Terp Topics. http://www.terptopics.com/GrammarASL.htm (accessed March 15, 2009).

Gallaudet University Press. 2005. *The Gallaudet dictionary of American Sign Language.* Washington, DC: Gallaudet University Press.

Valli, Clayton, Ceil Lucas, and Kristin J. Mulrooney. 2005. *Linguistics of American Sign Language: An Introduction.* 4th ed. Washington, DC: Gallaudet University Press.

Woodward, James. 1978. Historical basis of American Sign Language. In *Understanding language through sign language research,* ed. Patricia Siple, 333–48. New York: Academic Press.

The Manual Alphabet

A

B

C

D

E

F

G

H

I

J

K

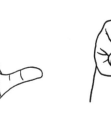

L

M

N

O

P

Q

R

S

T

U

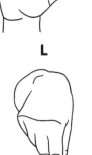

V

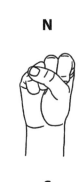

W

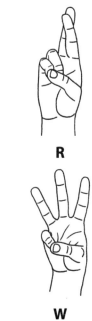

X

Y

Z

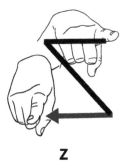

Numbers

 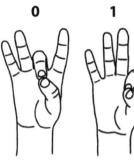  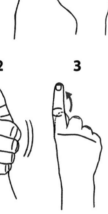 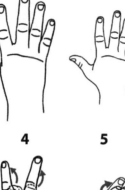 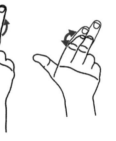 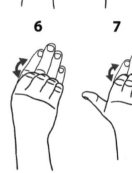

| 0 | 1 | 2 | 3 | 4 | 5 | 6 | 7 |

 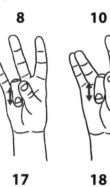 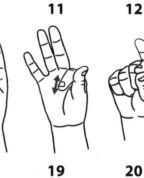 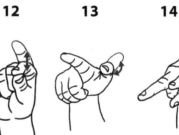 

| 8 | 8 | 10 | 11 | 12 | 13 | 14 | 15 |

| 16 | 17 | 18 | 19 | 20 | 21 | 22 |

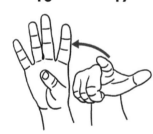 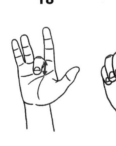  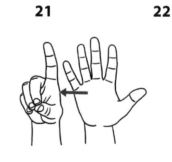

| 24 | 25 | 30 | 51 |

| 100 | 300 | 1000 | 1 million |

Signs of the Times

Lesson 1

Vocabulary

1 I, me
2 see, vision, sight
3 you
4 hear
5 think, mind, brain, sense, mental, thinker
6 good, well
7 now, this, present
8 go, going, attend, went
9 with, along with, amid, accompany
10 boy, male
11 girl, female
12 he, she, it, him, her, that, this, there, over there, point
13 they, those, them
14 us
15 we
16 that, this, it, which
17 come, come over, coming, return
18 look, look at, watch, observe
19 tree, trees, forest, woods, jungle
20 bird, chicken
21 in, within
22 drink, beverage, drinker
23 eat, food, eater
24 play, frolic, party, player
25 house, cottage, shed, barn, dwelling
26 time, o'clock, date
27 morning, dawn
28 night, evening
29 later, after awhile, after a bit

1
I, me

I
me

2
see, vision, sight

I see.
me see

3
you

I see you.
you, me see

4
hear

I hear you.
you, me hear

Deaf Culture Facts and Information

The population of the United States is just over 300 million people. About 10 percent of this population (30 million people) has some type of hearing loss, while 1 percent (3 million) is considered to be deaf. Approximately a quarter of the latter group uses sign language to communicate.

5
think, mind, brain, sense, mental, think<u>er</u>

I think I hear you.
you, me think me hear (you)

6
good, well

You hear well.
you, good hear

7
now, this, present

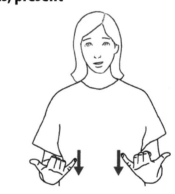

I see you now.
now, you me see

8
go, going, attend, went

I think you are going.
you go, me think

9

with, along with, amid, accompany

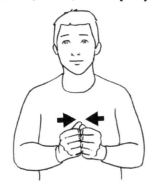

You go with me.
you with me go

10

boy, male

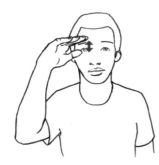

The boy is going now.
now boy go

11

girl, female

You go with the girl.
girl, you with go

12

he, she, it, him, her, that, this, there, over there, point

I see her now.
now girl there me see

13

they, those, them

They are going with her.
now, they with girl go

14

us

The girl sees us now.
now, girl there us see

15
we

We think you are good.
you good, we think

ASL Grammar Notes

When using a pronoun (*he*, *she*, *it*, *they*, *them*) for a person or object within your sightline, simply point to it. If the person or object is not within your sightline, fingerspell its name and then point to a space to your right. You can then point to that space to refer to it again.

16
that, this, it, which

That girl is going.
that girl go

17
come, come over, coming, return

I think he is coming.
now boy come, me think

18
look, look at, watch, observe

Look at that good girl.
girl good, look-at

19
tree, trees, forest, woods, jungle

Look at that tree.
tree there look-at

20
bird, chicken

The girl sees a bird.
bird, girl see

21
in, within

The bird is in the tree.
now, bird there in tree

22
drink, beverage, drink_er_

That is a good drink.
that drink good

23
eat, food, eat_er_

Look at the boy eating.
boy eat, look-at

24
play, frolic, party, play_er_

The boy plays in the tree.
boy in tree play++

25
house, cottage, shed, barn, dwelling

The bird is in the house.
now, bird in house

26
time, o'clock, date

Now it is time to go.
now, time go

27
morning, dawn

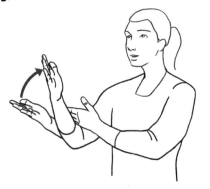

The girl saw you this morning.
now morning, girl see you

28
night, evening

The boy is eating with me tonight.
now night, boy with me eat

29
later, after awhile, after a bit

I am going to the barn later.
later, house me go

Mind Ticklers

Make the sign _____	and think about . . .
I, me	pointing to yourself
see, vision, sight	the eyes seeing outward
you	pointing at a person
hear	hearing with your ears
think, mind, brain	pointing to where your brain is
good, well	offering something good to someone
now, this, present	the present being in front of you
go, going, went	something moving away from you
with, along with, accompany	two things together
boy, male	touching the bill of a cap
girl, female	the string on a bonnet
he, she, him, her, it, that, this there, over there	pointing to a person, place, or thing
they, them, those	pointing to several things
us	me and all of you
we	me and all of you
this, that, it, which	something not present to point at
come, come over, coming	something moving toward you
look, look at, watch, observe	your eyes looking outward
tree	your arm as the tree trunk
bird	your fingers as the bird's beak
in, within	putting something in a box
drink	tipping a glass to drink
eat, food	putting food in your mouth
play, player	shaking Y hands as if carefree
house, shed, barn	making the roof and sides of a house
time, o'clock	tapping your watch
morning, dawn	the sun rising over the horizon
night, evening	the sun sinking over the horizon
later, after awhile	a minute hand showing 20 minutes past the hour

Practice Sentences

1. I think I hear a bird.
   me think me hear bird
2. Come with me to see the girl and boy.
   you with me come, boy girl see
3. Now is a good time to eat and drink.
   now time good eat drink
4. I'm coming over to eat with you this evening.
   now night me come with you eat
5. You can play with the girl later.
   later, girl you with play
6. Look at that bird in the tree.
   bird there in tree, look-at
7. I see the bird in the barn.
   bird in barn me see
8. She saw me in the house this morning.
   now morning, me in house girl see (me)
9. We will go to the forest with the boys later.
   later, forest with boy+ we go
10. Those girls go with the boys in the morning.
    morning those girl+ with boy+ go
11. Look at the bird playing now.
    now bird play look-at
12. Now is the time to go eat.
    now time go eat
13. This morning I heard the girls playing.
    now morning girl+ play, me hear
14. He is going home tonight to drink.
    now night boy go home drink
15. She hears the bird in the house.
    now bird in house girl hear

Class Activity

1. Have students pair up with a partner. The instructor signs the first six sentences in Lesson 1. Then the instructor reads each of the first six sentences while the partners sign the sentences to one another simultaneously. The instructor signs the next group of six sentences (7–12). Then she reads the sentences aloud (7–12) while the partners sign the sentences to one another simultaneously. Continue with groups of six sentences until the lesson is completed.

Student Activities

1. Which hand of yours is your dominant hand?

   _____

2. Which signs in Lesson 1 have no synonyms? _____ and

   _____

3. Your nondominant hand serves as the horizon for which signs?

   _____ and

   _____

4. How are all the signs for the pronouns alike?

   _____

   _____

5. What is the mind tickler for LATER?

   _____

   _____

6. Iconic signs are signs that resemble the object or action intended. What signs in Lesson 1 would be considered iconic?

_____

_____

7. Write six English sentences to sign to your classmates using the vocabulary in Lesson 1.

   1. _____

   _____

   2. _____

   _____

   3. _____

   _____

   4. _____

   _____

   5. _____

   _____

   6. _____

   _____

Lesson 2

Vocabulary

30 dog
31 cat
32 big, *great, huge, large
33 little, small, short
34 small, little, tiny
35 tall, high, height, adult
36 sit, sit down
37 like, favor, fond of
38 don't like
39 school
40 college
41 class, *family, *group, *organization, *team, *association, *society
42 noon
43 afternoon
44 day
45 all day
46 all night, overnight
47 daily, everyday, every day
48 tonight
49 today
50 weekend
51 this
52 these
53 my, mine
54 your, his, her, hers, its
55 yours, their, theirs
56 our, ours
57 myself
58 himself, herself, yourself, itself
59 ourselves
60 themselves, yourselves

30
dog

The dog is in the house.
now, dog in house

31
cat

Watch the cat in the tree.
cat tree there look-at

32
big, *great, huge, large

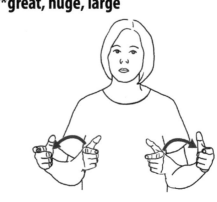

The dog plays in a big house.
dog in house large play++

33
little, small, short

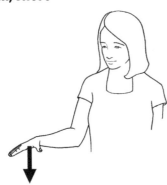

The little boy is playing now.
now, boy short play

34
small, little, tiny

I think I see the little cat.
cat tiny, me think (me) see

35
tall, high, height, adult

That girl is tall.
girl there tall

36
sit, sit down

Sit down with me to eat.
sit-down, with me eat

37
like, favor, fond of

I like sitting with you.
sit with you, me like

38
don't like

They don't like big cats.
cats large, they don't-like

39
school

That little girl likes school.
there girl short, school like

Deaf Culture Facts and Information

The rubella (German measles) epidemic of 1963–65 resulted in a significant increase in the number of children born deaf and those born deaf with additional disabilities, including a large number of deaf-blind children.

40
college

I hear that you like college.
college you like, me hear

41
class, *family, *group, *organization, *team, *association, *society

He likes going to class in the morning.
morning boy class go, like

42
noon

See me in the house at noon.
noon house (you) see me

43
afternoon

They like sitting in the afternoon.
afternoon they sit, like

44
day

We don't like day classes.
class day, we don't-like

45
all day

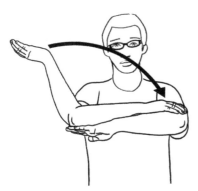

She doesn't like sitting all day.
all-day girl sit++ don't-like

46
all night, overnight

She likes playing all night.
all-night girl play++ like

47
daily, everyday, every day

The girl goes to school every day.
daily girl school go

48
tonight

Tonight we eat and drink.
now-night, we eat drink

49
today

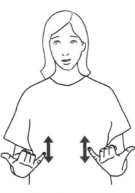

Today we go to school.
today, we school go

50
weekend

We don't like school on weekends.
weekend, school we don't like

51
this

This group plays every day.
daily group play

52
these

These dogs eat in the morning and at night.
morning, night, dog these eat

53
my, mine

We think this cat mine.
cat there mine we think

ASL Grammar Notes

Nonmanual signals (NMS) provide additional information that cannot be conveyed by the hands alone. They include facial expressions, head and body movements, and mouth movements.

54
your, his, her, hers, its

His bird likes the food.
bird boy his, eat like

55
yours, their, theirs

I think I see their college.
college their, me think (me) see

56
our, ours

Our girls go to college.
girl+ our, college go

57
myself

I go to school by myself every day.
daily myself school go

58
himself, herself, yourself, itself

He likes himself.
boy there like himself

59
ourselves

We think we are going ourselves.
we think ourselves go

60
themselves, yourselves

They are going by themselves.
they themselves go

Mind Ticklers

Make the sign _____	and think about . . .
dog	snapping your fingers for a dog to come
cat	your fingers as the cat's whiskers
big, great, huge, large	showing with your hands how big something is
little, small, short, tiny	showing with your hands the height of something
small, little	using your hands to show size
tall, high, height	your hand showing the height of something
sit, sit down	your feet hanging over a chair
like, favor	positive feelings from the heart
don't like	pushing away negative feelings
school	a teacher clapping for attention
college	a place of learning higher than school
class, family, group	people sitting around a table
noon	the sun high in the sky
afternoon	the sun beginning to set
day	the sun moving across the sky
all day	the sun moving slowly across the sky
all night, overnight	the sun below the horizon
daily, everyday	repeating the sign for **tomorrow** (see lesson 8)
tonight	signing **now** and **night** together
today	signing **now** twice
weekend	five days of the week coming to an end
this	pointing to something in your palm
these	pointing off to the side—there they are!
my, mine	holding what is yours to your chest
your, his, her, hers, its	an open hand means possessive
yours, their, theirs	pushing something towards several people
our, ours	yourself and several others
myself	indicating yourself
himself, herself, yourself, itself	indicating another person or thing
ourselves	indicating yourself and several people
themselves, yourselves	indicating several other people

Practice Sentences

1. That big dog is theirs.

   dog big there theirs

2. The little girl and boy go to school every weekend.

   weekend girl, boy short school go

3. I heard that your family is coming over in the morning.

   morning family your come-over me hear

4. They don't like sitting in school all day with us.

   all-day they with us school there sit++, don't-like

5. Later today our team goes out to eat and drink.

   today, later team our go eat drink

6. That tall boy is coming to look at our house today.

   today boy tall there, our house come look-at

7. The girl is coming to my house tonight to eat chicken.

   now-night girl my house come chicken eat

8. Every day we go to school by ourselves.

   daily ourselves school go

9. My little girl is coming to see me at noon.

   noon girl short my come see me

10. I don't like her big dog in my small house.

    dog big girl hers, in house small my, (me) don't-like

11. They ate in the small house with the girls and boys.

    house small they with boy+ girl+ eat

12. I like sitting with you morning, noon, and night.

    morning, noon, night, with you sit, me like

13. I saw your dog playing with my cat.

    dog your with cat my play++ me see

14. Now is the time to play with his family.

    now time with his family play++

15. This weekend the boys and girls are coming to eat.

    now weekend boy, girl come eat

Class Activities

1. In groups, go over the information you wrote for the student activities in Lesson 1.

2. In groups, take turns reading one of the English sentences you wrote in student activity 7 in Lesson 1. The person across from you will make an ASL sentence from your English sentence.

Student Activities

1. What part of speech is at the end of most ASL sentences in Lessons 1 and 2?

   _____

2. List the pronouns that use an Open B handshape.

   _____

   _____

   _____

3. The pronouns you listed in number two above are _____ pronouns.

4. A compound sign is two signs used together. What compound signs are shown in this lesson?

_____

_____

5. Which signs from Lessons 1 and 2 use the nondominant hand as the horizon?

_____

_____

6. In addition to the sign ALL-DAY moving slower than the sign DAY, what other distinction can be seen in the illustrations?

_____

_____

7. Write an ASL sentence for the following:
   a. I go to school every day.

   _____

   _____

   b. We don't like your brother.

   _____

   _____

   c. Look at the bird in the tree.

   _____

   _____

   d. You like big schools?

   _____

   _____

   e. My dog eats at noon.

   _____

   _____

Lesson 3

Vocabulary

61 bad
62 clean, nice, neat
63 clean up
64 into, enter, entrance
65 to
66 from
67 on, upon, onto, on top of
68 off
69 near, by, against, close
70 for
71 get, acquire, receive, obtain
72 without
73 not, don't, doesn't
74 no, refusal
75 yes, affirmative
76 work, task, *job, assignment, *industry, *function, *duty
77 want
78 don't want
79 sleep, asleep
80 water
81 soda, pop
82 Pepsi, Italy
83 Coca-Cola, Coke, vaccination, injection
84 tea
85 coffee, java
86 chocolate
87 vanilla

61
bad

We don't like bad boys.
boy bad, we don't-like

62
clean, nice, neat

Our little house is clean.
house our tiny, clean

63
clean up

Clean up and go to school.
clean-up, school go

64

into, enter, entrance

My dog went into your house.
dog my house your into

Deaf Culture Facts and Information

A small proportion of deaf children (around 10 percent) are exposed to Deaf culture in infancy by their Deaf parents. Most Deaf individuals learn about Deaf culture in residential schools for the deaf, and still others may not be exposed to Deaf culture until college or later in life.

65

to

He goes to your school all day.
all-day, boy to school your go

66

from

The girl and boy came from college.
boy, girl from college come

67

on, upon, onto, on top of

They sat on the tree by themselves.
they themselves on tree sit

68

off

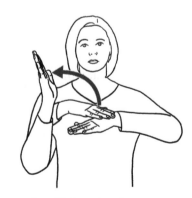

Now the cat is off the shed.
now cat off shed

69

near, by, against, close

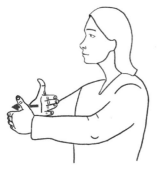

Come and eat near us.
come, near us eat

70

for

The boy likes cleaning up for me.
boy for me clean-up like

71

get, acquire, receive, obtain

Get a little cat for me.
cat tiny for me obtain

72

without

They went without you.
they, without you go

73

not, don't, doesn't

That is not my big house.
house there large, my not

74

no, refusal

No, it is not time to go.
now time go, no

75
yes, affirmative

Yes, we go there daily.
yes, daily we go

76
**work, task, *job, assignment, *industry,
   *function, *duty**

I don't like working all day.
all-day me work don't-like

77
want

The girl wants to see you.
now girl see you want

78
don't want

The boys don't want a big dog.
dog large, boy don't-want

79
sleep, asleep

The family is sleeping now.
now family sleep

80
water

They drink water all day.
all-day water they drink++

81
soda, pop

We see you drinking soda.
soda, you drink, we see

82
Pepsi, Italy

Yes, I want a Pepsi.
yes, pepsi me want

83
Coca-Cola, Coke, vaccination, injection

It is time to drink a Coca-Cola.
now time coke drink

84
tea

We think that the tea is bad.
tea, bad we think

ASL Grammar Notes

The preposition *to*, meaning a direction, is signed in most instances, although not always. For example, *Dad is going to the library* is signed NOW DAD TO LIBRARY GO; *Are you going to the movies?* is signed MOVIES YOU GO.

85
coffee, java

Our team likes coffee.
team our, coffee like

chocolate

I don't want chocolate now.
now, chocolate, me don't-want

vanilla

The girl wants vanilla Coke.
coke vanilla, girl want

Mind Ticklers

Make the sign _____	and think about . . .
bad	pushing something bad out of your mouth
clean, nice, neat	something neat and smooth
clean up	brushing the floor with a broom
into, enter, entrance	going into something
to	going from one place to another
from	moving away from a place
on, upon, onto	putting an object on something
off	the opposite of **on**
near, by, against, close	putting an object near another object
for	pointing outward to indicate something
get, acquire, receive	reaching out to get something and pulling it in
without	emptying your hands
not, don't	your head shaking
no, refusal	putting the letters *n* and *o* together
yes	nodding your head and fist
work, task, job, assignment, industry	using your hands to work
want	pulling something you desire to you
don't want	dropping what you do not want
sleep, asleep	your eyes closing and your head drooping
water	water trickling down your chin
soda, pop	the popping sound when the cap comes off
Pepsi, Italy	Italian words ending in *i*
Coke, vaccination, injection	giving blood and drinking Coke afterwards
tea	stirring tea with a spoon
coffee	using an old-fashioned coffee grinder
chocolate	mixing the ingredients for chocolate
vanilla	mixing the ingredients for vanilla

Practice Sentences

1. Today was a bad day all day.

   today all-day, bad

2. She doesn't want to clean the house without a drink of water.

   girl, house clean-up without drink water, she don't-want

3. Yes, I saw the girl sitting there drinking Pepsi.

   girl sit there drink pepsi me see, yes

4. We like drinking our vanilla coffee near that tree.

   coffee vanilla our, near tree there, we like drink

5. (You) go into the house and get the soda.

   now you into house, soda get

6. No, he doesn't like working without girls.

   no, boy work without girl, don't-like

7. That is not the tea that I want.

   tea that, me don't-want

8. The boys went to get vanilla Coke.

   coke vanilla, boy go get

9. I don't want you to drink coffee this morning.

   now morning, me don't-want you coffee drink

10. Yes, come with me to look at the little female dog.

    yes, dog girl small, you with me look-at

11. The entrance was bad; we heard you cleaned it.

    entrance bad you clean-up, we hear

12. I don't want him to drink water today.

    today boy water drink, me don't-want

13. I like to sit near her in school.

    girl in school, sit near me, me like

14. The team didn't want to drink in the house today.

    today team drink in house don't-want

15. The girl thinks it is bad to sleep all day.

    all-day sleep bad, girl (she) think

Class Activities

1. In small groups, go over the student activities from Lesson 2.

2. In small groups, one person starts by fingerspelling a food beginning with the letter A (apple). The next person picks a food starting with the letter B (banana), the next person uses the letter C (celery). Continue through the alphabet. Members in the group should voice the food being fingerspelled.

Student Activities

1. Go back and look at the seven sentences you wrote in Lesson 1. Now rewrite them as ASL sentences (if you wrote them in English) or English sentences if you wrote them in ASL.

   a. _____

   b. _____

   c. _____

   d. _____

   e. _____

   f. _____

   g. _____

2. Looking only at the vocabulary list for Lesson 3 (not the illustrations), write the signs that use only one hand. You should find nine signs.

   _____

   _____

   _____

3. Cover each English sentence in the practice sentences for Lesson 3 with a piece of paper. Looking only at the ASL sentences, say aloud what the English sentence should be, then check to see if you are right.

4. From memory write all the signs you can think of through Lesson 3 that are negative (for example, DON'T-WANT).

   _____

   _____

   _____

   _____

   _____

Lesson 4

Vocabulary

88 color, colorful, crayons
89 pink
90 black
91 brown
92 tan
93 red
94 white
95 yellow
96 purple
97 blue
98 green
99 orange
100 silver, shiny, sharp, bright
101 gold
102 person, *individual, figure, human
103 people, citizens
104 sister
105 brother
106 aunt
107 uncle
108 grandmother, grandma
109 grandfather, grandpa, granddad
110 cousin
111 baby, infant
112 father, dad, pop
113 mother, mom
114 step (mother, father), next, turn, your turn, go ahead
115 foster (mother, father), false, fake, copy
116 child, minor
117 children
118 wife, spouse
119 husband, spouse
120 mother and father, *parents

88
color, colorful, crayons

Yes, the big bird is colorful.
bird large color, yes

89
pink

Their house is not pink.
house their, pink not

90
black

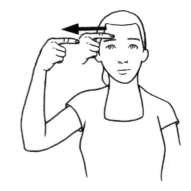

We like our coffee black.
coffee black, we like

91
brown

Their dog is black and brown.
dog their, black brown

92
tan

The girl wants a nice tan.
girl tan nice want

93
red

The red bird is asleep.
bird red sleep

94
white

Your white house is huge.
house white your large

Deaf Culture Facts and Information

When *Deaf* is capitalized, it refers to Deaf individuals who are members of the Deaf community and use American Sign Language as their preferred means of communication. When not capitalized, *deaf* refers to individuals who have a severe to profound hearing loss.

95
yellow

They don't want yellow tea.
tea yellow they don't-want

96
purple

The purple house is near us.
house purple near us

97
blue

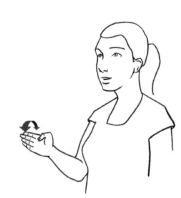

Look at the blue bird in the tree.
bird blue tree there look-at

98
green

Green tea is good for you.
tea green for you, good

99
orange (color and fruit)

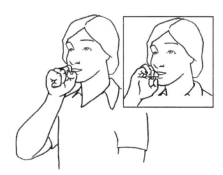

Yes, I like the color orange.
orange color, me like, yes

100
silver, shiny, sharp, bright

We cleaned the house so it shines.
we clean-up, now house shine

101
gold

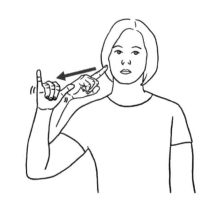

Gold is a nice color.
gold color, nice

102

person, *individual, figure, human

That person works every day.
daily person there work

103

people, citizens

Those people don't want coffee.
people those coffee don't want

104

sister

My sister went into the house.
sister my, house into

105

brother

Your brother likes my brown dog.
brother your, dog my brown, he like

106

aunt

I think your aunt is sleeping.
now aunt your sleep, me think

107

uncle

Get tea for your uncle.
tea for uncle your obtain

108
grandmother, grandma

Grandmother works near her son.
grandmother near son hers, work

109
grandfather, grandpa, granddad

Grandfather wants you to see him.
grandfather want you see him go

110
cousin

Your cousin doesn't want coffee.
cousin your, coffee don't-want

111
baby, infant

The baby slept all night.
all-night baby sleep

ASL Grammar Notes

Facial expressions and body movements are extremely important in communicating with Deaf people. ASL uses the shape, orientation, position, and movements of the hands, as well as subtle uses of facial expressions and head and body movements. In differing combinations, these make possible a considerable number of linguistic expressions.

112
father, dad, pop

Father likes the big brown house.
house large brown, father like

113

mother, mom

Your mother likes college.
mother your, college like

114

step (mother, father), next, turn, your turn, go ahead

My stepfather drinks white tea.
next father my, tea white (he) drink

115

foster (mother, father), false, fake, copy

Our foster mother is not bad.
foster mother our, bad not

116

child, minor

The child drinks Pepsi all day.
all-day child pepsi drink

117

children

The children want vanilla Coke.
children coke vanilla want

118

wife, spouse

My wife thinks it's time to go.
wife my think time go now

119
husband, spouse

Her husband works in that school.
husband hers, school there work

120
mother and father, *parents

Your parents like evenings.
evening, mother father your like

Mind Ticklers

Make the sign _____	and think about . . .
color, colorful, crayon	a child putting crayons in his mouth
pink	your lips being pink
black	eyebrows being black
brown	faces being brown
tan	faces being tan
red	lipstick making the lips red
white	wearing a white shirt
yellow, purple, blue, green	shaking the first letter of each color
orange	squeezing an orange at your mouth
silver, shiny, sharp	silver being shiny
gold	pointing to a gold earring and making a Y for *yellow*
person, individual, figure, human	outlining the shape of a person
people, citizens	signing **person** several times
sister	girls in the same family
brother	boys in the same family
aunt	an A handshape in the female position
uncle	a U handshape in the male position
grandmother, grandma	a mother in the past
grandfather, grandpa, granddad	a father in the past
cousin	a C handshape in the neutral position
baby, infant	rocking a baby in your arms
father, dad, pop	the male position at the top of the head
mother, mom	the female position at the bottom of the head
step (mother, father) next, turn	a second mother, father, brother, etc.
foster (mother, father), false, fake	not a biological mother or father
child	the height of a child
children	the height of several children
wife	a girl who is married
husband	a boy who is married
mother and father, parents	signing both **mother** and **father**

Practice Sentences

1. I like the color of your house.

   house your, color me like

2. My little sister likes the color pink.

   pink color sister my short like

3. Grandma and Grandpa don't want your black dog in the house.

   dog black your, grandma grandpa in house don't-want

4. Our cousin saw the black and brown cat this morning.

   now morning cat black brown, cousin our see

5. Our uncle's tan colored dog is not big.

   dog color tan our uncle his, huge not

6. The entrance to his sister's house is red and black.

   house entrance boy sister hers, red black

7. My aunt's yellow cat likes sitting in trees.

   cat yellow, my aunt hers, in tree sit like

8. My parents don't want to drink purple tea this morning.

   now morning parent my, tea purple drink don't-want

9. Yes, her stepmother likes the colors blue, pink, and red.

   next mother girl her color blue pink red like, yes

10. The people think the small green tree is in our house.

    tree short green in our house people think

11. Mom and Dad don't like eating oranges without water.

    orange without water mom dad eat don't-like

12. His wife and brother are coming with nice people.

    wife, brother, boy his with nice people come

13. My foster mother cleaned up her house.

    foster mother my house hers clean-up

14. Dad's aunt and uncle don't want the bad green tea.

    tea green bad, aunt uncle dad his, don't-want

15. Her stepfather drinks Coca Cola all day every day.

    daily, all-day next father girl hers coke drink

Class Activities

1. In small groups, students take turns signing a sentence they wrote for student activity 1 in Lesson 3. The other students in the group say what is being signed.

2. Divide students into groups of five, with four students facing the chalkboard and one with her back to the chalkboard. The instructor writes a sentence on the chalkboard for the four students to act out using gestures or pantomime until the lone student guesses the complete sentence. Rotate students after each sentence. **Do not use signs.** Here are some examples: The fat little boy is pulling the red wagon. My grandmother really enjoys smoking long cigars. The little girl and boy sat in the tree hiding from mother.

Student Activities

1. Write a gloss for the following descriptions:

   a. a child putting crayons in his mouth

   _____

   b. a girl who is married

   _____

   c. tapping your watch

   _____

   d. pushing away negative feelings

   _____

   e. people sitting around a table

   _____

   f. an open hand means possessive

   _____

   g. repeating the sign for *tomorrow*

   _____

   h. the opposite of *on*

   _____

2. Write the glosses for the colors that are initialized.

   _____

   _____

3. Write the glosses for the colors that are not initialized.

   _____

   _____

4. What is the difference in placement of male signs and female signs?

   _____

   _____

5. How would you sign *cousin Mary* and *cousin Joe*?

   _____

   _____

6. Write the number of immediate and extended family members you have (for example, *four uncles*).

   _____

   _____

   _____

   _____

Lesson 5

Vocabulary

121
daughter

Yes, their daughters are good.
daughter+ their good, yes

122
son

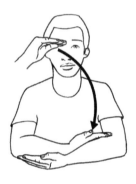

Our son is playing in the tree.
son our tree there play++

123
roommate

My sister's roommate slept overnight.
all-night roommate my sister hers sleep

124
share, divide up, partner

Dad doesn't like his partner.
partner father his (he) don't-like

125
single, *bachelor, *twins

My aunt doesn't like being single.
aunt my, single don't-like

126
deaf

Our deaf daughter is coming later.
later daughter deaf our come

127
hard of hearing

That hard of hearing person likes soda.
person there hard-of-hearing, soda like

128
American Sign Language, ASL

My roommate is in an ASL class.
now roommate my, class ASL there

129
senior citizen

My uncle is a senior citizen.
uncle my, senior citizen

130
friend, close

It is time for your friend to work.
now time friend your work

Deaf Culture Facts and Information

Approximately 7 percent of all deaf children have two deaf parents and approximately 3 percent have one deaf parent. In other words, 90% of deaf children have hearing parents.

131
kid

That kid is my little brother.
kid there short brother my

132
strange, strang<u>er</u> odd, peculiar, queer

That stranger is from my class.
stranger there from class my

133
boss, captain, coach, head, officer, employer

Her boss is coming at noon.
noon boss girl (there) hers come

134
nephew

Their nephew is my brother.
nephew their (he) brother my

135
niece

My niece didn't want to go with us.
niece my with us go don't-want

136
police, officer, policeman, cop, security, sheriff, *detective, guard

The police came with father.
police with father come

137
sweetheart, darling, girlfriend, boyfriend

My sweetheart likes gold.
sweetheart my, gold like

138
secretary, pencil

I think your secretary is sleeping.
secretary your sleep, me think

139
two of us, we

The two of us are fond of your grandfather.
grandfather your, two-of-us like

140
marry, wed, wedding, marriage

My aunt married your uncle.
aunt my, uncle your marry

141
divorce

Mother doesn't want a divorce.
mother, divorce don't-want

142
separate, apart, split up

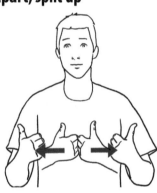

My husband and I are separated.
husband my, me, separate

143
man, male, guy, gentleman

That man is my father.
man there, father my

144
woman, female, lady

That woman is my mom.
woman there, mother my

ASL Grammar Notes

Questions requiring a yes or no response must include one of the following nonmanual signals: raising the eyebrows, widening the eyes, tilting the head and body forward, and /or raising the shoulders. Sometimes yes-no questions begin with a simple question mark directed at the person being questioned. For example,

ME-ASK-TO-YOU (simple question mark) MOTHER COME LATER
(ASL)

I have a question for you—is our mother coming later?
(English)

145
doctor, physician

Today the doctor came to see the infant.
today doctor come baby see

146
nurse

I hear the nurse coming now.
now nurse come me hear

147
fireman, firefighter

The fireman married his hard of hearing sweetheart.
fireman sweetheart hard-of-hearing his, he marry

148
social work, social work<u>er</u>

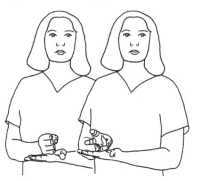

The social worker works with my husband.
social work<u>er</u> work with husband my

149
teach, taught, *educate, *instruct, *tutor, *education, teach<u>er</u>, profess<u>or</u>, *instruct<u>or</u>

My sister teaches in college.
sister my, college teach

150
judge, justice, jud<u>ge</u>, court

Grandfather likes judging us.
grandfather judge us like

Mind Ticklers

Make the sign _____	and think about . . .
daughter	a girl baby
son	a boy baby
roommate	two people coming together
share, divide up, partner	partners sharing everything
single, *bachelor, *twins	a person being alone
deaf	not hearing or speaking
hard of hearing	H–H handshape
ASL, American Sign Language	abbreviating American Sign Language
senior citizen	a person being alone
friend, close	two people linked together
kid	a child wiping his nose
strange, odd, stranger	seeing something twisted
boss, captain, coach, head, employer	the boss wearing epaulets
nephew	an N in the male position
niece	an N in the female position
police, policeman, cop, officer, security, sheriff	the badge a law officer wears
sweetheart	sweethearts whispering to one another
secretary, pencil	taking a pencil from your ear and writing
two of us, we	two fingers representing two people
marry, wed, wedding	coming together as one
divorce	two people going separate ways
separate, apart	pulling two things apart
man, male, guy	a man who is polite
woman, female, lady	a woman who is polite
doctor, physician	the doctor taking your pulse
nurse	the nurse taking your pulse
fireman, firefighter	the emblem on the fireman's hat
social work. social worker	social work is a helping profession
teach, instruct, teac<u>her</u>, profess<u>or</u>, instruct<u>or</u>	giving knowledge to someone
judge, justice, judge(er), court	the scales of justice

Practice Sentences

1. The doctor's son is a fireman and his daughter is a social worker.

   doctor son his fireman, daughter his social-worker

2. My roommate wants to marry her stepbrother.

   roommate my, next brother hers, (she) marry want

3. The deaf and hard of hearing people like playing with the children.

   children, deaf hard-of-hearing people play with like

4. My aunt and uncle are separated now.

   now aunt uncle my separate

5. The male nurse married my father's secretary.

   nurse man, secretary my father his, marry

6. The senior citizens went to see the police this morning.

   now morning senior citizen police go see

7. My nephew taught the big brown dog to sit.

   dog huge brown, nephew my teach sit

8. His bachelor brother drinks all day every day.

   daily all-day, brother his, bachelor drink++

9. The judge married the man and woman in his house.

   judge, man woman marry, judge house his

10. We don't like our friend's sweetheart.

    sweetheart our friend his, we don't-like

11. The two of us like the colors green and white on our house.

    color green white on house our, two-of-us like

12. The deaf people looked at the strange hearing person.

    hearing person strange, deaf people look-at

13. Dad's partner is not working today or tomorrow.

    today tomorrow, partner dad his work not

14. The coach's son doesn't want to go get sodas.

    soda son coach his get, don't-want

15. They think your niece's boy friend is nice.

    boy friend niece your, nice they think

Class Activities

1. In small groups, take turns telling each other about the immediate and extended family you wrote about in Lesson 4, number 6. For example, FAMILY MY, BROTHER FOUR, SISTER ONE, GRANDPARENT THREE.

2. Find a partner and interview him, asking general questions such as his name, where he's from, about his family, why he's taking ASL, if he has any deaf friends or family members, what activities he enjoys, etc. Write down his answers and then introduce your partner to the class using that information.

Student Activities

1. Write a paragraph (4 to 5 sentences) using the vocabulary for people in Lessons 4 and 5. Then rewrite the paragraph using ASL sentences.

_____

_____

_____

_____

_____

_____

_____

_____

_____

_____

_____

_____

_____

2. The -*er* or -*ist* agent sign was introduced in signs 132, 148, and 149. Compare the vocabulary that does not use the -*er* sign (DOCTOR, NURSE, and DAUGHTER) with vocabulary that does use the -*er* sign (e.g., TEACHER, STRANGER, and EATER) and write a general rule for use of the -*er* or -*ist sign*. Hint: STUDENT is an exception to your rule.

_____

_____

_____

_____

_____

Lesson 6

Vocabulary

151 warm, balmy
152 hot, stifling, muggy
153 cold, chilly, shiver
154 cold, virus, bug, head cold
155 stuck up, cold, snooty, aloof, sophisticated
156 help, assist, aid, give a hand
157 plenty, enough, sufficient, adequate
158 understand, get it, comprehend, see
159 have, has, had, possess, own
160 right, all right, privilege
161 right, correct, proper, appropriate, accurate
162 right, to the right, right side
163 happy, glad, joyful, cheerful
164 here, present
165 left, to the left, left side
166 left, abandon, leave behind, leave, rest, remain, drop off, leftovers
167 leave, depart, go, left
168 mistake, wrong, error
169 car, automobile
170 garage
171 drive, drove, steer
172 trailer, manufactured home
173 motorcycle, bike
174 train, railroad track, locomotive
175 subway
176 helicopter
177 airplane, plane, flight, air force, pilot
178 fly, take off, soar
179 fly, wing, flutter

151
warm, balmy

We like it warm every day.
daily warm, we like

152
hot, stifling, muggy

It is hot in the evening.
now evening hot

153
cold, chilly, shiver

Grandmother likes cold days.
day chilly, grandmother like

154

cold, virus, bug, head cold

My sweetheart's cold is bad.
sweetheart my, virus her bad

155

stuck up, cold, snooty, aloof, sophisticated

They think your aunt is stuck up.
aunt your, they think stuck-up

156

help, assist, aid, give a hand

It is time for me to help the bachelor.
now time bachelor me help

157

plenty, enough, sufficient, adequate

I think we saw enough.
we see enough, me think

158

understand, get it, comprehend, see

The twin understands her doctor.
twin, doctor hers, she understand

159

have, has, had, possess, own

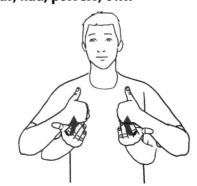

The woman and man have colds.
woman man, virus have

160
right, all right, privilege

You have the right to marry the nurse.
nurse you marry privilege have

Deaf Culture Facts and Information

A hearing child who has deaf parents is called a *coda* (child of a deaf adult). A coda can become a member of CODA, Inc. or a member of a state chapter.

161
right, correct, proper, appropriate, accurate

The fireman has the right time.
fireman correct time have

162
right, to the right, right side

The boss is sitting on the right.
now boss right-side sit

163
happy, glad, joyful, cheerful

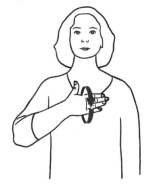

The deaf man is happy now.
now man deaf, happy

164
here, present

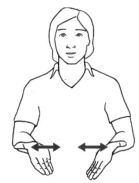

The doctor wants to sit here.
doctor want here sit

165

left, to the left, left side

The entrance is on your left.

entrance, your left-side

166

left, abandon, leave behind, leave, rest, remain, drop off, leftovers

My secretary left her coffee here.

secretary my, coffee hers here abandon

167

leave, depart, go, left

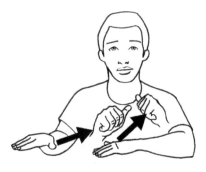

My roommate left this morning.

now morning, roommate my depart

168

mistake, wrong, error

Now he understands his mistake.

now man, mistake his, understand

ASL Grammar Notes

The nonmanual signal used with questions that require more than a yes or no response is squinting the eyes and lowering the eyebrows.

169

car, automobile

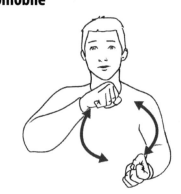

My doctor has a nice car.

doctor my, car his nice

170
garage

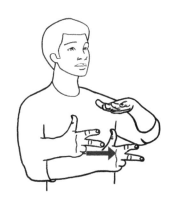

My roommate's car is in the garage.
roommate my, car hers there garage

171
drive, drove, steer

I'm happy I'm not driving today.
happy me, today me drive not

172
trailer, manufactured home

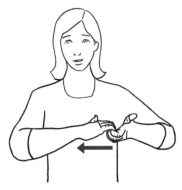

The policeman's trailer is red.
trailer police his red

173
motorcycle, bike

The teacher goes to school on a motorcycle.
teacher school motorcycle go

174
train, railroad track, locomotive

My house is near railroad tracks.
house my near train

175
subway

His sweetheart doesn't like the subway.
sweetheart his, subway don't-like

176
helicopter

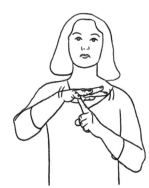

The helicopter is in the garage.
now helicopter there garage

177

airplane, plane, flight, air force, pil<u>ot</u>

The bachelor's flight is arriving now.
now airplane bachelor his arrive

178
fly, take off, soar

The airplane my foster mom was on took off on time.
**airplane, foster mother my there, right time
    fly-soar**

179
fly, wing, flutter

A red bird flew into the tall tree.
bird red tree tall there flutter

Mind Ticklers

Make the sign _____	and think about . . .
warm, balmy	warm air coming from your mouth
hot, stifling, muggy	taking something hot from your mouth
cold, shiver, chilly	the body shaking
cold, virus, bug	wiping your nose with a tissue
stuck up, cold, snooty	having one's nose in the air
help, assist, aid, give a hand	giving a helping hand
plenty, enough, sufficient, adequate	pushing away any more
understand, get it, comprehend, see	a lightbulb flicking on in your head
have, has, had, possess, own	pulling something owned to your body
right, all right, privilege	not stopping, but moving ahead
right, correct, proper, appropriate	emphasizing that something is correct
right, to the right, right side	the R handshape moving to the right
happy, glad, joyful, cheerful	your heart fluttering with happiness
here, present	indicating something is in front of you
left, to the left, left side	the L handshape moving to the left
left, abandon, leave behind, leave rest, remain	emptying the hands of what they held
leave, depart, go	going from one place to another
mistake, wrong, error	the mouth closing after a mistake
car, automobile	turning the steering wheel
garage	a vehicle going into a garage
drive, drove, steer	both hands on a steering wheel
trailer, manufactured home	the coupling on a trailer and car
motorcycle, bike	holding onto handlebars
train, railroad tracks	trains running on tracks
subway	a vehicle under ground
helicopter	the propellers on top of a helicopter
airplane, plane, flight, air force	the wings of a plane
fly, take off, soar	a plane flying through the air
fly, wing, flutter	a bird flapping its wings

Practice Sentences

1. My grandfather thinks that woman is stuck-up.

   woman there grandfather my think (she) stuck-up

2. Grandmother left this morning in a white and red car.

   now morning in car red white grandmother depart

3. My roommate goes to work on the subway every day.

   daily roommate my subway go work

4. That guy on the motorcycle lives in a silver trailer.

   man there on motorcycle in silver trailer live

5. The airplane took off at the wrong time.

   airplane time wrong fly-soar

6. The red bird flew to the tree on the right.

   bird red to tree right flutter

7. It's hot. It is a mistake to leave now.

   now hot, depart now mistake

8. My son left his purple motorcycle on the train.

   son my, motorcycle purple his, on train abandon

9. The married man was right; the plane took off on time with his wife.

   man married correct, airplane with wife correct time fly-soar

10. The boss heard that you came to work in a helicopter.

    you in helicopter come work, boss hear

11. Her sweetheart is cold. He has a bad cold.

    sweetheart girl hers himself cold, virus bad he have

12. There are plenty of people here happy to drive.

    here, plenty people happy drive

13. Go to the left and our mother is sitting there to the right.

    to-the-left you go, mother our to-the-right sit

14. People think that driving is a privilege.

    drive privilege, people think

15. The blue and white cars are now in the garage.

    now car+ blue white, in garage

Class Activities

1. In small groups, sign the paragraph you wrote in Lesson 5, activity 2. The other students in the group voice what is being signed.

2. In small groups, take turns fingerspelling modes of transportation starting with A and going through the alphabet.

Student Activities

1. Write an ASL sentence using the ASL equivalent used in this book for the conceptual sign/word underlined below.

   a. Mom has a bad cold.

   _____

   _____

   b. Grandma is cold.

   _____

   _____

   c. She is a very cold person.

   _____

   _____

d. Dad has the <u>right</u> to leave.

_____

_____

e. When you leave, go <u>right</u>.

_____

_____

f. The judge is always <u>right</u>.

_____

_____

g. That boy is <u>little</u>.

_____

_____

h. The fish is <u>little</u>.

_____

_____

i. <u>Get</u> me some food.

_____

_____

j. Grandpa doesn't <u>get</u> it.

_____

_____

k. Mom is glad the bird can <u>fly</u>.

_____

_____

l. My daughter is <u>flying</u> home.

_____

_____

2. Write the glosses for the signs that are iconic in Lesson 6.

_____

_____

_____

_____

_____

_____

Lesson 7

Vocabulary

180 truck, bus
181 traffic
182 gasoline, gas
183 will, *future
184 can, able, could
185 cannot, can't, unable
186 possible, can
187 impossible, not possible
188 maybe, perhaps, may, might, probably
189 do, doing, did, action, act, activity, *behave, *behavior
190 don't, doesn't, didn't, won't, isn't, not
191 sentence, *language, *captions
192 story, tale, mention, message
193 closed captions
194 say, said
195 move, relocate, shift, motion
196 put, place, lay
197 give, donate, hand, offer, grant, award, contribute
198 read, go through
199 who?, whose?, whom
200 when?
201 why?
202 how?
203 which?
204 where?
205 how much?, how many?
206 what?, pardon me?, come again?
207 what, itemize, what?

180
truck, bus

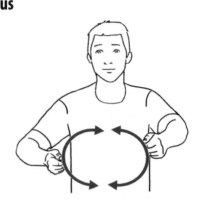

The driver left his truck in the garage.
driver truck his abandon there garage

181
traffic

Every day the traffic is bad.
daily, traffic bad

182
gasoline, gas

We got the gasoline ourselves.
gasoline we ourselves obtain

183
will, *future

Mom thinks the man will come later.
later man come, mother think will

184
can, able, could

The nurse can sleep now.
now nurse sleep can

185
cannot, can't, unable

My foster father cannot understand you.
foster father my, understand you cannot

186
possible, can

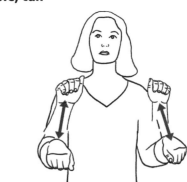

Yes, it is possible to leave now.
now possible depart, yes

187
impossible, not possible

It is impossible to leave on time.
correct time depart, impossible

188
maybe, perhaps, may, might, probably

Maybe the doctor and nurse will marry.
doctor, nurse marry, maybe will

189

do, doing, did, action, act, activity, *behave, *behavior

The two of us will do that tonight.
tonight, two-of-us do that, will

Deaf Culture Facts and Information

Members of Deaf communities around the world typically communicate using sign language. However, there is no universal sign language. France has French Sign Language, Germany has German Sign Language, and so on. Each has its own distinct grammar and vocabulary, making them mutually unintelligible. However, Deaf people from different countries are often able to communicate with one another on a superficial level using gestures.

190

don't, doesn't, didn't, won't, isn't, not

The firemen don't eat cold food.
fireman they, food cold eat, don't

191

sentence, *language, *captions

Her deaf daughter has good language.
deaf daughter, woman hers, language good

192

story, tale, mention, message

They like hearing happy stories.
story happy, they like hear

193

closed captions

The two of us watch TV with closed captions.
two-of-us, look-at C-C T-V

194
say, said

The pilot said it is time to leave.
now time depart, pi<u>lo</u>t say

195
move, relocate, shift, motion

Perhaps you can move your truck later.
later truck your, maybe move

196
put, place, lay

Put the gasoline near the house.
gasoline, near house (you) put

197
give, donate, hand, offer, grant, award, contribute

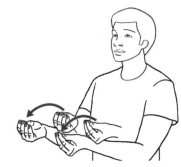

Give the cat a drink.
cat drink (you) give

ASL Grammar Notes

There are two signs for *what*. The sign most commonly used by ASL signers can mean *what, where, who, why,* and *when* (see 206). The other WHAT sign (see 207) is reserved for formal contexts. For purposes of clarity for beginning ASL signers, I have used the latter WHAT for nonquestioning forms and used the gloss ITEMIZE.

198
read, go through

The bachelor reads on the train in the morning.
train morning, bachelor read there

199
who?, whose?, whom

Who is your sweetheart now?
now sweetheart your who?

200
when?

When will the stranger come?
stranger come when?

201
why?

Why do you think that is impossible?
you think impossible why?

202
how?

How are your uncle and aunt going?
uncle aunt your go how?

203
which?

Which girl is your sister?
sister your which?

204
where?

Where did you put my motorcycle?
motorcycle my, (you) put where?

205

how much?, how many?

How much time is left?
time abandon how-much

206

what?, pardon me?, come again?

What time will the bus leave?
bus depart time what?

207

what, itemize, what?

What the man said is right.
itemize man say correct

Mind Ticklers

Make the sign _____   **and think about . . .**

Make the sign	and think about . . .
truck, bus	turning a large steering wheel
traffic	traffic going in both directions
gasoline, gas	putting gas into your tank
will, future	looking ahead to the future
can, able, could	both hands indicating a sure yes
cannot, can't, unable	the index finger unable to move
can, possible	both hands repeating **yes**
impossible, not possible	signing **that** several times with a head shake
maybe, perhaps, may, might, probably	weighing an action before doing it
do, doing, action, act, activity, behave	the hands doing something
don't, doesn't, didn't, won't, isn't	waving off everything and everybody
sentence, language, captions	stringing words together
story, tale, mention	stringing sentences together
closed captions	the CC symbol seen on television
say, said	pointing to your lower lip
move, relocate, shift	going from one place to another
put, place, lay	putting something down
give, donate, offer, grant	handing something to a person
read, go through	your eyes looking at a page
who?, whose?	circling pursed lips
when?	a point in time when something happens
why?	wanting to know
how?	opening your hands as if you are perplexed
which?	weighing two choices
where?	wanting to put your finger on where something is
how much?, how many?	throwing up your fingers to count "how many?"
what? pardon me? come again?	throwing up your hands to ask what's going on
what, itemize, what?	listing on the fingers what you want

Practice Sentences

1. Why does your brother have three red cars?

   brother your car three red have, why?

2. Which sentence do you think is wrong?

   sentence wrong, you think which?

3. Who put gasoline in the big tan truck?

   truck tan huge gas who?

4. Are you able to read that story now or later?

   you story read can now, later, which?

5. Who cannot understand why the boy left his house?

   house boy his depart why, understand cannot who?

6. Deaf people like it when stories have captions.

   story caption have, deaf people like

7. When do you think the plane takes off?

   fly-soar think you when?

8. Why do you think that is impossible to do?

   do that impossible, you think why?

9. How do you know that story has closed captions?

   story C-C have, you know how?

10. Where do you think the doctor put his airplane?

    airplane doctor his, you think (he) put where?

11. How much sleep did you get in the truck?

    you in truck sleep how-much?

12. What did you give your nephew tonight?

    now-night nephew your, you give what?

13. The fireman gave it to me, and I don't know what to do now.

    fireman give-me, now itemize me do, don't-know

14. It is impossible for me to understand that sentence.

    sentence that me understand impossible

15. When will you get gas for the blue car?

    gas for car blue, you obtain when?

Class Activities

1. With a partner, go over the ASL sentences you wrote using the conceptual sign/words in the Lesson 6 student activities. Take turns signing sentences to one another.

2. On a sheet of paper, write down an activity (flipping through the channels while watching television, driving a car on a curvy, bumpy road). In small groups, exchange papers and then act out the activity for the other students in the group to identify.

Student Activities

1. List the *wh-* words in this lesson.

   _____

   _____

2. What nonmanual signals should accompany the use of *wh-* words?

   _____

   _____

3. Write at least two synonyms for the following:

a. what?

_____

b. maybe

_____

c. house

_____

d. grandpa

_____

e. person

_____

f. strange

_____

g. teach

_____

h. boss

_____

4. Explain the differences between the two WHAT signs presented in this lesson.

_____

_____

_____

_____

_____

Lesson 8

Vocabulary

208 Monday
209 Tuesday
210 Wednesday
211 Thursday
212 Friday
213 Saturday
214 Sunday
215 long, long-time
216 past, before, ago, used to, ever, last
217 year
218 last year
219 next year
220 every year, yearly, annual, annually
221 month
222 calendar
223 last month
224 monthly
225 week
226 weekly, every week
227 next week
228 last week
229 yesterday
230 tomorrow
231 agree, think the same
232 look at me, watch me
233 please, like, appreciate
234 thank you, thanks, thank, you're welcome
235 hour
236 second
237 minute, in a minute, in a second, wait a minute

**208
Monday**

Monday morning they go to college.
morning Monday, they college go

**209
Tuesday**

Monday and Tuesday are good days for me.
Monday Tuesday for me good

**210
Wednesday**

It is impossible for me to sleep on Wednesday.
Wednesday, sleep me, impossible

211
Thursday

Grandmother sees the doctor on Thursday.
Thursday grandmother doctor there go

Deaf Culture Facts and Information

Many deaf individuals are exposed to Deaf culture at residential schools for the deaf, sporting events, or Deaf social clubs. All of these environments unite deaf people into communities of shared language and experience.

212
Friday

I have classes on Wednesday and Friday.
Wednesday Friday me class+ have

213
Saturday

This Saturday will be cold.
now Saturday, cold will

214
Sunday

Sunday the family eats at my house.
Sunday, house my, family (come) eat

215
long, long-time

How long will you see your grandfather?
grandfather your, you see how long-time will?

216
past, before, ago, used to, ever, last

This past Friday we saw our cousin.
ago Friday cousin our, we see

217
year

Father may fly to see you this year.
now year father soar see you maybe

218
last year

We did a big job last year.
last-year work huge we do

219
next year

Where will you go next year?
next-year you go where?

220
every year, yearly, annual, annually

Every year Mom gets a big car.
every-year mother car large obtain

221
month

Dad will help the school this month.
now month, father school help will

222
calendar

We got a calendar for next year.
calendar for next-year we obtain

223
last month

Whom did you see last month?
last-month you see who?

224
monthly

Can you go eat with us monthly?
monthly you with us eat can?

225
week

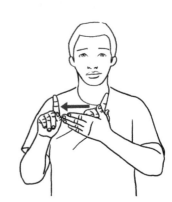

This week the cat and dog are here.
now week, cat dog here

226
weekly, every week

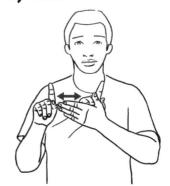

The fireman teaches a class weekly.
weekly, fireman class teach

227
next week

You think we are moving next week?
next-week we move think you?

228
last week

Was the traffic bad last week?
last-week traffic bad?

ASL Grammar Notes

Name signs are given to Deaf people and hearing people who interact with Deaf people on a regular basis. Name signs can be based on a physical characteristic, a particular interest, or a vocation; or they can be arbitrary.

229
yesterday

Yes, you're right, yesterday was Monday.
yesterday Monday, you correct, yes

230
tomorrow

Can you come over tomorrow?
tomorrow, you come can?

231
agree, think the same

The family cannot agree on a time.
family agree time, cannot

232
look at me, watch me

Why are you looking at me?
you look-at-me, why?

233
please, like, appreciate

Please come to see me on Saturday.
Saturday you come see me please

234
thank you, thanks, thank, you're welcome

Which man did you thank?
man you thank, which?

235
hour

Can you see me for two hours today?
today, you see me, two-hour possible?

236
second

The bus leaves here in 45 seconds.
45 second bus here depart

237
minute, in a minute, in a second, wait a minute

Mom saw Dad for a minute yesterday.
yesterday, mother see father minute

Mind Ticklers

Make the sign _____	and think about . . .
Monday, Tuesday, Wednesday, Thursday, Friday, Saturday	signing the first letter of each day
Sunday	Sunday being a wonderful day
long, long-time	measuring the length of time on your arm
past, before, ago, used to, ever, last	motioning to a time in the past
year	the earth going around the sun
last year	a year in the past
next year	a year in the future
every year, yearly, annually	signing **next-year** several times
month	all the days on a calendar
calendar	flipping the pages of a calendar
last month	a month in the past
monthly	signing **month** several times
week	the days across the calendar
weekly, every week	signing **week** several times
next week	a week in the future
last week	a week in the past
yesterday	a day in the past
tomorrow	a day in the future
agree, think the same	two people thinking the same thing
look at me, watch me	another person's eyes watching you
please	circling the heart to show a need
thank you, thanks, thank, you're welcome	putting your hand out to someone
hour	the minute hand going around a clock
second	the second hand on a clock moving
minute, in a minute, in a second, wait a minute	the minute hand on a clock moving

Practice Sentences

1. His family cannot go next week on Monday.

   next-week Monday family his go cannot

2. Whose niece goes to school on Tuesday and Thursday?

   Tuesday Thursday niece who school go?

3. My sister agrees that next week on Wednesday it will be cold.

   next week Wednesday sister my agree cold will

4. Please look at me for five seconds.

   for five-second, look-at-me please

5. Friday is a good day for us to leave.

   Friday for us good day depart

6. Thanks for coming today; I am happy that you are here.

   today you come thank-you, me happy you here

7. Last year Mom worked 47 weeks with Dad.

   last-year mom with dad 47 week work

8. Last month had five Sundays; that is strange.

   last-month five Sunday have, that strange

9. Is it possible for me to leave next week?

   next-week possible me depart?

10. Why can't you sleep here with me tomorrow?

    tomorrow you here sleep with me cannot why?

11. The nurse left her job three months ago.

    three-month ago nurse job her depart

12. In the past, people worked on Saturday and Sunday.

    ago Saturday Sunday people work

13. How do you know which week Dad is leaving?

    which week dad depart, you know how?

14. Yesterday, Monday, Dad said that we will move.

    yesterday Monday dad say we move will

15. Do we agree that Sunday is the day to leave?

    Sunday, we depart, we agree correct?

Class Activity

1. In small groups, go over the student activities in Lesson 7.

Student Activities

1. As a review, fill in the blanks for the topic-comment format shown below (topic-comment is explained in the Introduction).

   English   The black dog is big.

topic	comment

   ASL   _____   _____

   English   I see the big black dog.

topic	comment	action

   ASL   _____   _____   _____

   English   I saw the big black dog yesterday.

time indicator	topic	comment	action

   ASL   _____   _____   _____   _____

   English   I didn't see the big black dog yesterday.

time indicator	topic	comment	action	negation

   ASL   _____   _____   _____   _____   _____

   English   Why didn't you see the big black dog yesterday?

time indicator	topic	comment	action	negation	interrogative

   ASL   _____   _____   _____   _____   _____   _____

2. Rewrite the paragraph below into ASL sentences. Use the format above as an aid.

   Yesterday the family agreed to take a summer vacation. Last year and the year before last we didn't go anywhere. No one wanted to be in our big house all year. Dad is a doctor and Mom is a nurse, so time off is possible for them. When we go, I think we will drive as Mom doesn't like flying. We will leave on Friday and return one week later on Saturday or Sunday.

   _____

   _____

   _____

   _____

   _____

Lesson 9

Vocabulary

238 while, during
239 former, previous, old, once upon a time
240 first week (of the month)
241 second week (of the month)
242 third week (of the month)
243 fourth week (of the month)
244 every now and then, periodically
245 since, up to now, has been, all along, ever since
246 late, not yet, have not, yet
247 guess, assume, estimate
248 hide, hid, conceal
249 find, discover, locate, find out
250 learn, student
251 keep, save, store
252 continue, last, keep, permanent, maintain
253 still, on going
254 sometimes, once in a while, occasionally
255 once, one time
256 some, *part, *piece, section, portion
257 cut, scissors, cut out
258 fire, cut, expel, terminate
259 cut, wound, scratch
260 cut, miss, absent, gone, skip, not attend
261 gone, missing, disappeared, not here
262 break, intermission, halftime
263 send, mail, *refer
264 paper, tissue
265 file, folder
266 write, *note, writer
267 pen

238
while, during

Don't drive while eating.
drive while eat, don't

239
former, previous, old, once upon a time

My former boss didn't like men.
boss my former, men, she don't-like

240
first week (of the month)

The first week of the month I'm moving.
first-week-of-the-month, me move

241

second week (of the month)

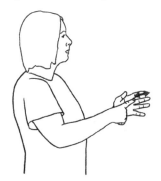

The second week of August I'm leaving.
A-U-G-U-S-T, second-week, me depart

242

third week (of the month)

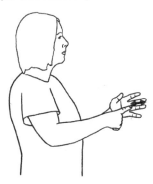

Eat with me the third week of June.
J-U-N-E third-week you with me eat

243

fourth week (of the month)

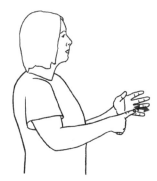

My bike arrives the fourth week of May.
M-A-Y fourth-week motorcycle my arrive will

244

every now and then, periodically

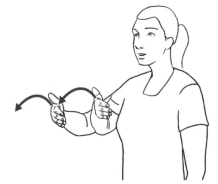

Every now and then my aunt comes over.
every-now-and-then aunt my come

245

since, up to now, has been, all along, ever since

Dad has been here for three months.
three-month father since here

246

late, not yet, have not, yet

I have not seen my sister tonight.
now night sister my, (me) see, not-yet

247
guess, assume, estimate

I guess I can go next week.
next-week me go, guess can

Deaf Culture Facts and Information

The leading advocate for deaf people in the United States is the National Association of the Deaf (NAD), which has chapters in almost every state.

248
hide, hid, conceal

Who hid my little green car?
car my tiny green, hide who?

249
find, discover, locate, find out

It is impossible to find your brother.
brother your find, impossible

250
learn, student

Where did you learn to do that?
you learn do that where?

251
keep, save, store

I want to save the leftovers for tomorrow.
for tomorrow abandon me want keep

252
continue, last, keep, permanent, maintain

My secretary continued to help all day.
all-day secretary my continue help

253
still, on going

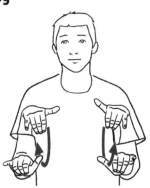

Are you still with your boyfriend?
sweetheart your with on-going?

254
sometimes, once in a while, occasionally

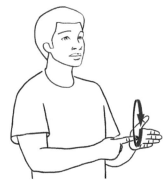

Sometimes I don't like Mondays.
sometime Monday me don't-like

255
once, one time

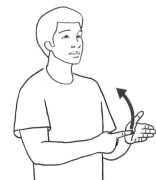

The doctor sees children once a week.
weekly, children, doctor see once

256
some, *part, *piece, section, portion

I guess some people are not coming.
guess me, people some come, not

257
cut, scissors, cut out

The teacher hid the students' scissors.
scissor, student their, teacher hide

258
fire, cut, expel, terminate

The policeman was fired last week.
last-week, policeman fired

259
cut, wound, scratch

Don't cut me with those scissors.
scissors (you) wound me, don't

260
cut, miss, absent, gone, skip, not attend

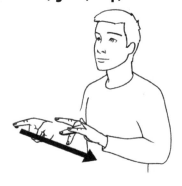

Who cut class last week?
last-week class skip who?

261
gone, missing, disappeared, not here

My car has been missing since Saturday.
since Saturday car my gone

ASL Grammar Notes

Prosody uses body movement, facial expressions, timing, pausing, and changes in the size and manner of articulation to add information not encoded in the grammar or choice of vocabulary. Prosody can indicate whether a sentence is a question, statement, or command; the emotional state of the signer; and whether the signer is expressing irony, sarcasm, or emphasis.

262
break, intermission, halftime

The green team was on break.
team green, intermission

263
send, mail, *refer

Send your sweetheart to my house.
sweetheart your here my house send

264
paper, tissue

Don't cut the paper right now.
now, paper scissors, don't

265
file, folder

My file is in your car.
file my in car your

266
write, *note, writer

Write to me some time next week.
next-week, you write me

267
pen

Who has my black and white pen?
pen my, black white, have who?

Mind Ticklers

Make the sign _____	and think of . . .
while, during	two events occurring simultaneously
former, previous, old, once upon a time	indicating an event in the past
first week, second week, third week, fourth week	pointing to one of the four weeks in a month
every now and then, periodically	moving into the future a little at a time
since, up to now, has been, all along, ever since	moving from a point in the past to the present
late, not yet, have not, yet	being behind in time
guess, assume, estimate	trying to grasp what is in your head
hide, conceal	putting something under cover
find, discover	pulling something out of a hiding place
learn, student	putting knowledge in your head from a book
save, keep, store,	keeping your eyes on something
continue, last, keep, permanent	moving steadily into the future
still, on going	continuing into the future
sometimes, once in a while, occasionally	something happening once in a cycle
once, one time	showing one finger for one time
some, part, piece, section, portion	cutting a section of something
cut, scissors, cut out	scissor blades opening and closing
fire, cut, expel, terminate	severing the hold a person has on something
cut, wound	cutting yourself with a knife
cut, miss, absent, gone, skip, not attend	missing one of the five days of school or work
gone, missing, disappeared	something dropping out of your view
break, intermission, halftime	the time between quarters of a game or show
send, refer	sending an item into the future
paper, tissue	paper running through a machine
file, folder	putting paper into a folder
write, note, writer	writing several sentences with a pen
pen	holding a pen while writing

Practice Sentences

1. The first week of May the boss fired three people.

   M-A-Y first-week three people boss terminate

2. Sometimes the man cuts class to write his father.

   sometimes man skip class why? write his father

3. During the third week of April, Grandpa will get an orange car.

   A-P-R-I-L third-week grandpa car orange obtain will

4. Dad and Mom have been married for twenty years.

   up-to-now dad mom 20 years, marry

5. I guess you have not sent what you found last week.

   last week what you find, me guess you late send

6. When did you cut yourself, yesterday?

   you cut yourself when? yesterday?

7. Your sister still thinks I am keeping her car.

   sister your, (she) still think car hers me keep

8. They assume the doctor will begin working the fourth week.

   doctor begin work fourth-week will, they guess

9. Your pen and my pencil are blue and green.

   pen your pencil my, blue green

10. My boss has been missing for six weeks.

    boss my missing up-to-now six-week

11. Please locate my friend's silver car by today.

    today friend my, car silver his, (you) find please

12. The black paper we like cutting is gone.

    paper black we like cut missing

13. I guess my former doctor is still working.

    doctor my former still work me guess

14. Look at the bad cut that your dog has.

    dog your cut bad look-at

15. People are sleepy, when is the break?

    now people sleep++, intermission when?

Class Activities

1. In groups of three, go over the paragraph each student wrote in ASL sentences in Lesson 8.

2. In small groups, one student from each group looks at the board. The instructor writes an emotion on the board (scared, happy, sad). The student makes a facial expression for the emotion to those in her group, and they guess the emotion. Continue until every student has portrayed two emotions.

Student Activities

1. Looking only at the vocabulary list at the beginning of Lesson 9, write glosses for the signs that use only the dominant hand.

   _____

   _____

2. Looking only at the vocabulary list at the beginning of Lesson 9, write glosses for the signs in which both hands move.

   _____

   _____

3. Looking only at the vocabulary list at the beginning of Lesson 9, write glosses for the signs that are made above the shoulders.

   _____

   _____

4. How are these groups of signs similar relative to your body?

   a. CONTINUE, ON-GOING, NEXT WEEK, TOMORROW, NEXT YEAR

   _____

   _____

   _____

   b. AGO, LAST YEAR, LAST WEEK, LAST MONTH, PAST, YESTERDAY, FORMER

   _____

   _____

   _____

   c. NOW, TODAY, MONTH, WEEK, HERE

   _____

   _____

   _____

5. Write a general rule incorporating the information that you wrote in number 4.

   _____

   _____

   _____

   _____

   _____

Lesson 10

Vocabulary

268 most
269 course, subject, lesson
270 Internet
271 e-mail
272 fax, faxed
273 message, send e-mail
274 computer
275 keyboard, type
276 mouse
277 calculator
278 text, text message, texting
279 scan, scanner
280 download
281 video relay
282 divide, split
283 subtract, take away, deduct, eliminate, remove
284 negative, subtract, minus
285 positive, plus, add, advantage, cross
286 add, addition, additional
287 sum, total, all, comes to, add
288 no, none, not any
289 nothing
290 talk, chat, chatting, conversation
291 communication, communicate, *negotiation, *negotiate
292 communication breakdown, miscommunication
293 license, permit
294 license expired, date expired, expired
295 certification, certificate, certified

268
most

Most people don't go to college.
people most, college go, not

269
course, subject, lesson

Which course do you have on Friday?
Friday, course you have which?

270
Internet

Most people like the Internet.
people most, internet like

271
e-mail

Mom sent me four e-mails today.
today four e-mail, mother sent-me

Deaf Culture Facts and Information

A distinction is made between organizations consisting of and managed by deaf people and organizations consisting of and managed by mainly hearing people. The distinction is in the words *of* (managed by deaf people) and *for* (managed by hearing people). Some examples are the National Association of the Deaf, Communication Services for the Deaf and Hard of Hearing, Registry of Interpreters for the Deaf, National Theatre of the Deaf, Union League of the Deaf, and Teletypewriters for the Deaf Inc.

272
fax, faxed

Dad faxed that to me yesterday.
yesterday that, father fax-me

273
message, send e-mail

Who wrote the message to the police?
message to police, write who?

274
computer

Most of us now have computers.
now computer, most us have

275
keyboard, type

Where did you find your keyboard?
keyboard your, find where?

276
mouse

The woman's mouse is missing.
mouse, woman hers gone

277
calculator

Help me find Dad's calculator.
calculator father his, help-me find

278
text, text message, texting

Dad texts me every day.
daily father text me

279
scan, scanner

Scan most of that today.
today most that scan

280
download

What do you want to download?
download you want what?

281
video relay

Who likes the video relay service?
video-relay, like who?

282
divide, split

Who knows how to divide?
divide, know how who?

283
subtract, take away, deduct, eliminate, remove

They are learning how to subtract.
now, subtract how, they learn

284
negative, subtract, minus

Granddad is a negative person.
grandfather himself negative+

285
positive, plus, add, advantage, cross

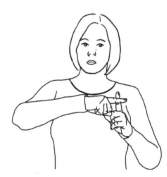

Grandma is a positive person.
grandmother herself positive+

286
add, addition, additional

We can add eleven people.
eleven people we add, can

287
sum, total, all, comes to, add

How many people are there in total?
people, sum how-many?

288
no, none, not any

The man has no paper for you.
man, paper for you, none

289
nothing

There is nothing to download today.
today, download nothing

290
talk, chat, chatting, conversation

I talk with my friends all day.
all-day friend my, me chat++

291
communication, communicate, *negotiation, *negotiate

Some communication is not good.
communication, some good not

ASL Grammar Notes

Signers emphasize that something is true (assertion) by nodding the head and tightening closed lips. They show that something is not true by shaking the head and tightening closed lips.

292
communication breakdown, miscommunication

Communication breakdowns are bad.
communication-breakdown, bad

293
license, permit

Where is your driver's license?
license drive your, where?

294
license expired, date expired, expired

He thinks his license expired last year.
last-year man license-expire, he think

295
certification, certificate, certified

Are you certified to drive a truck?
truck-drive, you certificate have?

Mind Ticklers

Make the sign _____	and think of . . .
most	one item being higher than the other
course, subject, lesson	the lesson in a book
Internet	making contact from one place to another
e-mail	sending an e-mail over an invisible wire
fax, faxed	sliding paper into a fax machine
message, send e-mail	sending a message over a wire
computer	tape reels on the first computers
keyboard, type	typing something
mouse	moving the computer mouse around
calculator	keying in some numbers
text message, text, texting	typing a message with your thumbs
scan, scanner	the light passing beneath the paper
download	pulling an item from place to another
video relay	the cameras at both ends taking pictures
divide, split	separating something into two parts
subtract, take away, deduct, remove, eliminate	taking something off the paper
negative, subtract, minus	a minus sign
positive, plus, add, advantage, cross	a plus sign
add, addition, additional	putting something with the rest
sum, total, all, comes to	bringing everything together
no, none, not any	O handshapes meaning *none*
nothing	shaking zeros to indicate nothing is there
talk, chat, chatting, conversation	waving your hands in the air while talking
communication, negotiate	people talking back and forth
communication breakdown	part of the communication process not working
license, permit	framing the shape of a license with L handshapes
license expired	part of the license being gone
certificate, certification, certified	framing the shape of a certificate

Practice Sentences

1. Most of the people here didn't understand the lesson.

   lesson, most people here understand not

2. Which do you like, faxing or e-mailing messages?

   message, fax, e-mail, you like which?

3. I don't like a computer without a mouse.

   computer without mouse me don't-like

4. Download the message and e-mail it to Mother.

   you message download, to mother e-mail

5. The nurse and the deaf person had a communication breakdown.

   nurse, deaf person, communication-breakdown

6. Most deaf people like having a video relay in their house.

   video-relay most deaf people in house like have

7. The teacher added a mouse to the keyboard.

   keyboard, teacher add mouse

8. Mom is negative one day and positive the next day.

   one day mom positive, next day mom negative

9. My deaf friends like chatting all night.

   all-night deaf friend my chat++ like

10. She said a total of 210 permits were scanned yesterday.

    yesterday, 210 license scan, woman say

11. When will your driver's license expire?

    drive license-expire your when?

12. There is no communication in my family.

    communication my family none

13. The little child can't divide the oranges.

    orange, child short divide can't

14. The sum is not what I thought it would be.

    sum itemize me think, not

15. Her addition was wrong.

    sum, girl there hers, wrong

Class Activities

1. In small groups, go over the answers to questions 1 though 5 from the Lesson 9 student activities.

2. In small groups, take turns signing all the numbers from 1–100, leaving out all twos (12, 20–29, 32, and so forth). If someone signs a 2, the group starts over again at 1.

Student Activities

1. Use the vocabulary in each grouping below to write an ASL sentence. Be creative! (You can also choose one or two other vocabulary entries from Lesson 10.)

   a. MOTHER SON TEXTING DON'T HOW TALK

   _____

   _____

   _____

b. NOTHING COMPUTER INTERNET MOST DOWNLOAD RUN

_____

_____

_____

c. FIREMAN LICENSE-EXPIRED COMPANY CHAT TOTAL MOST

_____

_____

_____

d. NOTHING SUM GRANDMA BROTHER HIDE LICENSE INTERNET

_____

_____

_____

e. VIDEO-RELAY SCAN MOUSE FAX INTERNET POSITIVE CONVERSATION

_____

_____

_____

2. Without looking at the Mind Tickler section, write what you think the rationale is for the following signs.

a. LICENSE-EXPIRED

_____

_____

_____

b. KEYBOARD

_____

_____

_____

c. DIVIDE

_____

_____

_____

d. COMMUNICATION

_____

_____

_____

Lesson 11

Vocabulary

296 empower, empowerment
297 automatic
298 suspend, hold up, suspension
299 allow, admit, *permit, *let, *permission
300 admit, confess, grant
301 welcome, invite, hire, admit
302 long, length, long-measure
303 buy, purchase, bought
304 sell, sold, get rid of
305 store, shop, market, storehouse, warehouse, clerk
306 home, residence, habitat
307 name, person's name
308 call, named, nickname
309 call, call on, summon, get
310 call, telephone, phone
311 call, yell, scream, shout, howl
312 cell phone, mobile phone
313 visit, visitor
314 improve, improvement, progress, advance, gain
315 smell, odor, scent
316 awful, terrible, horrible, danger, ugly, horrific, terrific
317 pretty, beautiful, lovely
318 ugly, awful
319 make, *create, *produce, form, manufacture
320 make, force, made
321 make, cause
322 blind, sightless, visually impaired
323 few, several, a number of

296
empower, empowerment

The class was to empower people.
class for people empower learn

297
automatic

The secretary automatically leaves at 5:00.
5:00 secretary depart automatic

298
suspend, hold up, suspension

My daughter was suspended for three months.
three-month daughter my, suspend

299
allow, admit, *permit, *let, *permission

Allow the judge to see your computer.
computer your, judge see, allow

300
admit, confess, grant

Who admitted that they had your calculator?
calculator your, confess have who?

301
welcome, invite, hire, admit

Admit fifteen men in two hours.
two-hour, fifteen man, welcome

302
long, length, long-measure

The long truck had computers in it.
truck long-length computer in have

303
buy, purchase, bought

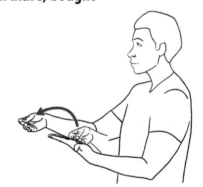

Who bought a computer last week?
last week, computer buy who?

304
sell, sold, get rid of

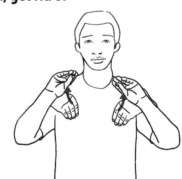

My uncle has a license to sell buses.
uncle my, license have for bus sell

305
**store, shop, market, storehouse, warehouse,
    cle<u>rk</u>**

That store sends faxes.
store there fax send

Deaf Culture Facts and Information

Within American Deaf culture, there
is African American Deaf culture, Gay
and Lesbian Deaf culture, Deaf Women
culture, Latino American Deaf culture,
and American Indian Deaf culture,
among several others.

306
home, residence, habitat

We moved into our home two years ago.
two year ago, home our, we move

307
name, person's name

What is your brother's name?
brother your, name what?

308
call, named, nickname

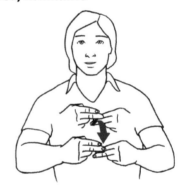

What do you call your dog?
dog your, named what

309
call, call on, summon, get

The teacher called on me this morning.
now morning teacher summon me

310
call, telephone, phone

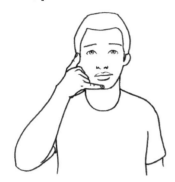

I called Mom last Wednesday.
last-week Wednesday, mother, me phone

311
call, yell, scream, shout, howl

Who was yelling last night?
ago night yell++, who?

312
cell phone, mobile phone

My cell phone is white and blue.
cell-phone my color white blue

313
visit, visit<u>or</u>

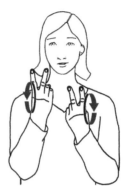

The police let me visit Dad.
police allow me father visit

ASL Grammar Notes

Rhetorical questions are used to introduce and draw attention to the information about to be presented. Nonmanual signals (NMS) are raised eyebrows and a tilt of the head or slight shaking of the head (different from NMS for wh-questions). In addition to WHY, other signs used in rhetorical sentences are: WHO, WHAT, WHERE, FOR-FOR, REASON, and WHEN.

314
improve, improvement, progress, advance, gain

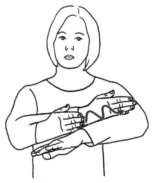

My son's communication improves every day.
daily son my, communication (his) improve

315
smell, odor, scent

Do you smell coffee in the house?
coffee in house, you smell?

316
awful, terrible, horrible, danger, ugly, horrific, terrific

The senior citizen slept terribly last night.
ago night, senior-citizen sleep awful

317
pretty, beautiful, lovely

You have a pretty name.
name your pretty

318
ugly, awful

We think your dog is ugly.
dog your ugly, we think

319
make, *create, *produce, form, manufacture

The deaf man made beautiful houses.
house beautiful, deaf man produce

320
make, force, made

Mom made us leave home.
mother my force us, home depart

321
make, cause

The yelling made the dog hide.
yell++ cause dog hide

322
blind, sightless, visually impaired

The blind man has two secretaries.
blind man, two secretary have

323
few, several, a number of

We received several calls this morning.
now morning, several phone+ we get

Mind Ticklers

Make the sign _____	and think about . . .
empower, empowerment	giving power to someone
automatic	the automatic shift on a car
suspend, hold up, suspension	holding something up
allow, admit, permit, let, permission	opening your hands to something
admit, confess, grant	getting something off your chest
welcome, invite, hire, admit	extending an inviting hand
long, length, long-measure	showing length with your hands
buy, purchase, bought	giving money from your hand to someone else
sell, sold, get rid of	passing something you have to someone else
store, shop, storehouse, warehouse, clerk	shaking clothes taken off the rack
home, residence	where you eat and sleep
call, named, nickname	the name you give someone
call, call on, summon	tapping someone then pulling her toward you
call, telephone, phone	putting the telephone receiver to your ear
call, yell, scream, shout	cupping your hands so the sound carries
cell phone, mobile phone	a small telephone
visit, visitor	moving V handshapes toward where you are going to or have visited
improve, improvement, progress,	getting better in small increments
smell, odor, scent	pulling an odor toward your nose
awful, terrible, horrible, danger, ugly	your hair standing on end
pretty, beautiful, lovely	outlining a pretty face
ugly, awful	a face that is distorted
make, create, produce, form	putting something together with your hands
make, force, made	pushing someone into doing something
make, cause	showing the result in your hands
blind, sightless, visually impaired	your eyes being closed and not seeing
few, several, a number of	not one, but more than one

Practice Sentences

1. Some teachers use ASL to communicate.

   teacher some communicate how? A-S-L

2. Mom admitted that she sold our white car.

   car white our, mom confess sell

3. The teacher calls on me several times a day.

   several time daily teacher summon me

4. Please allow the blind child to sit near you.

   blind child sit near you allow please

5. Admitting his mistake, the man was put on suspension.

   man confess mistake, he suspension

6. Mom made me buy a car that I didn't want.

   car, mom force me buy, me don't-want

7. Call the dog; it is time to come into the house.

   dog you yell, now time into house

8. Mom's cell phone is pretty blue, Dad's is ugly orange.

   cell-phone mom hers blue pretty, cell-phone dad his orange ugly

9. The girl was not invited so she cried a lot.

   girl cry a-lot why? welcome not

10. My parents named their dog "Smelly."

    parents my dog their name smell

11. Good communication made the family happy.

    family happy why? communication good

12. Several old homes were sold the first week of the month.

    first-week several home old sell

13. The visitor thought that the dog and cat were ugly.

    dog cat ugly, visitor think

14. My nephew's language improved with closed captions.

    nephew my, language his improve how? C-C

15. How many pens does that store sell monthly?

    monthly store there pen+ sell how-many?

Class Activities

1. With a partner, compare what you wrote for the two student activities in Lesson 10.

2. In small groups, write all the signs the group can think of in three minutes that start with an A handshape (for example, MOST, CONTINUE). Report the number each group has written to the instructor. The instructor writes the number on the board. Have the person in the group with the highest number share his list with the class. Continue the activity with other handshapes. The group with the largest total wins the game and receives a prize.

Student Activities

1. Write a short joke that you have heard recently.

   _____

   _____

   _____

   _____

   _____

2. Now write the same joke in ASL sentences.

   _____

   _____

   _____

   _____

3. What are some of the problems/difficulties you encountered in the ASL version?

   _____

   _____

   _____

   _____

   _____

4. Write a definition for simultaneous communication.

   _____

   _____

   _____

   _____

   _____

5. Explain whether you can or cannot use simultaneous communication while signing in ASL.

   _____

   _____

   _____

   _____

Lesson 12

Vocabulary

324 again, repeat, over
325 problem, difficult, hard, rough
326 kidding, tease, playing with, joking, kid
327 fool, trick, take advantage of
328 in front of, before, confront, face
329 before, prior to, previous to
330 from now on, after, henceforth
331 fix, repair
332 meet, confront, met, face, address
333 next, after
334 believe
335 don't believe, doubt, unsure, skeptical
336 mad, angry, anger, cross
337 furious, hot
338 sad, unhappy, morose, tragic
339 I love you
340 love, lov__er__
341 chase, after
342 finish, did, over, done, complete, already, through
343 over, finish, done, *end, *conclusion, *result
344 city, town, community, village
345 hotel, motel
346 live, life, *address, residence
347 many
348 act, play, drama, show, performance, theater, act__or__, act__ress__
349 through, passage
350 first, original
351 new, original, *fresh

324
again, repeat, over

Can you call Mom again?
mother you phone again can?

325
problem, difficult, hard, rough

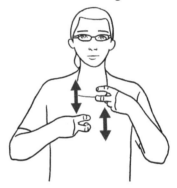

The student has several problems.
problem, student himself several have

326
kidding, tease, playing with, joking, kid

Why is the visitor teasing the boy?
visitor tease boy why?

327

fool, trick, take advantage of

Don't trick them.
(you) trick them, don't

Deaf Culture Facts and Information

Mainstreaming of deaf children into public schools first started after World War II. It escalated tremendously after the passage of Public Law 94-142 (Education for All Handicapped Children Act) in 1975. About 82 percent of all deaf children are now mainstreamed.

328

in front of, before, confront, face

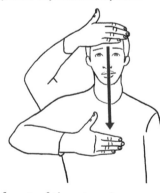

Who is in front of the store?
in-front-of store who?

329

before, prior to, previous to

Call the teacher before you leave.
prior-to depart, teacher you phone

330

from now on, after, henceforth

From now on, call on your cellphone.
from-now-on cell-phone your phone

331

fix, repair

He knows how to fix computers.
computer, man know how fix

332
meet, confront, met, face, address

Yesterday your mom met my sweetheart.
yesterday, mother your, sweetheart my, meet

333
next, after

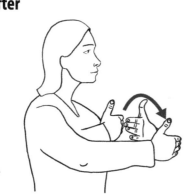

Call the doctor next month.
next month, you phone doctor

334
believe

My uncle believes what you said.
uncle my, (he) believe itemize you say

335
don't believe, doubt, unsure, skeptical

I don't believe Grandpa is here.
grandfather here, me doubt

336
mad, angry, anger, cross

Why is the visitor mad?
visitor mad why?

337
furious, hot

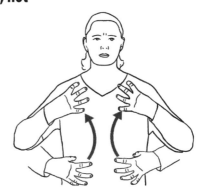

They fooled Dad, he is furious.
father furious why? they fool (him)

338
sad, unhappy, morose, tragic

The sad girl is still going home.
girl sad, on-going home go

339
I love you

I love you.
I-love-you

340
love, lov<u>er</u>

I think you love your dog.
dog your, you love me think

341
chase, after

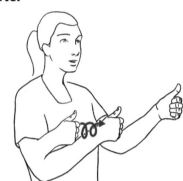

The brown dog is chasing the cat.
now, dog brown, chase cat

342
finish, did, over, done, complete, already, through

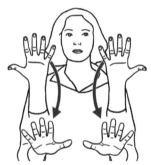

Your brother finished his paper.
brother your, paper finish

343
over, finish, done, *end, *conclusion, *result

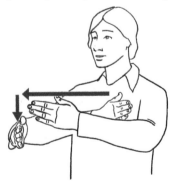

My sister ended the communication.
sister my, communication end

344
city, town, community, village

The big city is nice to visit.
city large, nice visit

345
hotel, motel

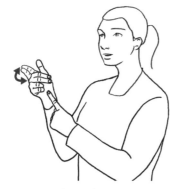

The city has seven hotels.
city, seven hotel have

346
live, life, *address, residence

How long have you lived in the city?
you here city live since?

347
many

I believe you have many friends.
you friend many have, me believe

ASL Grammar Notes

Listing is making a visual list of information, (for example, names, places, options, ages, etc.). It is used most often when providing information about the examples above and when going back and forth from items in the list. See vocabulary **first, second, third,** etc., for how to use listing.

348
act, play, drama, show, performance, theater, act*or*, act*ress*

Our show is the third week of May.
performance our, M-A-Y third-week

349
through, passage

They saw birds flying through the woods.
passage woods they see bird flutter

350
first, original

Mom is the first person to leave.
mother first person depart

351
new, original, *fresh

My roommate has a new sweetheart.
roommate my, sweetheart new have

Mind Ticklers

Make the sign _____	and think about . . .
again, repeat, over	putting something in your hand again
problem, difficult, hard, rough	hitting knuckles together is rough
kidding, tease, joking, playing with	not really giving anything
fool, trick, take advantage of	tapping someone on the back to fool them
in front of, before, confront, face	something in front of you
before, prior to, previous to	the area behind a stationary point
from now on, after, henceforth	the area after a stationary point
fix, repair	using your hands to fix something
meet, face, confront, address	the hands coming together to solve something
next, after	moving over one object to become next
believe	a thought that you hold onto
doubt, don't believe, unsure, skeptical	not believing your eyes
mad, angry, anger, cross	your face wrinkling in anger
furious, hot	all your emotions leaping out
sad, morose	a sad face
I love you	making the I, L, and Y handshapes together
love, lover	someone close to your heart
chase, after	one hand chasing the other hand
finish, did, over, done, after, complete, already, through	nothing left in your hands to do
end, over, finish	your fingers at the end of your arm
city, town, community, village	the rooftops of a town
hotel, motel	a flag flying on top of a hotel
live, life, address, residence	life flowing up through your body
many	the many fingers you have
act, play, drama, show, performance, theater, actor, actress	putting on clothes for a performance
through, passage	your hand going through two fingers
first, original	being number one
new, original, fresh	shining up something new

Practice Sentences

1. I saw your dog chasing my cat again.

   dog your chase cat my again, me see

2. Many people wanted to see the first show again.

   first performance, many people want again see

3. From now on we cannot believe what you say.

   from-now-on itemize you say, we believe cannot

4. Father tricked Grandfather in front of the group.

   front-of group father trick grandfather

5. Many of us lead a very good life.

   good life many us have

6. My partner said that he loved your daughter.

   partner my, love your daughter, he say

7. When do you think the show will be over?

   performance finish you think when?

8. I don't believe she is mad, she is teasing you.

   girl mad, me doubt, she tease (you)

9. Mom loves Dad because he shops with her.

   mom love dad why? he with her shopping

10. My uncle's address is at that hotel.

    uncle my, address his there hotel

11. My sister was sad at the end of the play.

    performance end finish, sister my sad

12. The group at the hotel said, "I love you."

    I-love-you, group there hotel say

13. Why is your little brown dog angry?

    dog brown little your, angry why?

14. Many of the people here have a difficult time believing you.

    people many here, difficult (time) believe you

15. The new visitor didn't know where to go first.

    visitor new, where go first, don't-know

Class Activities

1. As a class, briefly discuss simultaneous communication and Total Communication.

2. In small groups, each student signs her joke from Lesson 11 to the group in ASL. Then the group figures out the joke in English. Pick the best joke in each group to be signed to the entire class.

Student Activities

1. From the twelve interesting cultural facts read thus far, choose three that are most fascinating for you. Be prepared to explain, in ASL, to your classmates why you are fascinated.

   a. _____

   _____

   b. _____

   _____

   c. _____

   _____

2. Listing is an ASL technique for making a visual list of information you are sharing. Write three sentences using listing.

a. _____

_____

_____

b. _____

_____

_____

c. _____

_____

_____

3. What is a rhetorical question?

_____

_____

_____

_____

4. Which sentence in Lesson 12 is rhetorical?

_____

_____

_____

_____

5. Rewrite three sentences from Lesson 12 to make them rhetorical.

a. _____

_____

_____

b. _____

_____

_____

c. _____

_____

_____

Lesson 13

Vocabulary

352 interest, interested, interesting, appeals
353 fascinating, fascinated
354 bored, boring, boredom
355 dry, towel, not wet, not interesting, bored, *desert
356 place, position, *location, *area, *region, where, locale, setting, site
357 ask, request, inquire
358 question
359 word
360 vocabulary
361 need, necessary, should, supposed to
362 must, have to
363 wish, long for, desire
364 hungry, starve
365 listen
366 listen, hear something, taking in, auditory, take in auditorally
367 take in visually, visually
368 speech, oral, speechreading, lipreading, read lips
369 hearing aid, aid (behind-the-ear)
370 hearing aid, aid (in-the-ear)
371 earmold
372 cochlear implant
373 loud, noise, sound
374 under, beneath, below
375 less than, under, below
376 increase, raise, gain, jump, add to
377 look for, search, hunt
378 look, appear, appearance, face, look-like
379 more

352
interest, interested, interesting, appeals

You have an interesting first name.
first name your, interest

353
fascinating, fascinated

The show last week was fascinating.
last-week performance fascinating

354
bored, boring, boredom

My teacher's class is not boring.
teacher my, class hers, bored not

355

dry, towel, not wet, not interesting, bored,*desert

My afternoon class is not interesting.
afternoon class my, dry

356

place, position, *location, *area, *region, where, locale, setting, site

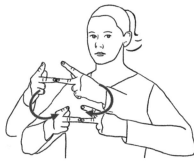

The place near the hotel is nice.
location near hotel nice

357

ask, request, inquire

Ask Dad for some food.
food some father you request

358

question

My boss has a computer question.
boss my computer question (he) have

359

word

Communication is a long word.
word communication, long-length

360

vocabulary

How much vocabulary have you learned?
vocabulary you learn finish, how-much?

361
need, necessary, should, supposed to

We need to finish this before tomorrow.
prior-to tomorrow we need that finish

Deaf Culture Facts and Information

State residential schools for the deaf were generally located in areas of low population density. The prevalent thinking at the time regarding children and adults who were "different" was that they were better off "out of sight, out of mind."

362
must, have to

Father must leave before next week.
prior-to next-week father depart must

363
wish, long for, desire

I wish to go to an interesting place.
location interest, wish me go

364
hungry, starve

Ask the boy if he is hungry.
boy hungry, you ask

365
listen

Listen, the white dog is howling.
listen, dog white now howl.

366
listen, hear something, taking in, auditory, take in auditorally

We heard a fascinating story.
story fascinating we take-in-auditorally finish

367
take in visually, visually

The woman sat down and took in the beautiful woods.
woman sit-down, take-in-visually woods pretty

368
speech, oral, speechreading, lipreading, read lips

Most Deaf people cannot speechread well.
deaf people most, speechread good, cannot

369
hearing aid, aid (behind-the-ear)

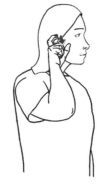

My mother used to have a hearing aid.
ago, mother my, hearing-aid have

370
hearing aid, aid (in-the-ear)

Granddad has a new hearing aid.
now grandfather hearing-aid new have

371
earmold

What color is your new earmold?
earmold your new, color what?

372
cochlear implant

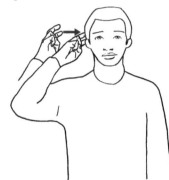

Maybe a cochlear implant will help him.
boy, cochlear-implant maybe help

ASL Grammar Notes

Pluralization is shown by using numbers (THREE PIGS), placing a sign in different locations (CAR, CAR, CAR), using classifiers (VEHICLE LONG-LINE), indexing (pointing to indicate how many), and using distributional aspect with verbs (ME HELP-YOU, HELP-HIM, HELP-HER) to represent repetition of an action.

373
loud, noise, sound

Listen, you can hear a noise.
listen, noise you hear can

374
under, beneath, below

I wish to sit under a big tree.
tree tall, wish me beneath sit

375
less than, under, below

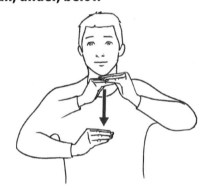

A hearing aid is less than I thought.
hearing-aid less-than me think

376
increase, raise, gain, jump, add to

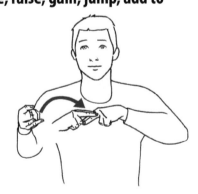

Dad wants to increase the sound.
sound father increase want

377
look for, search, hunt

They will look for a good hearing aid.
hearing-aid good, they look-for, buy

378
look, appear, appearance, face, look-like

Mom's happy you don't' look bored.
mother happy you appearance bored not

379
more

The nurse wants to ask more questions.
nurse want more question++

Mind Ticklers

Make the sign _____	and think about . . .
interest, interesting	liking something twice as much
fascinating	your interest being pulled forward
bored, boredom	what some people do when they are bored
dry, towel, not wet, bored	wiping your chin with a towel
place, position, location, site	drawing a location with your hands
ask, request	pleading for what you want
question	outlining a question mark in the air
word	the approximate length of a word
vocabulary	the words on a page
need, necessary, should	trying to put your hooks in something
must, have to	hooking something you want
wish, long for, desire	something near to your heart
hungry, starve	the path food takes to the stomach
listen	cupping the ear to hear better
hear something, listen	taking in all the sounds around you
take in visually	taking in all the sights around you
speech, oral, speechreading, lipreading	looking at the lips
hearing aid, aid (behind the ear)	where a behind-the-ear hearing aid goes
hearing aid, aid (in the ear)	the small hearing aid that fits in the ear
earmold	what goes in the ear to help listening
cochlear implant	the hearing device behind the ear
loud, noise, sound	the ear hearing vibrations
under, beneath, below	something below the horizon
less than, under, below	less than the average
increase, raise, gain, jump	adding onto what already exists
look for, search, hunt	peering out to find something
look, appear, appearance, face	outlining what the face looks like
more	adding one amount to another

Practice Sentences

1. Do you know who lives in that interesting house?

   person live interesting house there you know?

2. Most of the time in class are you bored or interested?

   class, most time you bored, interest, which?

3. My hearing aid doesn't work well in groups.

   hearing-aid my, in group work good, not

4. My sister wishes she looked good.

   sister my, appearance good she wish

5. My father saw language visually, he was deaf.

   father my deaf, language take-in-visually+

6. Speechreading is difficult.

   speechread problem

7. More police came to help search for the little girl.

   girl short, more police come help search

8. Your teacher's earmold looks new.

   earmold, teacher hers appearance new

9. Many deaf people don't like cochlear implants for children.

   cochlear-implants for children many deaf people don't-like

10. My uncle became bored sitting there a long time.

    uncle my bored why? sit++ long time

11. The stuck up woman had a very interesting vocabulary.

    vocabulary, stuck-up woman hers, interesting

12. The children were fascinated watching the firemen work.

    firemen work, children look-at fascinated

13. Listen to me, I have to eat, I am starving.

    take-in-auditorally, me eat must, starve

14. Dad's pay increase was less than he wanted.

    pay increase dad his less-than want

15. My son needs to learn more vocabulary every day.

    daily son my vocabulary more need learn

Class Activity

1. In small groups, share the information you wrote in student activities 1–5 in Lesson 12.

2. As a refresher, just before the end of class, have the class sign and sing the ABC song ending with, "now I've signed my ABC's, next time please sign with me."

Student Activities

1. In the thirteen lessons covered so far, there are probably several signs that are different from what you have learned previously or seen someone using. Write the glosses for these signs.

   _____

   _____

   _____

   _____

2. Now create Mind Ticklers for the signs you came up with above.

_____

_____

_____

_____

_____

3. Speechreading and lipreading have the same sign but not the same meaning. How do they differ?

_____

_____

_____

_____

_____

4. Without looking at the vocabulary in Lesson 13, write five signs that use only one hand and five signs that use both hands.

One-hand signs

1. _____

2. _____

3. _____

4. _____

5. _____

Two-hand signs

1. _____

2. _____

3. _____

4. _____

5. _____

Lesson 14

Vocabulary

380 regardless, anyway, nevertheless, it doesn't matter, anyhow, still

381 each, every

382 everything

383 everyone, everybody

384 obey, mind

385 think about, *wonder, think over, consider

386 complain, object, mind, care, grievance, objection, protest

387 stop, halt, cut it out, quit

388 hope, expect, anticipate

389 any

390 heavy

391 light, not-heavy

392 light, bulb

393 give up, surrender, quit

394 write down, document, record, put down

395 clear, obvious, light, bright

396 bright, clever, smart, intelligent, gifted

397 smart, sharp

398 hair

399 cheek

400 skin

401 foot, feet

402 hand

403 chest

404 head

405 body, *health, *physical

406 heart

407 back, back-anatomy

408 breast

409 arm

410 voice

The following signs are made by simply pointing to the body part.

411 abdomen

412 butt

413 chin

414 elbow

415 eye

416 eyebrow

417 finger

418 forehead

419 knee

420 nose

421 shoulder

422 teeth

423 thigh

424 thumb

425 wrist

380
regardless, anyway, nevertheless, it doesn't matter, anyhow, still

Please go regardless of what Mom says.
mother say, regardless, please go

381
each, every

Every person I meet is interesting.

every person me meet interest

382
everything

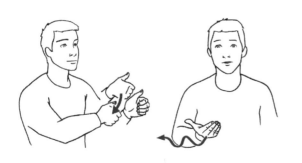

They wish they knew everything.
every-thing, they wish know

383
everyone, everybody

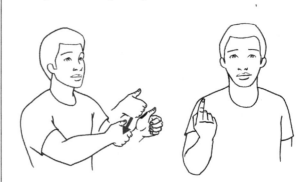

Everyone thought he speechread well.
speechread he every-one think (he) good

384
obey, mind

They took it in visually and obeyed.
they take-in-visually, obey finish

385
think about, *wonder, think over, consider

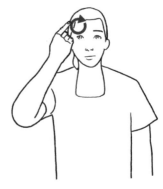

The girl thinks about boys all day.
all-day, girl think-about boy

386
complain, object, mind, care, grievance, objection, protest

They complained that the boy signed.
boy signing, they complain

Deaf Culture Facts and Information

The ability of a deaf person to speak and speechread is dependent upon the degree of deafness, the age at onset of deafness, and mastery of the spoken language. Most deaf individuals do not depend on speechreading for communication.

387
stop, halt, cut it out, quit

Stop listening to your friends.
friend your, (you) listen stop

388
hope, expect, anticipate

I hope to get a big raise.
increase large me hope obtain

389
any

My big dog obeys any individual.
dog large my, person any obey

390
heavy

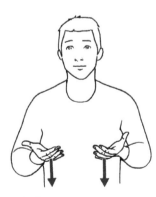

My computer is heavy.
computer my heavy

391
light, not-heavy

Hearing aids are light.
hearing-aid, not-heavy

392
light, bulb

Where is the new light?
light new where?

393
give up, surrender, quit

Father gave up any hope of fixing his hearing aid.

hearing-aid father his, he fix surrender

394
write down, document, record, put down

Write down what the man says.
man say, (you) put-down

395
clear, obvious, light, bright

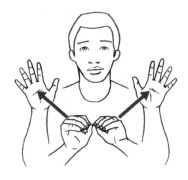

Today will be a clear day.
today, clear will

396
bright, clever, smart, intelligent, gifted

Your son is a bright boy.
son your, bright

397
smart, sharp

You have three sharp children.
children your three, smart

398
hair

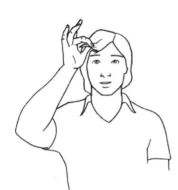

She has light colored hair.
girl hair color not-heavy

399
cheek

You have red cheeks.
cheek your red

400
skin

My skin looks yellow
skin my yellow appearance

ASL Grammar Notes

Classifiers are specific handshapes that show the movement, location, or appearance of an object. After a signer indicates a person or thing, he will use a classifier in place of the ASL sign or referent. For example, the 3 handshape with the thumb sticking up represents a vehicle; signing ROW, ROW, ROW using this handshape means *parking lot*. Classifiers may also be used to embody the actions of a person or other animate being, such as using a Bent 3 to indicate throwing a baseball.

401
foot, feet

My aunt has little feet.
aunt my, feet hers, tiny

402
hand

Your uncle has big hands.
uncle your hand large

403
chest

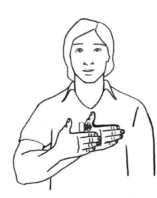

The doctor listened to my chest.
chest my doctor hear-something

404
head

Think with your head.
head your for-for, think

405
body, *health, *physical

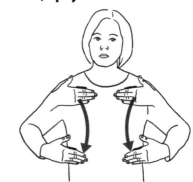

Whose body is black and blue?
body black blue who?

406
heart

Listen, I hear your heart.
listen, heart your me hear

407
back, back-anatomy

You cannot see your back.
back your you see cannot

408
breast

She has small breasts.
breast hers small

409
arm

The doctor looked at my arm.
arm my doctor look-at

410
voice

We are fascinated listening to her voice.
voice girl hers we listen fascinating

The following signs are made by simply pointing to the body part.

411 abdomen	419 knee
412 butt	420 nose
413 chin	421 shoulder
414 elbow	422 teeth
415 eye	423 thigh
416 eyebrow	424 thumb
417 finger	425 wrist
418 forehead	

Mind Ticklers

Make the sign _____	and think about . . .
regardless, anyway, nevertheless, it doesn't matter, anyhow	not wanting to handle a problem
each, every	your thumbs representing one
everything	**every** plus **thing**
everyone, everybody	**every** plus **one**
obey, mind	moving the hands out to show respect
think about, wonder, think over	mulling something over in your head
complain, object, mind, care, grievance, objection, protest	getting something off your chest
stop, halt, cut it out, quit	putting up a barrier to stop something
hope, expect, anticipate	thinking with high hopes
any	pointing your thumb to a number of things
heavy	straining at the weight of something
light, not heavy	something light enough to float
light, bulb	an overhead light coming on brightly
give up, surrender, quit	throwing your hands up in frustration
write down, document, record, put down	putting something down on paper
clear, obvious, light, bright	something opening before your eyes
bright, clever, smart, intelligent, gifted	showing that your brain shines
smart, sharp	your brains beyond your head
hair	holding a piece of your hair.
cheek	holding your cheek
skin	pinching a piece of skin on your arm
foot, feet	pointing to your foot
hand	indicating the hand starts at the wrist
chest	patting your chest
head	outlining the head
body, health, physical	outlining the body
heart	touching the heart
back	patting yourself on the back
breast	touching each breast
arm	rubbing your arm
voice	speech coming out your mouth

The following signs are made by pointing to the body part:

411 abdomen

412 butt

413 chin

414 elbow

415 eye

416 eyebrow

417 finger

418 forehead

419 knee

420 nose

421 shoulder

422 teeth

423 thigh

424 thumb

425 wrist

Practice Sentences

1. Regardless how interesting the play, everyone looked bored.

   performance interest, regardless, every-one appearance bored

2. Each person in the group had high hopes.

   hope high each person in group have

3. My uncle gave up because everything was too heavy.

   uncle my surrender, why? every-thing heavy

4. Each person wrote down what he thought was right.

   correct, person each think itemize, put-down

5. Everyone liked his green eyes.

   boy, eyes green, every-one like

6. Who complains about his shoulder every day?

   shoulder, complain daily who?

7. His abdomen, chest, and neck were red.

   ago boy, abdomen, chest, neck his, red

8. Please obey your father and write what he said.

   please, father your, obey, write itemize (he) say

9. Whom do you know who is gifted?

   bright, you know who?

10. We hope that our children will be smart.

    children our we hope smart will

11. The nurse was furious when she thought about her husband.

    nurse furious, why? she think-about husband

12. The four H's in the 4-H Club stand for *health*, *heart*, *head*, and *hand*.

    four H group, H four what? health heart head hand

13. The light in here is not bright enough.

    light here clear enough, not

14. Complaining while being mad is not good.

    mad you complain, good not

15. Her right eye is blue, and her left eye is brown. Fascinating.

    girl her, eye to-the-right blue, eye to-the-left brown, fascinating

Class Activities

1. In small groups, go over the student activities in Lesson 13.
2. In small groups, students take turns signing the following sentence in ASL filling in the blanks alphabetically with signs or fingerspelled words.

First student:

MY FRIEND ___(A) *Art*___ WHO LIVES IN ___(A) *Austin*___ IS ___(A) *angry.*___
              (person)   (town)   (adjective)

Next student:

MY UNCLE ___(B) *Ben*___ WHO LIVES IN ___(B) *Boise*___ IS ___(B) *brilliant.*___
              (person)   (town)   (adjective)

Student Activities

1. What are the compound signs in this lesson?

   _____

   _____

2. The following signs are paired with their nonmanual signals (NMS). Write at least two other signs for each NMS. Practice signing each sign with its NMS.

1. FINALLY	pah (voice)	_____	_____
2. DISAPPROVE	frown	_____	_____
3. WHAT-FOR	fo	_____	_____
4. VERY FAR	tongue flap	_____	_____
5. HAPPY	smile	_____	_____
6. VERY LARGE	puffed cheeks	_____	_____
7. CAN'T STAND SOMETHING	pursed lips/eye squint	_____	_____
8. DELICIOUS	wipe lips	_____	_____
9. LAZY	half-lip press/blow	_____	_____

Lesson 15

Vocabulary

426 silly, foolish, cut up, ridiculous, fo<u>ol</u>
427 fault
428 responsible, obligation, charge, duty, in charge of
429 funny, humorous
430 fun
431 hold, grip, keep
432 favorite, prefer, rather, preference
433 little bit, little
434 kill, murder
435 feel, emotions, sense, figure, sensation
436 refuse, won't, decline
437 decline, turn down, reject
438 good, way to go, yes
439 gray
440 order, command, direct
441 dismiss, lay off, excused, release
442 excuse, excuse me, pardon, forgive
443 a lot, much, lots, amount
444 small amount, small quantity
445 large amount, large quantity
446 stand, on your feet
447 kneel, kneel down
448 jump for joy, excited
449 get up, stand up
450 great, fantastic, wonderful, marvelous, terrific
451 enthusiasm, enthusiastic, anxious, motivated, eager, industrious
452 nervous, anxious
453 worry, anxious

426
silly, foolish, cut up, ridiculous, fo<u>ol</u>

Who is your silly friend?
friend your silly who?

427
fault

The nurse said it was not her fault.
fault nurse hers, she say not

428
responsible, obligation, charge, duty, in charge of

The detective was not responsible.
detective responsible, not

429
funny, humorous

He writes funny stories.
stories funny, he write

Deaf Culture Facts and Information

ASL, like all living languages, changes over time. New signs are created when new inventions appear on the market. Examples include signs for *microwave*, *cell phone*, *texting*, *computer*, *Internet*, and *laptop*. Some old ASL signs have been adapted as everyday items have been modernized. For example, the old sign for *telephone* required two hands—one to hold the candlestick base up to the mouth and one to hold the receiver up to the ear. The modern sign is made with one hand in a Y handshape that mimics the shape of a telephone handset.

430
fun

Go to college to have fun.
go college why? fun have

431
hold, grip, keep

Hold the boy's head while I get Dad.
boy head his you hold, me father summon

432
favorite, prefer, rather, preference

What is your favorite color?
color favorite your what?

433
little bit, little

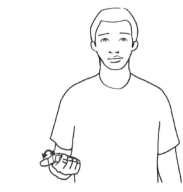

The nurse has a little time.
nurse time little-bit have

434
kill, murder

Don't kill the little bird.
bird tiny kill, don't

435
feel, emotions, sense, figure, sensation

My sister feels silly now.
now sister my silly feel

436
refuse, won't, decline

Don't refuse to go with Mom.
you with mother go, refuse don't

437
decline, turn down, reject

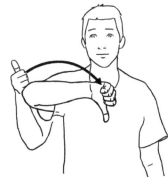

The family turned down the old car.
car old, family reject

438
good, way to go, yes

The player said, "way to go."
player say, way-to-go

439
gray

My favorite daughter has gray hair.
daughter favorite my hair gray have

440

order, command, direct

Who ordered the men to stop?
men stop, order who?

441

dismiss, lay off, excused, release

The school laid him off for one month.
one-month, man, school dismiss

442

excuse, excuse me, pardon, forgive

Excuse me, we have to leave now.
excuse (me), we depart now must

443

a lot, much, lots, amount

We have a lot of time left.
time abandon, we a-lot have

444

small amount, small quantity

A small amount of food was eaten.
food, small-amount eat finish

445

large amount, large quantity

A large amount of coffee was left.
coffee abandon large-amount

446
stand, on your feet

Grandpa is standing over there.
now grandfather over-there stand

447
kneel, kneel down

We kneel a lot in church.
church there we a-lot kneel

448
jump for joy, excited

Yesterday they were jumping for joy.
yesterday they jump-for-joy

449
get up, stand up

The girls refused to get up.
girl they get-up, refuse

ASL Grammar Notes

Transliteration is the process of providing a word-for-word signed account of what a hearing person says.

450
great, fantastic, wonderful, marvelous, terrific

We had a great time yesterday.
yesterday we wonderful time have

451
enthusiasm, enthusiastic, anxious, motivated, eager, industrious

The boss likes your enthusiasm.
enthusiasm your, boss like

452
nervous, anxious

Look, Dad is obviously nervous.
look-at, father, he nervous clear

453
worry, anxious

Don't worry, you are not laid off.
worry (you) don't, dismiss not

Mind Ticklers

Make the sign _____	and think about . . .
silly, foolish, cut up, ridiculous, fool	a silly person playing around
fault	letting your responsibility down
responsible, obligation, duty, charge	the burden being on your shoulders
funny, humorous	a clown with a funny nose
fun	fun as something to sit and think about
hold, grip, keep	the gesture of holding something
favorite, prefer, rather, preference	your taste in things
little bit, little	shooting small marbles
kill, murder	putting a knife into something
feel, emotions, sense, figure, sensation	feelings coming from the heart
refuse, won't, decline	not wanting to touch anything
decline, turn down, reject	the thumbs-down gesture
good, way to go, yes	the thumbs-up gesture
gray	mixing black and white together
order, command, direct	saying something toward someone
dismiss, lay off, excused, release	wiping a name off a list
excuse, pardon, forgive	wiping away a mistake
a lot, much, lots, amount	a gesture showing how much
small amount, small quantity	a small amount of something
large amount, large quantity	a large amount of something
stand	the legs in a standing position
kneel	the legs bent in a kneeling position
jump for joy, excited	a person jumping up and down
get up, stand up	moving from lying down to standing
great, fantastic, wonderful, marvelous	throwing your hands up in celebration
enthusiasm, enthusiastic, anxious, motivated, eager, industrious	rubbing your hands together to get ready for a task
nervous, anxious	the hands and arms shaking
anxious, worry	a lot of confusion going on in the head

Practice Sentences

1. Excuse me, your son is acting silly.

   excuse-me, son your silly behave

2. Mom jumped for joy when she heard that you were coming.

   you come, mom hear (she) jump-for-joy

3. The class had a fantastic time and they are anxious to go again.

   class, fantastic time have, again they enthusiastic go

4. A small amount of food is enough for the baby.

   baby, eat small-amount, enough

5. Don't worry; you are not going to be laid off.

   you worry don't, laid-off will, not

6. Way to go; we all had great fun.

   way-to-go, great fun we have

7. The paper my brother worked on for weeks was turned down.

   week++ brother my, paper (he) work++, turn-down

8. The policeman is responsible for bringing a large amount of food.

   food large-amount, policeman responsible bring

9. Hold on to your car and sell it in three weeks.

   three-weeks-future, car your sell

10. What will you order when we go to the store?

    store, we go, you order what?

11. We don't understand why he refused to marry her.

    man refuse marry woman, why? we understand, not

12. When do you think the man was killed?

    man kill, you think when?

13. How did you feel when Mom was laid off last week?

    last-week mom lay-off, you feel how?

14. Get up and go see your funny brother in school.

    brother funny your, school there, you get-up go see

15. Everyone was enthusiastic the new boss was coming to visit.

    boss new come visit, every-one enthusiastic

Class Activities

1. In groups of three, go over the three student activities in Lesson 14.

2. Several students go to the chalkboard and write two glosses that are used with nonmanual signals (NMS). Have each student demonstrate his or her NMS with the signs. The whole class imitates. Repeat the same activity several times.

Student Activities

1. What are the glosses used in the text for the conceptual signs listed below?

   a. big dog _____

   b. big hands _____

   c. bright day _____

   d. bright child _____

   e. head cold _____

   f. cold outside _____

   g. she's cold _____

   h. he is light _____

   i. broken light _____

   j. little feet _____

   k. little boy _____

   l. little time _____

2. Looking at the glosses for body parts in Lesson 15, write an ASL paragraph incorporating as many body parts as you can.

   _____

   _____

   _____

   _____

   _____

   _____

   _____

   _____

   _____

   _____

Lesson 16

Vocabulary

454 fine, well, good health
455 don't care, don't mind
456 nosy, prying
457 young, youthful
458 old, age, elderly
459 hard, solid, intense
460 soft, spongy, tender
461 fall, autumn
462 spring
463 summer
464 winter
465 wet, moist, damp, humid
466 clouds, cloudy
467 sunshine, sunny, sunlight
468 sun
469 moon
470 weather
471 snow, snowfall
472 rain, rainfall, drizzle
473 wind, windy, breeze
474 smoke, fog
475 hurricane
476 storm
477 thunder, rumble
478 lightning
479 tornado
480 dark, darkness
481 sunset, twilight
482 sunrise, dawn
483 early

454
fine, well, good health

The teacher feels fine now.
now teacher feel good-health

455
don't care, don't mind

They don't care what you ordered.
your order, they don't-care

456
nosy, prying

Her aunt is a nosy person.
girl, aunt hers, nosy (person)

457
young, youthful

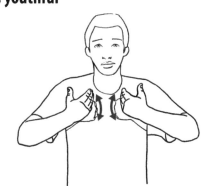

The young people are leaving now.
now people young they depart

458
old, age, elderly

Who laid off the old man?
man old, lay-off, who?

459
hard, solid, intense

The young boy has a hard head.
boy young, head his hard

460
soft, spongy, tender

The doctor said to eat soft food.
food soft doctor say eat

461
fall, autumn

Fall is a pretty time of year.
fall pretty time during year

462
spring

Dad prefers springtime.
spring, father prefer

463
summer

The family visits us every summer.
every summer, family us visit

Deaf Culture Facts and Information

Contact signing, traditionally known as Pidgin Sign English, is a result of contact between English and ASL, and it combines features of both languages. Contact signing is used by deaf and hearing people when communicating with one another.

464
winter

Winter driving makes me nervous.
drive during winter, me nervous

465
wet, moist, damp, humid

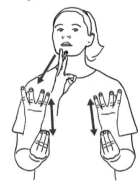

It is humid during the summer.
during summer, wet

466
clouds, cloudy

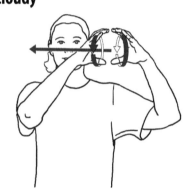

Tomorrow is supposed to be cloudy.
tomorrow cloudy maybe

467
sunshine, sunny, sunlight

Yesterday it was sunny.
yesterday sunny

468
sun

The sun is huge.
sun huge

469
moon

The moon is bright sometimes.
moon sometimes clear

470
weather

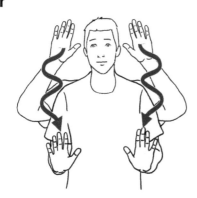

The weather here has been nice.
here, weather nice since

471
snow, snowfall

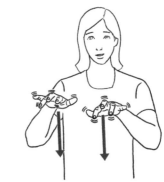

The children played in the snow.
snow, children play

472
rain, rainfall, drizzle

The rain makes everything wet.
rain, cause every-thing wet

473
wind, windy, breeze

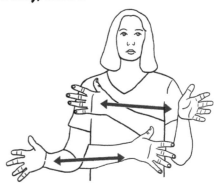

Summer winds feel good.
wind summer good feel

474
smoke, fog

The smoke in the house was bad.
smoke in house bad

ASL Grammar Notes

Backchannel feedback consists of nonmanual signals (laughing, head nodding/shaking, etc.) or response signs (OH-I-SEE, REALLY? NO!, etc.) that a person will use in a conversation to show the signer (the person "talking") that she is paying attention, understanding the signer, responding to what the signer is saying, reinforcing communication, and/or showing emotional involvement.

475
hurricane

Summer is the time for hurricanes.
hurricane, summer time come

476
storm

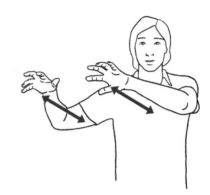

The storm lasted five hours.
five-hour storm continue

477
thunder, rumble

I heard the thunder all night.
all-night thunder me hear

478
lightning

The evening lightning was beautiful.
lightning night beautiful

479
tornado

When did you see the tornado?
tornado you see when?

480
dark, darkness

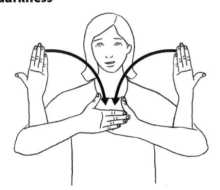

Inside the house was dark.
house in dark

481
sunset, twilight

Sunset above the water is beautiful.
water there, sunset beautiful

482
sunrise, dawn

Sunrise is at 6 o'clock tomorrow.
tomorrow sunrise time 6

483
early

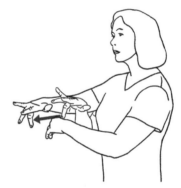

See me early tomorrow morning.
tomorrow morning early (you) see me

Mind Ticklers

Make the sign _____	and think about . . .
fine, well, good health	extending your hand in a strong manner
don't care, don't mind	not putting your nose in someone's affairs
nosy, prying	putting your nose into another's affairs
young, youthful	excitable children
old, age, elderly	the beard on an old man
hard, solid	tapping on something hard
soft, spongy, tender	squeezing a soft object
fall, autumn	the leaves falling from trees
spring	the time when things grow
summer	wiping the perspiration from your brow
winter	the idea of shivering
wet, moist, damp, humid	feeling water in an object
clouds, cloudy	the shape of a cloud moving overhead
sunshine. sunny, sunlight	drawing the sun and showing the rays
sun	the sun as a circle of light
moon	the crescent shape of the moon
weather	snow, rain, and wind coming down
snow	snowflakes fluttering down
rain, rainfall, drizzle	raindrops falling
wind, windy, breeze	wind blowing back and forth
smoke, fog	smoke swirling up from a fire
hurricane	H handshapes outlining a hurricane shape
storm	large moving winds
thunder	a ground-shaking noise
lightning	the shape of a lightning bolt
tornado	the funnel depicting a tornado
dark	covering the eyes to depict darkness
sunset, twilight	the sun going below the horizon
sunrise, dawn	the sun coming up over the horizon
early	getting off the mark before anyone else

Practice Sentences

1. Are your grandmother and grandfather in good health?

   grandmother, grandfather your fine now?

2. Which do you want to see tomorrow, rain or snow?

   tomorrow, you want see rain, snow, which?

3. During the spring we have many hard rains.

   during spring many awful rain++ have

4. Sunset is early during the winter months.

   during winter month, sunset early

5. Mom doesn't care who killed Grandma's cat.

   cat grandma hers, who kill, mom don't-care

6. That young man is nosy, he wants to see everything.

   man young there, nosy, see every-thing he want

7. The sunset last night was beautiful.

   ago night sunset beautiful

8. The lightning and thunder lasted all night and all day.

   all-night, all-day, lightning, thunder continue

9. Hurricanes can cause a lot of problems.

   hurricane, a-lot problem cause able

10. The clouds in summer look soft.

    summer cloud soft appearance

11. A blue moon is the second full moon in one month.

    one-month two full moon name what? blue moon

12. The rain and wind continued for six days.

    six-day rain wind continue++

13. During the winter, it gets dark early.

    during winter, dark early

14. How early do you think your mother will leave?

    mother your, time depart early you think?

15. The sunshine made the house very warm.

    house very warm why? sunshine

Class Activity

1. In small groups, have one student read another student's paragraph from Lesson 15. The writer of the paragraph signs it. Continue until all the paragraphs have been read and signed.

Student Activities

1. Explain how these pairs of glosses are similar.

   a. SUNNY/SUN

   _____

   _____

   b. MOON/SUN

   _____

   _____

   c. SUNSET/SUNRISE

   _____

   _____

   d. TORNADO/HURRICANE

   _____

   _____

   e. WINDY/STORM

   _____

   _____

f. RAIN/SNOW

_____

_____

g. WINTER/COLD

_____

_____

h. NOSY/DON'T CARE

_____

2. What nonmanual signals would be used with the following signs?

a. DON'T-CARE

_____

_____

b. YOUNG

_____

_____

c. THUNDER

_____

_____

d. HARD/SOLID

_____

_____

e. REFUSE

_____

_____

f. JUMP FOR JOY

_____

_____

g. LIGHTNING

_____

_____

Lesson 17

Vocabulary

484 check, check off, mark
485 check, bank check, draft
486 check, investigate, inspect
487 cancel, correct, criticize, call off, check
488 both
489 together
490 run away, escape, flee, take off, run off, flight, sprint
491 run, manage, control, direct, govern, in charge, rule, manager
492 run, jog
493 run, runny nose, running
494 run, liquid, drip
495 run, compete, contest, race, competition, athletics, sports
496 run, running, operate, work
497 recycle
498 wine
499 beer, brew
500 never, not at all
501 happen, occur, event
502 walk, stroll, step
503 willing, offer
504 sick, disgusting, nauseous
505 high, stoned, altitude
506 cry, cries, tears, weep
507 then, *or, *nor
508 than
509 ticket
510 unfair, worthless, insignificant
511 frustrated, frustration
512 vicinity, approximately, about, around, near, in the area

484
check, check off, mark

My paper has four checks on it.
paper my, four check have

485
check, bank check, draft

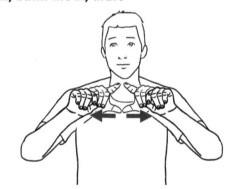

You can write me a check later.
later you draft for me write

486
check, investigate, inspect

The police checked the house.
house, police inspect finish

487
cancel, correct, criticize, call off, check

When will you cancel my license?
license my, you cancel when?

Deaf Culture Facts and Information

Deaf individuals are represented in almost all occupations listed in the *Dictionary of Occupational Titles*. There are medical doctors, dentists, teachers, printers, professors, laborers, postal workers, and scientists who are deaf.

488
both

Both sisters received a check.
sister+, both draft receive

489
together

The brothers go to school together.
brother+, school together go

490
run away, escape, flee, take off, run off, flight, sprint

Who ran away from home last week?
last-week home flee who?

491
run, manage, control, direct, govern, in charge, rule, manager

Who runs the store at night?
night store manage who?

492

run, jog

Mom likes running every day.
daily mother jog like

493

run, runny nose, running

My son has a runny nose.
son my runny-nose have

494

run, liquid, drip

The water ran all day.
all-day water drip

495

run, compete, contest, race, competition, athletics, sports

The race lasted a long time.
race long time continue

496

run, running, operate, work

My car is running well.
car my good operate

497

recycle

My aunt recycles everything.
aunt my every-thing recycle

498
wine

You prefer white or red wine?
wine you prefer, white red which?

499
beer, brew

Don't drink beer all night.
all-night (you) beer drink, don't

500
never, not at all

My sister never writes checks.
sister my draft write, never

501
happen, occur, event

What happened to Dad last week?
last-week, father happen what?

502
walk, stroll, step

Mom and Dad walk every day.
daily mother father walk

503
willing, offer

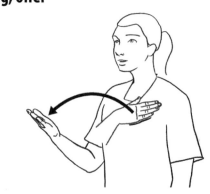

The bachelor is willing to race.
now bachelor, race, willing

504
sick, disgusting, nauseous

The old wine smelled disgusting.
wine old smell disgusting

505
high, stoned, altitude

Your brother is acting like he's stoned.
brother your stoned behave

506
cry, cries, tears, weep

The baby cries morning, noon and night.
morning noon night, baby cry++

507
then, *or, *nor

You run, then I will run.
first you jog, then me jog will

ASL Grammar Notes

Directional verbs change their movement to indicate the location of the subject and/or object of a sentence. For example, in the sentences YOU-GIVE-ME/ME-GIVE-YOU and HE-TELL-ME/ME-TELL-HIM, the verb moves away from or toward the signer depending on who is giving or telling. Some directional verbs can also be used in sentences such as HE-GIVE-HER where the signer is neither the subject nor object.

508
than

My friend has more than ten dogs.
friend my more than ten dog have

509
ticket

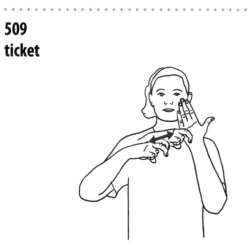

Where did you put my ticket?
ticket my (you) put where?

510
~~unfair, worthless, insignificant~~ simple

That ticket is worthless now.
now ticket that worthless

511
frustrated, frustration

They both looked frustrated.
he+ both appearance frustrate

512
vicinity, approximately, about, around, near, in the area

That happened in this vicinity.
that happen approximately here

Mind Ticklers

Make the sign _____	and think about . . .
check, check off, mark	putting a checkmark on paper
check, draft	the size of a bank check
check, investigate, inspect	looking closely at something
cancel, correct, criticize, call off, check	putting an X on something cancelled
both	putting two things together
together	two objects side by side
run away, escape, flee, take off, run off, flight	a person fleeing something
run, manage, control, direct, govern, in charge, rule	taking the reins in hand to take control
run, jog	your legs moving as if running
run, runny nose	having a runny nose
run, liquid, drip	water coming from a faucet
run, compete, contest, race, competition	two people running against one another
run, working, operate	parts working together
recycle	the symbol for recycled materials
wine	drinking wine makes your cheeks red
beer, brew	beer foam dripping down your chin
never	saying never is always questionable
happen, occur, event	something turned over
walk, stroll	your feet moving along
willing, offer	extending your heart to someone
sick, disgusting, nauseous	something that makes your stomach turn
high, stoned, altitude	an H hand moving upward
cry, tears	tears coming from the eyes
then, or, nor	something first then second
than	what is above is more than below
ticket	someone punching your ticket
unfair, worthless, insignificant	removing something unimportant
frustrated, frustration	being slapped down
vicinity, approximately, about, around, near, in the area	outlining an area

Practice Sentences

1. My nephew checks his cancelled checks every month.

   monthly, nephew my cancel draft+ his, (he) inspect

2. My two friends and I run early two days a week.

   two-day week, two friend, me, early jog

3. Both people ran away without leaving a note.

   people both escape, abandon write not

4. She can manage the store better than her brother.

   store girl manage can better than brother

5. The water ran all day and my father was mad.

   father my mad why? all-day water drip

6. That never happens when Grandma is watching.

   grandmother look-at, that happen never

7. My parents are good when it comes to recycling.

   parent my, good recycle

8. My brother never drinks beer.

   brother my beer drink never

9. Dad is willing to say what needs to be done.

   do need, dad willing say

10. Don't become frustrated and cry, try it again.

    you frustrate cry, don't, again try

11. Your ticket is worthless, it was for last week.

    ticket your worthless why? for last-week

12. Do it together first, then do it individually.

    first together do, then individual do

13. Something strange is happening near here.

    something strange near here happen

14. At my aunt's wedding, she had only wine and beer.

    wedding aunt my, only beer wine have

15. My brother looked stoned yesterday at work.

    yesterday, work, brother my high appearance

Class Activities

1. With a partner, go over the student activities in Lesson 16.

2. In small groups, take three minutes for everyone to remember the details of a recent conversation. Now in front of your group retell the conversation, taking on the different roles by moving your body appropriately in the space around you (remember to use NMS).

Student Activities

1. Use the two glosses below in an ASL sentence.

   a. CHECK OFF/NEVER

   _____
   _____
   _____

   b. WALK/SICK

   _____
   _____
   _____

   c. DRIP/VICINITY

   _____
   _____
   _____

   d. WINE/BEER

   _____
   _____
   _____

   e. OPERATE/HAPPEN

   _____
   _____
   _____

   f. JOG/TOGETHER

   _____
   _____
   _____

   g. TICKET/FRUSTRATED

   _____
   _____
   _____

2. Draw the side view of a person below. Using the body as a time line, add the glosses related to time in the appropriate places around the drawing. You should have at least eight time glosses.

Lesson 18

Vocabulary

513 about, concerning, regarding
514 arrive, get, reach
515 art, artwork, draw, illustration, art<u>ist</u>
516 know, recognize
517 don't know, unknown
518 aware, knowledge, familiar
519 away, go away
520 wall, barrier
521 become, get
522 drop, let go of, let fall
523 better
524 best
525 blood
526 tell, told, reveal
527 tell me, told me
528 busy, business
529 close, shut
530 open
531 insult, put one down
532 laugh at, ridicule, make fun of, mock
533 nothing to it, insignificant, minor
534 different, differ, differently, not the same
535 disobey, militant, strike
536 either, neither
537 vote, elect, election
538 evidence, proof, confirmation
539 what's up, what's going on, event
540 even, fair, tie, equal, just, draw

513
about, concerning, regarding

They talked about the bad checks.
bank-check bad, they talk concerning

514
arrive, get, reach

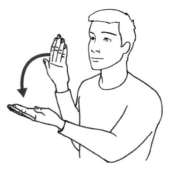

Two faxes arrived before ten o'clock.
prior-to time ten, two fax arrive

515
art, artwork, draw, illustration, art<u>ist</u>

The artwork arrived early this morning.
now morning early, art arrive

516
know, recognize

The artist knows that person.
person there artist know

517
don't know, unknown

I don't know when that happened.
that happen when? me don't-know

518
aware, knowledge, familiar

Are you aware he arrives today?
today he arrive you aware?

519
away, go away

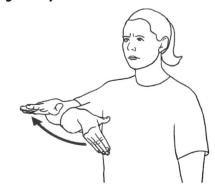

Mom shouted at the dog to go away.
dog, mother shout him away

Deaf Culture Facts and Information

Long conversations and interactions are valued in Deaf culture. It is common for Deaf people to stay for extended periods of time at Deaf social events. Because the Deaf community is spread throughout the entire country, people often have a lot of "catching up" to do. They also enjoy communicating in sign language, an opportunity they typically don't get with their colleagues at work.

520
wall, barrier

The new wall is not high.
wall new high not

521
become, get

Dad becomes mad when I drink.
me drink, father become mad

522
drop, let go of, let fall

Please don't drop that here.
that drop here please don't

523
better

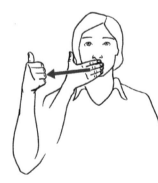

That wine is better than mine.
wine there better than my

524
best

They play best when together.
they (when) together best play

525
blood

Who saw blood on the cat?
blood cat have, see who?

526
tell, told, reveal

Tell the woman when to arrive.
woman there, (you) tell time arrive

527
tell me, told me

Tell me before you leave.
prior-to you depart, tell-me

ASL Grammar Notes

ASL verbs do not change to show past, present, or future tense. Instead, time adverbs (e.g., BEFORE, YESTERDAY, NOW, LATER) generally occur at the beginning of an ASL sentence or are established at the beginning of a conversation or story. If a time is not specified, the story is generally assumed to be in the present tense.

528
busy, business

The man you know is busy.
man you know, busy

529
close, shut

Tell me when the store closes.
store close time tell-me

530
open

How do I open the Internet?
internet, me open how?

531
insult, put one down

You insult my wife, she will cry.
wife my, (you) insult she cry will

532
laugh at, ridicule, make fun of, mock

Don't make fun of the strange person.
person strange, (you) laugh-at, don't

533
nothing to it, insignificant, minor

I'll write that, there's nothing to it.
write that me will, nothing-to-it

534
different, differ, differently, not the same

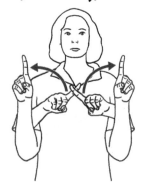

The two sisters act different.
two sister different behave

535
disobey, militant, strike

The little boy disobeys everyone.
boy short, every-one he disobey

536
either, neither

You can have either hot or iced tea.
have can (you) either hot cold tea

537
vote, elect, election

Send your vote by email.
vote your, send how? email

538
evidence, proof, confirmation

The police needed more evidence.
proof more, police need

539
what's up, what's going on, event

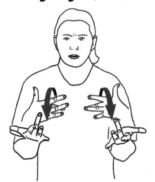

What's going on tomorrow?
tomorrow what's-up?

540
even, fair, tie, equal, just, draw

Tell me when the vote is tied.
vote equal (you) tell-me

Mind Ticklers

Make the sign _____	and think about . . .
about, concerning, regarding	talking around something
arrive, get, reach	going from one place to another
art, artist	drawing on a canvas
know, recognize	tapping the head to indicate you know
don't know, unknown	turning your hand out for a negative gesture
aware, knowledge, familiar	patting the head to indicate you know a lot
away, go away	gesturing for someone to go away from you
wall, barrier	indicating something is blocking your vision
become, get	the top becoming the bottom
drop, let go of, let fall	the act of dropping something
better	**good** with the comparative ending
best	**good** with the superlative ending
blood	the sign **red** plus the sign **liquid**
tell, told, reveal	words coming from your mouth
tell me, told me	words coming from someone to you
busy, business	**work** with a moving B handshape
close, shut	closing the lids on a box
open	opening the lids on a box
insult, put down, offend	poking your finger at someone
laugh at, ridicule	poking fingers at someone
nothing to it, insignificant, minor	zeros on both hands
different, differ, differently	the opposite of **same**
disobey, militant. strike	turning your head to ignore what's going on
either, neither	one or the other
vote, elect, election	putting your ballot into the voting box
evidence, proof	putting proof in your hand to be seen
what's up, what's going on	moving your hands up as if excited
even, fair, equal, tie, just, draw	being on an even playing field

Practice Sentences

1. The story was about a little girl who ran away.

   story concerning what? girl short run-away

2. When the artist arrived late everyone made fun of him.

   artist arrive late, every-one made-fun-of

3. The police needed more proof than they had.

   proof, police have, need more

4. The doctor became mad when the nurse insulted her.

   nurse insult doctor, doctor become mad

5. The boss wants to know what's up.

   boss want know what's-up

6. Our teacher is open and understanding.

   teacher our, open, understand

7. People became militant when they couldn't vote.

   people vote cannot, they militant finish

8. Tell me where you think you dropped the ticket.

   ticket you let-fall, tell-me place you think let-fall

9. The artist remains busy most of the time.

   most time artist busy continue

10. Your daughter looks a lot different than her brother.

    daughter your, brother her appearance a-lot different

11. They told me to go away now and come again tomorrow.

    they tell-me now go-away, tomorrow again come

12. We don't know how to tell Dad what happened.

    itemize happen, tell dad how, we don't-know

13. We will clean up; there is nothing to it.

    two-of-us clean up will, nothing-to-it

14. Neither person told me about my daughter's behavior.

    daughter my, behavior her, neither person tell-me

15. No one understood why the boy insulted his mother.

    boy insult mother his why? none one understand

Class Activity

1. In a small group, go over the student activities from Lesson 17.

Student Activities

1. Write eight words from the Mind Ticklers in this lesson and either write the "and think about" mnemonic or create one of your own.

   a. _____
   _____

   b. _____
   _____

   c. _____
   _____

   d. _____
   _____

   e. _____
   _____

f. _____

_____

g. _____

_____

h. _____

_____

2. Looking only at the vocabulary list for Lesson 18 write a gloss for all the signs that use a B or Open B handshape.

_____

_____

_____

_____

_____

3. Write an ASL sentence for each of the glosses below.

a. ELECT

_____

_____

b. DISOBEY

_____

_____

c. TELL

_____

_____

d. KNOW

_____

_____

e. REACH

_____

_____

Lesson 19

Vocabulary

541 incline, tendency, inclined, tend
542 whiskey, liquor
543 take, remove, take you
544 take, take up, start, begin
545 drop, give up, discontinue, quit
546 microphone, public address system
547 rest, relax
548 very
549 until, pending
550 surprise, amazed, astonished
551 start, begin, commence, initiate
552 blow up, blow one's top, temper, mad
553 all, whole, total, complete, entire
554 sorry, apologize, unfortunate
555 enjoy, pleasure, enjoyable, joy, appreciate
556 full, fill, complete, total
557 last, final
558 prize, award, trophy
559 predict, foretell, forecast, prophesy, foresee
560 forget, forgot, disregard
561 slipped my mind, a thought disappeared
562 waste, throw away, squander
563 second
564 third
565 fourth
566 fifth
567 slow, slowly
568 take me
569 tie, knot
570 trust, faith, confidence, confident

541
incline, tendency, inclined, tend

The fireman's tendency is to arrive late.
fireman tendency his late arrive

542
whiskey, liquor

Where did Dad put the whiskey?
whiskey, father put where?

543
take, remove, take you

Take the whiskey with you.
whiskey you remove

544
take, take up, start, begin

When did you take up drawing?
art, (you) take-up when?

Deaf Culture Facts and Information

Deaf culture has developed out of Deaf people's shared experiences. They share a unique heritage of education, storytelling, poetry, the arts, sports, and social organizations. Unlike most cultures, Deaf culture is rarely passed from parent to child; instead it is passed from deaf generation to deaf generation using ASL as the major means of communication.

545
drop, give up, discontinue, quit

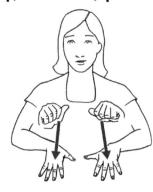

Why did you drop the class?
class, (you) discontinue why?

546
microphone, public address system

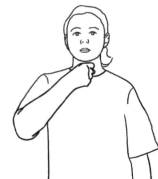

Who is speaking on the microphone?
microphone, speak now who?

547
rest, relax

Come and relax with me.
come with me relax

548
very

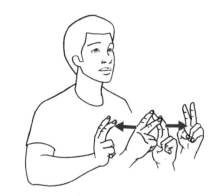

The young man looks very busy.
man young appearance very busy

549
until, pending

Sit here until sunset.
until sunset, here sit

550
surprise, amazed, astonished

Your niece looks surprised.
niece your, surprise appearance

551
start, begin, commence, initiate

What time does the voting start?
vote, time start?

552
blow up, blow one's top, temper, mad

We have never seen Dad blow up.
father blow-up, we see ago, never

553
all, whole, total, complete, entire

All the beer was taken yesterday.
yesterday beer all remove

554
sorry, apologize, unfortunate

My niece is sorry you left early.
niece my, sorry you early depart

555

enjoy, pleasure, enjoyable, joy, appreciate

They enjoyed their time together.
time together they enjoy

556

full, fill, complete, total

I'm surprised the house is full.
house full me surprise

557

last, final

Tuesday is the last day in the month.
final day month, Tuesday

558

prize, award, trophy

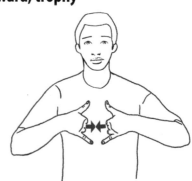

Father got six awards this year.
now year, father award six obtain

ASL Grammar Notes

Every sign has four parameters (parts): *handshape*—the configuration of the hands; handshapes come from the manual alphabet; *movement*—how the hands move while making the sign; *orientation*—the direction the palm faces while making the sign; and *location*—the place where a sign is produced

559

predict, foretell, forecast, prophesy, foresee

Who can predict the weather?
weather predict, who?

560
forget, forgot, disregard

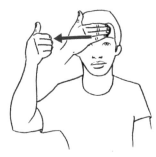

They forgot when classes start.
class start when, they forget

561
slipped my mind, a thought disappeared

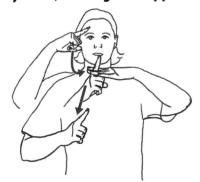

I think it slipped his mind.
boy slipped-his-mind, me think

562
waste, throw away, squander

I don't like you wasting my whiskey.
whiskey my, you waste, me don't-like

563
second

This is the second time I saw you.
now second time me see you

564
third

She is the third of five children.
five children girl third

565
fourth

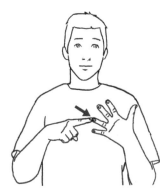

This is my fourth surprise party.
me now fourth party surprise

566
fifth

The fifth message came late.
message fifth late come

567
slow, slowly

You need to speak slowly.
you speak need slow

568
take me

Take me with you next week.
next-week me, you take-me

569
tie, knot

Who forgot to tie your surprise?
surprise your, forget tie who?

570
trust, faith, confidence, confident

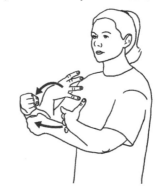

We believe you trust us.
you trust us, we believe

Mind Ticklers

Make the sign _____	and think about . . .
inclined, tendency, incline, tend	your heart reaching out
whiskey, liquor	measuring a drink with your fingers
take, remove, take you	reaching out and physically taking something (for example, a hat, a chair, etc.)
take, take up, start, begin	something you cannot physically hold (for example, a class, a bath, etc.)
drop, give up, discontinue, quit	opening your hands to drop something
microphone, public address system	holding a microphone
rest, relax	hands over your chest in repose
very	**much** with V handshapes
until, pending	waiting until a point in time
surprise, amazed, astonished	the look of surprise
start, begin, commence, initiate	putting a key in a keyhole and turning it
blow up, blow one's top, temper, mad	the top popping off after an explosion
all, whole, total, complete	gathering everything and putting it in a pile
sorry, apologize, unfortunate	rubbing near your heart to indicate sorrow
enjoy, pleasure, enjoyable, enjoyment, appreciate	everything in your body tingling
full, fill, complete, total	leveling off a full container
last, final, lastly	your pinkie finger being your last finger
award, prize, trophy	the shape of a trophy
predict, foretell, forecast, prophesy	looking into the future
forget, forgot, disregard	wiping away knowledge you had
slipped my mind, (my) thought disappeared	your thought falling and disappearing
waste, throw away	throwing something from your hand
second, third, fourth, fifth	counting your fingers two through five
slow, slowly	the hand moving slowly up the hand and arm
take me	pulling yourself to be taken
tie, knot	the act of tying a knot
trust, faith, confidence, confident	holding onto a belief

Practice Sentences

1. When the fourth person arrives we will begin.

   fourth person arrive, we begin will

2. I apologize, I forgot to tell you when to vote.

   time vote, me sorry (me) forget tell-you

3. The whole group was surprised when you blew up.

   you blow-your-top, group all surprise

4. Please take me with you when you leave.

   you depart, you take-me please

5. We started slowly until he understood what to do.

   until man understand itemize do, we slow start

6. Father made a prediction, but it slipped my mind.

   father predict make finish, me slip-my-mind

7. Sorry, the last person received the award.

   award, sorry, person last get

8. Dad took up running after giving up beer and wine.

   beer, wine, dad discontinue, he take-up jog now

9. Grandma looks very relaxed after drinking beer all day.

   all-day grandma beer drink, appearance very relax

10. I'm surprised how my son learned to tie that.

    son my, tie that learn how, me surprise

11. The store's old public address system is thirty years old.

    public-address-system old, store its, now thirty year old

12. The second week of May is my daughter's third art class.

    second-week M-A-Y, daughter my, third class art hers

13. You will enjoy taking that class with us.

    class you take-up with us, you enjoy will

14. The parents have trusted their children for a long time.

    long-time time parents their children trust

15. Taking all the children will fill my car.

    children me take all, car my full will

Class Activity

1. In small groups, take turns reading a mnemonic written for the first student activity in Lesson 18. The other students must guess the gloss/sign.

Student Activities

1. How would you describe the handshape used for the following signs? There may not be a "right" answer.

   a. GIRL

   _____

   _____

   b. MOTHER

   _____

   _____

   c. WHISKEY

   _____

   _____

   d. TAKE

   _____

   _____

e. SURPRISE

_____

_____

f. PRIZE

_____

_____

g. SLOW

_____

_____

h. TAKE-ME

_____

_____

2. Write four English sentences from the practice sentences for Lesson 19. Then rewrite each sentence into an ASL sentence. Go back to the practice sentences to see how well you did.

a. _____

_____

_____

_____

b. _____

_____

_____

_____

c. _____

_____

_____

_____

d. _____

_____

_____

_____

Lesson 20

Vocabulary

571 pay, payment
572 dollar, buck
573 credit card
574 money, *funds, *finance, *budget, *economy
575 cents
576 twenty-five cents, quarter
577 ten cents, dime
578 fifty cents, half-dollar
579 expensive, costly, high
580 spend, pay out
581 shopping, shop
582 interest (money)
583 idea, opinion
584 inside, indoors
585 out, outside, outdoors, exterior, external
586 turn off
587 turn on
588 preach, preach<u>er</u>, minist<u>er</u>
589 pray, prayers, worship
590 heaven
591 church, place of worship
592 temple, place of worship
593 religion, religious
594 Jesus
595 God
596 Christ, Christian
597 Jewish, Judaism

571
pay, payment

Who will pay for the Pepsi?
Pepsi, pay who?

572
dollar, buck

The bachelor has ten dollars.
bachelor ten dollar have

573
credit card

Do you always pay with a credit card?
credit-card, (you) pay always with that

574
money, *funds, *finance, *budget, *economy

Where do you put your money?
money your put where?

575
cents

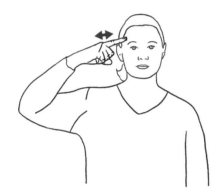

We cannot find any cents.
cent any, we find cannot

576
twenty-five cents, quarter

A bus ticket is a quarter.
now ticket bus quarter

577
ten cents, dime

Father gave the baby ten cents.
finish, father ten-cent baby give

Deaf Culture Facts and Information

Approximately 60 percent of old ASL signs are French in origin because of Laurent Clerc, the first deaf teacher of deaf children in the United States. The other 40 percent evolved from signs that children who came from Martha's Vineyard, New Hampshire, Maine, and other areas brought to the American School for the Deaf.

578
fifty cents, half-dollar

The Coke was about 50 cents.
Coke approximately 50-cent

579
expensive, costly, high

That new beer is expensive.
that beer new expensive

580
spend, pay out

My sister spends a lot of money.
sister my a-lot money spend

581
shopping, shop

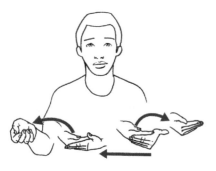

The man and woman enjoy shopping.
man woman they shopping enjoy

582
interest (money)

We received no interest this month.
this month interest obtain none

583
idea, opinion

I forgot your idea.
idea your me forget

584
inside, indoors

Go inside and play.
(you) go inside play

585

out, outside, outdoors, exterior, external

The bird is out of the house.
now bird out house

586

turn off

Turn off the television now.
now T-V turn-off

587

turn on

Dad turned on my lights.
light, my, father turn-on

588

preach, preacher, minister

The preacher's wife likes shopping.
wife preacher his, she shopping like

ASL Grammar Notes

Dropping the hands after a comment is an indication that you are through "talking." Not dropping your hands after a comment could indicate that you are not finished with your turn, or, when combined with nonmanual features, it could indicate that you are asking a question.

589

pray, prayers, worship

Don't forget to pray for me.
(you) pray for me, forget don't

590
heaven

Who wants to go to heaven?
heaven, want go, who?

591
church, place of worship

Where is the community church?
church community where?

592
temple, place of worship

The temple is near here.
temple near here

593
religion, religious

Grandpa is very religious.
grandfather very religion

594
Jesus

The people prayed to Jesus.
people to Jesus pray

595
God

God is in heaven.
God up-there heaven

596
Christ, Christian

The Christians are in church.
now Christians there church

597
Jewish, Judaism

Jewish people go to temple.
people Jewish there temple (go)

Mind Ticklers

Make the sign _____	and think about . . .
pay, payment	pushing money out of the hand
dollar, buck	counting out dollar bills
credit card	the old way of imprinting a credit card
money, funds, economy, finance, budget	money piling up in your hand
cents	*cents* sounding like *sense*
quarter, twenty-five cents, dime, ten cents, fifty cents	**cent** plus the appropriate numerical sign
expensive, costly, high	the cost making money fly away
spend, pay out	the idea of throwing money away
shopping, shop	buying several different things
interest (money)	money in your hand
idea, opinion, view	an idea coming from your head
inside, indoors	doubling the sign **in** to make it a noun
out, outside, external, exterior	pulling something out of a box
turn off	the act of turning something off
turn on	the act of turning something on
preach, preacher, minister	a minister gesticulating
pray, prayers, worship	holding the hands reverently
heaven	the vastness of heaven
church, place of worship	the C handshape on a rock
temple, place of worship	the T handshape on a rock
religion, religious	religious feelings coming from the heart
Jesus	the spikes put through his hands
God	the idea of God being in heaven
Christ, Christian	Christ wearing a robe
Jewish, Judaism	the beards worn by some Jewish men

Practice Sentences

1. Don't pay everything with your credit card.

   credit-card your, pay every-thing, don't

2. He is inclined to spend money that he doesn't have.

   man money spend he not have, his tendency

3. Our minister enjoys visiting friends at the temple.

   minister our visit friend there temple, (he) enjoy

4. Turn off the TV before you fall to sleep.

   T-V, turn-off prior-to you sleep

5. My mom and aunt enjoy shopping at expensive stores.

   mom, aunt my, shopping store expensive (they) enjoy

6. The group has an idea how you can spend your interest.

   interest your how spend? group idea have

7. I'm sorry; I cannot find four dollars and fifty cents for you.

   sorry, four dollar fifty cent for you, me find cannot

8. The preacher predicted that all of us would go to heaven.

   heaven, preacher predict all us go will

9. Take me to church with your family next Sunday.

   next Sunday, me church with family your take-me

10. My uncle donated most of the money for the new church.

    new church, uncle my most money (he) give

11. The exterior of our house doesn't look very good.

    house our outside, appearance good not

12. The Jewish man prayed morning, noon, and night.

    morning, noon, night, man Jewish pray

13. God is in heaven and all is right with the world.

    God there heaven, every-thing all-right now

14. The second Monday of each month we have religious studies.

    Monday, second-week, we religious class have

15. Our minister has an idea of how to pay for the new church.

    church new, how pay-for, minister our idea have

Class Activities

1. In small groups, share your descriptions of the handshapes from student activity 1 in Lesson 19, and discuss how you came up them.

2. In small groups, students watch the instructor sign an interesting fact about deaf history, culture, or signing. The first student to raise his hand and sign the correct answer gets a point for his team. The first team to reach five points wins.

Student Activities

1. Use the vocabulary in Lesson 20 to write an English paragraph about religion or going shopping (write four or five sentences).

   _____

   _____

   _____

   _____

   _____

   _____

   _____

   _____

2. Rewrite the paragraph above in ASL sentences.

   _____

   _____

   _____

   _____

   _____

   _____

   _____

3. Write the glosses in this lesson that might be considered iconic.

   _____

   _____

   _____

   _____

   _____

Lesson 21

Vocabulary

598 chair, seat
599 couch, sofa
600 bed
601 drawer
602 closet
603 floor, level
604 ceiling, overhead
605 toilet, commode
606 shower
607 hair dryer
608 toothbrush
609 toothpaste
610 door
611 doorbell
612 window
613 curtains
614 wash face
615 wash hands
616 table, desk
617 lamp
618 oven, stove, bake
619 refrigerator
620 microwave
621 steps, step, stairway
622 wash, laundry
623 restroom
624 furniture
625 television, TV
626 room, *box, *office

598
chair, seat

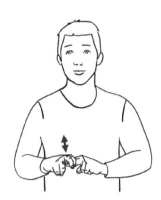

The chairs here are not soft.
chair+ here soft not

599
couch, sofa

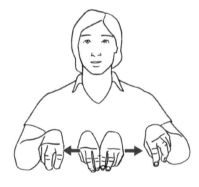

Our sofa is red, white, and black.
sofa our, red white black

600
bed

How much was the bed?
bed how-much?

601
drawer

Put my money in the drawer.
money my drawer there put

602
closet

It is dark in the closet.
closet inside dark

603
floor, level

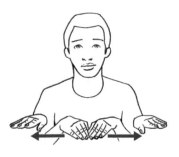

Our bed is on the third floor.
bed our third floor there

604
ceiling, overhead

The church ceiling is very high.
ceiling there church, very high

605
toilet, commode

Grandpa has a toilet outside.
toilet outside grandfather have

606
shower

He showers morning and night.
morning night man shower

607
hair dryer

Her hair dryer is orange and yellow.
hair-dryer girl hers, orange yellow

Deaf Culture Facts and Information

Sixty percent of English words are visually indistinguishable on the lips. That is, the mouth movements look the same. For example, it is almost impossible to see the difference between the words *mat, mad, man, pat, pad, pan, bat, bad,* and *ban*. The identical physical appearance of so many words represents a major challenge to speechreading.

608
toothbrush

My red toothbrush is missing.
now toothbrush red my missing

609
toothpaste

What color is your toothpaste?
toothpaste your, color what?

610
door

Which door do you want brown?
door want you brown which?

611
doorbell

The new house had an old doorbell.
house new, doorbell old have

612
window

Sunshine is coming in the window.
now sunshine through window

613
curtains

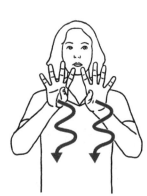

Mom put the old curtains in the closet.
curtain old closet there mother put

614
wash face

Wash your face before bedtime.
prior-to bed, (you) face-wash

615
wash hands

Wash your hands before eating.
prior-to eat, (you) wash-hand

616
table, desk

The orange is on the table.
orange, table there

617
lamp

The small lamp is on the table.
lamp tiny, table there

618
oven, stove, bake

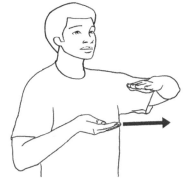

I think the oven is white.
oven white me think

619
refrigerator

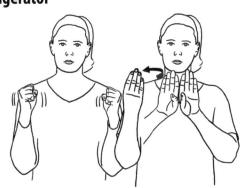

Is the refrigerator still working?
now refrigerator work still?

620
microwave

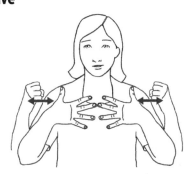

Grandma doesn't know how to turn on the microwave.
microwave, grandmother turn-on don't-know

621
steps, step, stairway

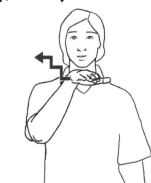

The house has no steps.
house step have, none

ASL Grammar Notes

Eye contact in ASL is very important and almost continuous, unlike when hearing people are speaking to one another. Not maintaining eye contact in Deaf culture is considered impolite. Keeping eye contact with the person with whom you are signing will take time and practice.

622
wash, laundry

Dad does all of our laundry.
laundry our, father himself all do

623
restroom

Which is correct, toilet or restroom?
toilet, restroom, accurate which?

624
furniture

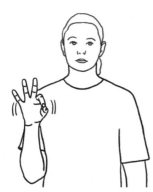

Most of our furniture is black.
furniture our most black

625
television, TV

The new TV is on the table.
T-V new, table there

626
room, *box, * office

Our house has five rooms on the first floor.
house our, first floor room+ five

Mind Ticklers

Make the sign _____	and think about . . .
chair, seat	your feet dangling over the seat's edge
couch, sofa	several people sitting on a couch
bed	where you put your head to rest
drawer	pulling out or opening a drawer
closet	the place where clothes hang behind a door
floor, level	showing that the floor is level
ceiling, overhead	what is over your head
toilet, commode	the shaking T handshape for _toilet_
shower	water coming from the shower head
hair dryer	a hair dryer shaped like a gun
toothbrush	brushing your teeth
toothpaste	putting paste on a toothbrush
door	a door opening and closing
doorbell	pushing the button on the door jam
window	a window opening and closing
curtains	curtains hanging down from a window
wash face, wash hands	the gesture of washing your hands and face
table, desk	the top of a table
lamp	a lamp on a table with the light on
oven, stove, bake	putting something into an oven
refrigerator	a door keeping the cold air inside
microwave	microwaves shooting out
steps, step, stairway	making the outline of steps
wash, laundry	rubbing clothes together to get them clean
restroom	the handshapes R-R for _restroom_
furniture	the shaking F handshape for _furniture_
television	the handshapes T-V for _television_
room, box, office	making the shape of a room with your hands

Practice Sentences

1. Who paid for the chairs in our living room?

   chair+ there our living room, buy who?

2. The toilet and shower are not working right.

   toilet, shower, work correct not

3. The blue bedroom has a couch, but no TV.

   bed room blue, couch have, T-V, none

4. Close the refrigerator door after you get your food.

   refrigerator, finish you get food your, close door

5. Why did Mother forget our toothbrushes and toothpaste?

   toothbrush, toothpaste our, mother forget why?

6. The room on the third floor has no furniture.

   furniture, third floor room none

7. Why does Dad have a microwave in his bathroom?

   microwave, father bathroom his have there, why?

8. Look on the table for the hair dryer and lamp.

   hair-dryer, lamp, on table (you) search

9. The ceiling is not the right color for a small bedroom.

   color ceiling for bed room small correct not

10. Close the window before going to bed tonight.

    now night prior-to you bed go, window-close

11. Who do you think washed all the cars today?

    today car+, think you wash all who?

12. Wash your hands and face before coming to eat.

    wash-hand, wash-face, your, prior-to come eat

13. The oven door doesn't open right.

    door oven open correct, not

14. I had no idea that you had all that furniture.

    furniture yours a-lot have, me idea none

15. The overhead lights in church are very bright.

    church light ceiling very clear

Class Activities

1. In groups of three, one person signs his or her ASL paragraph from student activity 2 in Lesson 20 while the other two voice it. Then rotate until each person has signed his or her paragraph. Remember to maintain eye contact.

2. As a class, quickly go over student activity 3 in Lesson 20.

Student Activities

1. Use the vocabulary in Lesson 21 to write an English paragraph about the furniture in your house. Use some color glosses in your four to five sentences.

   _____

   _____

   _____

   _____

   _____

   _____

2. Rewrite the paragraph above in ASL sentences.

_____

_____

_____

_____

_____

_____

3. Write the five glosses for the signs in this lesson that are made above your neck.

_____

_____

_____

_____

_____

Lesson 22

Vocabulary

627 up
628 upstairs
629 down
630 downstairs
631 knife
632 bowl
633 bathroom
634 bedroom
635 living room
636 dining room
637 soap
638 bath, bathe
639 dance
640 bell, alarm, ring, ringing
641 always, ever
642 against, sue, oppose, opposed to
643 opposite, oppose, contrast, contrary, enemy
644 far, distance, distant
645 ahead, in front, go ahead of
646 other, another, else
647 grow, grown, raise, grow-up
648 grow, raise (plant)
649 lead, guide, head, led
650 success, finally, achievement, at-last, hit, succeed, works, successful
651 shoot, gun
652 rifle, hunt, hunting
653 pull, draw
654 broke, bankrupt, no money

627
up

Go up four steps and stop.
(you) up four step, stop

628
upstairs

Go upstairs and get the dog.
(you) upstair, dog obtain

629
down

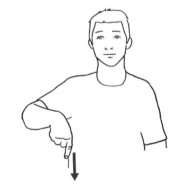

Put the black dog down.
dog black down put

630
downstairs

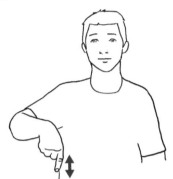

I hear the cat downstairs.
cat downstairs, me hear

631
knife

A little knife is on the floor.
knife tiny, there floor

632
bowl

Who took my new bowl?
bowl my new remove who?

633
bathroom

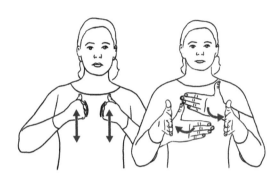

The school's bathroom is closed.
bath-room school close

634
bedroom

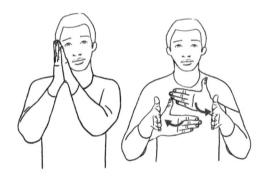

We cannot find the bedroom.
bed-room we find cannot

635
living room

Our living room is large.
living-room our large

636
dining room

The dining room has six lamps.
dining-room six lamp have

Deaf Culture Facts and Information

Some deaf people, especially those who were mainstreamed or isolated from other deaf people, thought that they would eventually become hearing or they would die before becoming an adult. This is because they never saw deaf adults.

637
soap

Leave the soap in the bathroom.
soap there bath-room abandon

638
bath, bathe

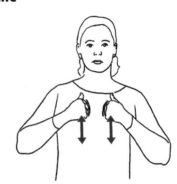

After your bath, go to bed.
bath finish, you bed go

639
dance

When is the college dance?
dance college when?

640
bell, alarm, ring, ringing

The church bell is very loud.
bell church very loud

641
always, ever

My sister is always slow in the morning.
morning sister my slow always

642
against, sue, oppose, opposed to

Grandma is against drinking liquor.
drink whiskey grandmother opposed-to

643
opposite, oppose, contrast, contrary, ene<u>my</u>

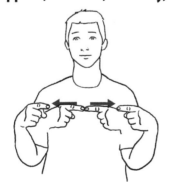

My bedroom is opposite the bathroom.
bed-room my opposite bath-room

644
far, distance, distant

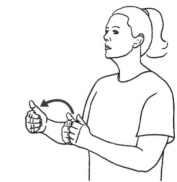

How far is it to the party?
party how far?

ASL Grammar Notes

A gerund is the form of a verb that acts as a noun. In English, gerunds end in *ing*; for example, *Swimming* is good exercise. ASL does not have a sign that means *ing*. When a verb is used as a noun, the function is understood from its position in the sentence (i.e., topic-comment) and repetition of the sign. For example, *Playing* is good exercise.   *Painting* is something I enjoy.

PLAY-PLAY GOOD EXERCISE   PAINT-PAINT ITSELF ME ENJOY

645
ahead, in front, go ahead of

Don't run ahead of the red car.
car red (you) run ahead don't

646

other, another, else

The other bedroom is blue and red.
bed-room other, color blue red

647

grow, grown, raise, grow-up

That woman has five grown children.
woman there children five grow-up have

648

grow, raise (plant)

Mom's favorite tree is growing slowly.
tree favorite mother hers slow grow

649

lead, guide, head, led

Her aunt led the group home.
girl aunt hers group home there lead

650

**success, finally, achievement, at-last, hit,
succeed, works, successful**

The man had good success at work.
man work success good have

651

shoot, gun

The small gun is in the drawer.
gun small where? there drawer

652
rifle, hunt, hunting

Put the rifle near the door.
rifle, near door put

653
pull, draw

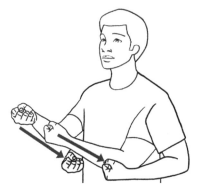

We pulled the oven outside.
oven, outside we pull

654
broke, bankrupt, no money

The preacher is always broke.
preacher himself broke always

Mind Ticklers

Make the sign _____	and think about . . .
up	pointing up
upstairs	double motion for a noun
down	pointing down
downstairs	double motion for a noun
knife	sharpening a knife on a strop
bowl	making the shape of a bowl with your hands
bathroom	a room for bathing
bedroom	your bed in a room
living room	a room you live in
dining room	a room for eating
soap	the slippery feel of wet soap
bath, bathe	a pantomime of washing your body
dance	moving your feet as you dance
bell, alarm, ring, ringing	the clapper hitting the side of a bell
always, ever	a never-ending circle
against, sue, oppose	an object encountering a barrier
opposite, contrast, contrary, enemy	two things at extreme ends
far, distance, distant	one hand far in front of the other
ahead, in front, go ahead of	one hand moving ahead of the other
other, another, else	pointing to one person and then another with your thumb
grow, raise, grow up	the continuous growth of a child
grow, raise (plants)	a plant emerging from the ground
lead, guide, head, led	taking someone by the hand to lead them
success, finally, achievement, at last, hit, succeed, works	success at a high level
shoot, gun	the act of shooting a gun
rifle, hunt, hunting	carrying a rifle while hunting
pull, draw	the act of pulling something
broke, bankrupt, no money	your head being chopped off

Practice Sentences

1. My parents searched upstairs and downstairs for my little brother.

   brother my short, parent my, upstairs downstairs look-for

2. Her brother grew up hunting with their father.

   brother her with father their raise hunting

3. Right now another person is ahead of me.

   person other ahead me now

4. Grandma is against drinking and dancing.

   drink, dance, grandmother my oppose

5. The downstairs bedroom has finally been cleaned.

   at-last bedroom downstairs clean-up finish

6. There is no soap or toilet paper in the upstairs bathroom.

   bath-room upstairs, soap, toilet paper, have none

7. Go up and see if the children are still sleeping.

   children sleep on-going you up see

8. Mom grows several different small trees in the sun room.

   tree+ small, several different, mom there sun-room grow

9. Our living room is too small for a large party.

   living room our small, party large cannot

10. We all saw another car far ahead of us.

    car other far-ahead we see

11. The guide had no idea who heard the ringing.

    bell, guide idea none who hear

12. Father refused to declare bankruptcy, and Mother agreed with him.

    broke, father announce refuse, mother agree refuse

13. Go down and see if you can find my old rifle.

    rifle my old (you) go down see possible find

14. We felt successful when we finished that job.

    finish job, success we feel

15. My brother and sister always do the opposite of what I do.

    me do, brother sister my always opposite me do

Class Activities

1. In groups of three, one person signs his or her ASL paragraph from student activity 2 in Lesson 21 while the other two voice it. Then rotate until each person has signed his or her paragraph. Remember to maintain eye contact.

2. In small groups, students write their names vertically on a piece of paper. Then they write one of their personality traits after each letter. Share the information written with the group. For example:

   S implistic
   U nderstanding
   E nergetic

Student Activities

1. Rewrite the following English sentences into ASL sentences.

   a. Mom ran into Jim yesterday.

   _____

   _____

   b. Mary is ahead of everyone in class.

   _____

   _____

   c. Don't be stupid, grow up.

   _____

   _____

   d. I fell asleep in the car.

   _____

   _____

   e. They think he broke the bank.

   _____

   _____

   f. Dad can pull a lot of weight.

   _____

   _____

   g. Don't shoot the old horse.

   _____

   _____

   h. Mike has gone too far.

   _____

   _____

2. Cross out the glosses that are not compound signs.

   a. GROW-UP

   b. UPSTAIRS

   c. BATHROOM

   d. DOWNSTAIRS

   e. BEDROOM

   f. CLOSE THE DOOR

   g. FORETELL

   h. SLIPPED MY MIND

   i. TRUST

   j. MOIST

   k. SUNRISE

   l. EVERYONE

Lesson 23

Vocabulary

655 not my responsibility, out of my hands
656 train-gone, you missed out, cannot be repeated, already gone
657 use, utilize, apply, wear
658 shoes, *boots
659 dress
660 socks
661 pants
662 shirt
663 clothes, dress
664 hat
665 cap
666 pocketbook, purse, handbag
667 suitcase, luggage
668 necklace
669 ring
670 bracelet
671 shorts
672 handkerchief, tissue
673 underwear
674 flip flops, sandals
675 hoodie
676 short sleeves
677 long sleeves
678 glasses, eyeglasses
679 bra, brassiere
680 coat, jacket

655
not my responsibility, out of my hands

That mistake is not my responsibility.
mistake there, not-my-responsibility

656
train-gone, you missed out, cannot be repeated, already gone

Sorry, you missed out.
sorry, train-gone

657
use, utilize, apply, wear

Mom uses the downstairs toilet.
toilet downstairs mother use

658
shoes, *boots

Your shoes are under the table.
shoe your where? under table

Deaf Culture Facts and Information

By the 1860s, nearly 40 percent of all teachers of deaf children were deaf themselves. After the Milan Congress of 1880, which promoted an oral-only education for deaf children, the number of deaf teachers dropped to about 14 percent in the United States because they were "unable" to teach speech.

659
dress

That looks like a new dress.
dress there, appearance new

660
socks

The boy's socks are different colors.
sock boy his, color different

661
pants

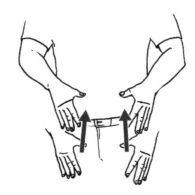

Put your pants in the closet.
pants your there closet put

662
shirt

I don't like wearing a pink shirt.
shirt pink, me use don't-like

663
clothes, dress

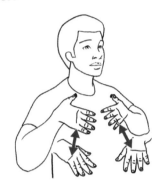

Her mother dresses nicely every day.
daily mother hers nice clothes

664
hat

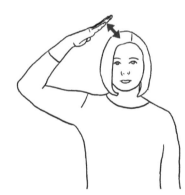

Where did he put my hat?
hat my man put where?

665
cap

Most boys like caps.
cap, most boy like

666
pocketbook, purse, handbag

Your red purse is on the steps.
purse red your steps there

667
suitcase, luggage

The dark blue suitcase is full.
suitcase dark blue full

668
necklace

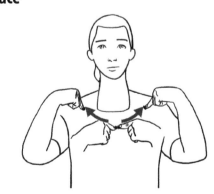

Her necklace is gold and silver.
necklace, girl hers, gold silver

669
ring

She left her ring in the bathroom.
girl ring hers, bath-room there abandon

ASL Grammar Notes

Fingerspelling includes a class of signs known as "loan signs" or "borrowed signs." These signs have evolved from fingerspelling the individual letters of an English word and are sometimes defined as *lexicalized* (like a word) fingerspelling. Some features of the individual letter signs have changed over time, so that a new sign is created. For example, the sign NO began as the fingerspelling of N-O, but the handshapes have changed and the movement is reduplicated (repeated). In the lexicalized sign that began as Y-E-S, the E has been dropped and the palm orientation and movement have changed.

670
bracelet

That bracelet is very pretty.
bracelet there very pretty

671
shorts

His shorts need to be washed.
now boy shorts his need wash

672
handkerchief, tissue

I forgot my handkerchief.
handkerchief my (me) forget

673
underwear

Underwear comes in different colors.
underwear color different+ have

674
flip flops, sandals

The black flip flops are too big.
flip-flop black, a-lot big

675
hoodie

Your hoodie is on the chair.
hoodie your, chair there

676
short sleeves

Short sleeves are fine in the summer.
summer short-sleeves fine

677
long sleeves

Mom always wears long sleeves.
long-sleeves mother use always

678
glasses, eyeglasses

My brother needs other glasses.
brother my glasses other need

679
bra, brassiere

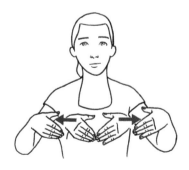

Bras can be very expensive.
bra very expensive can

680
coat, jacket

Always wear a coat in the winter.
during winter coat always use

Mind Ticklers

Make the sign _____	and think about . . .
not my responsibility, out of my hands	flicking the responsibility from your shoulders
train gone, you missed out, cannot be repeated, already gone	literally signing **train gone**
use, utilize, apply, wear	signing **work** with a U handshape
shoes, boots	hitting your shoes together to knock off dirt
dress	the outline of a dress
socks	knitting socks
pants	pulling up your pants
shirt	holding up your shirt
clothes, dress	brushing off your clothes
hat	what goes on your head
cap	touching the bill of a cap
pocketbook, purse	holding on to your purse
suitcase, luggage	carrying a suitcase
necklace	outlining the shape of a necklace
ring	placing a ring on your finger
bracelet	placing a bracelet on your wrist
shorts	showing the length of your shorts
handkerchief, tissue	wiping your nose
underwear	what is under your pants
flip flops, sandals	the strap between your toes
hoodie	pulling your hood over your head
short sleeves, long sleeves	indicating the length of your sleeves
glasses, eyeglasses	the shape of eyeglasses
bra, brassiere	where the bra is worn
coat, jacket	putting on a coat

Practice Sentences

1. Raising that child is not my responsibility.

   child there me raise, not-my-responsibility

2. Sorry, you missed out, there is nothing more to say.

   sorry, train-gone

3. Wear your hoodie when going out in the cold weather.

   weather cold you outside hoodie use

4. Your socks, shorts, and underwear are on the bed.

   sock shorts underwear your, on bed now

5. Can you put my hat in your purse?

   hat my your purse in possible?

6. I wear flip-flops and shorts every day during the summer.

   daily during summer flip-flop, shorts, me use

7. The nurse has a new bracelet and necklace.

   bracelet, necklace new, nurse have

8. We finally got Mom to wear blue shorts.

   at-last shorts blue mom use

9. My uncle cannot see very far with his new glasses.

   uncle my, eyeglasses new, see far cannot

10. Put all your clothes in the suitcase upstairs.

    clothes your all, suitcase upstairs put

11. Your red ring looks nice with your beautiful red dress.

    ring red your, with dress red beautiful your, appearance nice

12. Wear short sleeves in the summer and long sleeves in the winter.

    summer short-sleeves, winter long-sleeves, use

13. They wanted to lead the group; it is out of my hands.

    group lead they want, me not-my-responsibility

14. My aunt always wears white pants to work.

    aunt my work there, pants white use always

15. My brother wore his cap while hunting with Dad.

    brother my, cap his use when? with father hunt

Class Activities

1. In small groups, go over the student activities in Lesson 22.

2. After introducing Lesson 23, students get into groups of three. They then line up and number themselves. Students one and two face each other, while student three faces the back of student two. Student one signs to student two what student three is wearing. Student two then voices what is signed. Rotate positions until each student's clothing has been described.

Student Activities

1. Using twelve of the glosses for articles of clothing, write ASL sentences to describe what an imaginary person is wearing.

   _____

   _____

   _____

   _____

   _____

   _____

   _____

   _____

   _____

2. Below are some examples of verb/noun pairs. Fill in the missing verb or noun then practice signing each pair.

   a. FLY/AIRPLANE

   b. PUT-GAS-IN/_____

   c. OPEN-DOOR/_____

   d. PUT-ON-CLOTHES/CLOTHES

   e. LICK-ICE-CREAM/ICE CREAM

   f. PRINT/_____

   g. OPEN BOOK/BOOK

   h. USE BROOM/BROOM

   i. _____/NAME

   j. SELL/_____

   k. GO-BY-BOAT/BOAT

   l. SIT/CHAIR

   m. PAINT/_____

   n. DRESS/DRESS

3. The signs for the glosses NOT-MY-RESPONSIBILITY and YOU-MISSED-OUT are often described as "sign idioms." Why do you think this is so?

   _____

   _____

   _____

   _____

   _____

   _____

   _____

   _____

   _____

   _____

Lesson 24

Vocabulary

681 go ahead, get along, proceed, go on, continue, onward

682 toward, approach

683 test, exam, quiz, examination

684 movie, film, cinema, show

685 show,* illustrate, *represent, reveal, *demonstrate, *example, *symbol

686 confuse, mixed up, mix

687 ignore, neglect

688 ignore me

689 around, round

690 policy, principle

691 catch, apprehend, arrest, capture, caught

692 blanket, cover

693 cover, go over, look over

694 review, go over, look over

695 cover up, vague, unclear, obscure

696 street, *road, *path, *way, trail, procedure, method, course

697 bury, cemetery, buried

698 book, textbook, album

699 magazine, brochure, flyer, pamphlet

700 stay, remain, don't move

701 west, western

702 east, eastern

703 north, northern

704 south, southern

681

go ahead, get along, proceed, go on, continue, onward

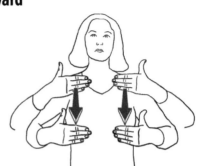

Go ahead, finish your work.
go-ahead work your finish

682

toward, approach

Don't go toward the bad dog.
dog bad (you) toward don't

683

test, exam, quiz, examination

Who took the exam yesterday?
yesterday exam take-up who?

684
movie, film, cinema, show

Last night's movie was funny.
ago night movie funny

685
show,* illustrate, *represent, reveal,
*demonstrate, *example, *symbol

Show the man your necklace.
necklace your, man show

686
confuse, mixed up, mix

Your question confused me.
question your, me confuse

687
ignore, neglect

Go ahead and ignore what I say.
go-ahead me say (you) ignore

Deaf Culture Facts and Information

In the southern states, schools for the deaf kept Black and white students segregated for many years. The last segregated school, the Louisiana School for the Colored Deaf and Blind in Baton Rouge, remained open until 1978.

688
ignore me

You cannot ignore me.
ignore-me (you) cannot

689
around, round

Dad is running around the house.
now father around house jog

690
policy, principle

The old man ignored the policy.
policy, man old ignore

691
catch, apprehend, arrest, capture, caught

The police arrested the two men.
finish two man police arrest

692
blanket, cover

Put a blanket on the bed.
blanket, bed there put

693
cover, go over, look over

The teacher looked over the new car.
car new teacher go-over

694
review, go over, look over

Who reviewed the classes' work?
class work review who?

695
cover up, vague, unclear, obscure

The stranger's story was vague.
stranger story vague

696
street, *road, *path, *way, trail, procedure, method, course

Drive to the third street.
you third street drive

697
bury, cemetery, buried

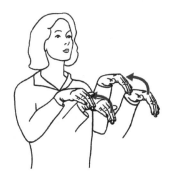

My house is near the cemetery.
house my, cemetery near

698
book, textbook, album

Read what is in the book.
(you) itemize in book you read

ASL Grammar Notes

A gloss is the basic form of an English word that represents a sign concept. Glosses are written in small capital letters, and they are used to transcribe signs on paper. In ASL, signs have no prefixes or suffixes attached to them, so the gloss takes only one form. For example, *run* and *running* are both glossed as RUN, *slow* and *slowly* are glossed as SLOW, etc. The change in meaning is accomplished by modifying certain features of the sign.

699
magazine, brochure, flyer, pamphlet

Mom likes gardening magazines.
magazine concerning grow-plant mother like

700
stay, remain, don't move

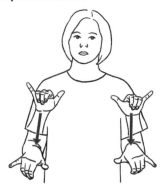

You stay here with the books.
(you) with book them here stay

701
west, western

Go west young man.
man young west go

702
east, eastern

I became confused and went east.
me become confuse, east go

703
north, northern

The North is very cold.
north very cold

704
south, southern

The book is about the South.
book this concerning south

Mind Ticklers

Make the sign _____	and think about . . .
go ahead, get along, proceed, go on, continue, onward	moving ahead into the future
toward, approach	one hand approaching the other hand
test, exam, quiz, examination	the questions on a test or quiz page
movie, film, show	the film flickering before your eyes
show, illustrate, represent, reveal, demonstrate, example, symbol	pointing to and showing what is in your hand
confuse, mix up, mix	moving your hands as if mixing something
ignore, neglect	turning your head away from something
ignore me	someone turning their nose from you
around, round	going around something
policy, principle	listing policies on paper
catch, apprehend, arrest	grabbing someone
blanket, cover	pulling a blanket up to your neck
cover, go over, look over	looking over something thoroughly
review, go over	going back over a page
cover up, vague, unclear, obscure	rubbing something to make it unclear
street, road, path, way, trail, method	indicating the width of a road, path, etc.
bury, cemetery, buried	the mound over a grave
book, textbook, album	the act of opening a book
magazine, brochure, flyer, pamphlet	the binding of a magazine
stay, remain, don't move	holding something down with the hands
west, western	moving a W handshape to the west
east, eastern	moving an E handshape to the east
north, northern	moving an N handshape up to the north
south, southern	moving an S handshape down to the south

Practice Sentences

1. Go ahead with your plans to finish your book today.

   today plan your book finish, proceed

2. The test the teacher gave us was very confusing.

   test teacher give-us very confuse

3. Grandma made the blanket on the bed in the front bedroom.

   blanket on bed, bedroom front, grandma make

4. How can you ignore him? He doesn't have on a shirt?

   man shirt none, you ignore-him how?

5. The magazine covers the West in the old days.

   west, long-ago, magazine now go-over

6. He forgot to wear shoes when he went to the movies.

   man movie go (he) forget shoe use

7. Can you tell me which way is east?

   east, able (you) tell-me where?

8. Stay here with your brother for several more hours.

   several more hour (you) with brother your here stay

9. Who can show me where the teacher put the test?

   test teacher put where, show-me who?

10. All of us need to review before tomorrow's test.

    prior-to tomorrow test, all us need review

11. The stranger was a little vague in her message to the police.

    message for police, stranger write, little-bit vague

12. Walk toward the open window and ignore what people say.

    people say (you) ignore, toward window-open you walk

13. Go west past three streets, then turn left at the fourth street.

    you west three street, then fourth street left-direction

14. The police had a difficult time catching the little boy.

    boy short, police catch problem

15. Go around the house and see if you can find your sister.

    sister your, around house go, see find

Class Activities

1. In small groups, sign what you wrote for student activity 1 in Lesson 23 while the others in your group voice for you.

2. Students form rows with five students in each row, and the instructor stands behind the students. The first student in each row turns to watch the instructor sign a sentence. The student then signs the same sentence to the next person in line. Continue until all five students in each row have signed the sentence, and then compare the last sentence from each row.

Student Activities

1. List the glosses in this lesson that have similar handshapes.

   _____

   _____

   _____

   _____

2. Write the glosses for the signs in this lesson that are above the neck.

   _____

   _____

   _____

   _____

3 Write the glosses for the signs in this lesson that touch the body.

   _____

   _____

   _____

   _____

4. Write the glosses for the signs in this lesson that use nonmanual signals (NMS) and what the NMS are for each sign.

   _____

   _____

   _____

   _____

5. For the next class, bring a nursery rhyme to sign in ASL.

Lesson 25

Vocabulary

705 wide, expand, general, broad, width
706 reduce, slim down, lose weight
707 weigh, pound, weight
708 shortly, soon, before long, in a little bit
709 no clue, no idea, just don't know
710 expert, gifted, can-do
711 major, field, profession, line of work, trade, straight
712 majority
713 minority
714 bureaucrat
715 line, string, *rope, wire
716 hate, dislike
717 expression, facial expression, make faces
718 easy, simple, gentle
719 break, broken
720 appear, seem, apparently
721 appear, show up, come up, emerge, pop up
722 disappear, vanish
723 ready, all set, prepared
724 often, frequent, frequently, habitually
725 prepare, plan, ready, in order, organize, arrange, make
726 profit, benefit, gain, advantage, benefits
727 breakdown, collapse, cave in
728 give out, pass out, disseminate, contribute
729 technology, technician
730 seal, *approve, authorize

705
wide, expand, general, broad, width

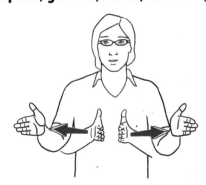

The street to my house is wide.
house my, street wide

706
reduce, slim down, lose weight

The magazine was about losing weight.
magazine concerning what? slim-down

707
weigh, pound, weight

He ignores his weight.
man weight his ignore

708
shortly, soon, before long, in a little bit

Come to see me soon.
(you) soon come see me

Deaf Culture Facts and Information

Members of the Deaf community generally prefer the terms *Deaf* or *hard of hearing*, as opposed to older terms such as *mute*, *deaf-mute*, *hearing impaired*, *handicapped*, *disabled*, *the deaf*, or *deaf and dumb*.

709
no clue, no idea, just don't know

Dad has no clue about how to lose weight.
slim-down how?, father no-clue

710
expert, gifted, can-do

The girl is gifted in music.
girl herself music gifted

711
major, field, profession, line of work, trade, straight

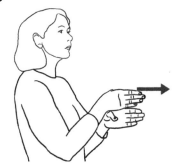

My son has two majors.
son my, two major have

712
majority

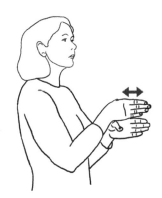

The majority refuses to give up.
now majority surrender refuse

713
minority

My uncle voted with the minority.
uncle my with minority vote

714
bureaucrat

The bureaucrat was an expert.
bureaucrat himself expert

715
line, string, *rope, wire

Who put my string in the garage?
string my put there garage who?

716
hate, dislike

They hate bad people.
people bad, they hate

717
expression, facial expression, make faces

The dog has funny expressions.
dog expression funny

718
easy, simple, gentle

The doctor has an easy job.
doctor job easy

719
break, broken

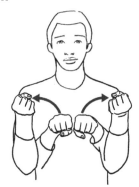

Tell me what you broke today.
today you break what? tell-me

720
appear, seem, apparently

Seems like a beautiful day.
day beautiful seem

721
appear, show up, come up, emerge, pop up

Her sister showed up at the movies.
sister girl hers movie show-up

722
disappear, vanish

The nurse seemed to disappear.
nurse seem disappear

ASL Grammar Notes

Pronouns in ASL are formed by pointing in the direction of a person, place, thing, or the space assigned to a referent. Unlike English, ASL makes no distinction between subject and object pronouns. That is, the sign for *I* is the same as the sign for *me*, *he* is the same as *him*, and *she* is the same as *her*.

723
ready, all set, prepared

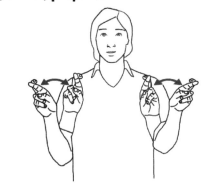

Who is ready to go now?
now ready depart who?

724

often, frequent, frequently, habitually

The man frequently stays with us.
man with us frequent stay

725

prepare, plan, ready, in order, organize, arrange, make

The majority did not like the plan.
majority like plan not

726

profit, benefit, gain, advantage, benefits

The store always made a profit.
store profit always have

727

breakdown, collapse, cave in

My aunt's breakdown was awful.
breakdown aunt my, hers awful

728

give out, pass out, disseminate, contribute

The bureaucrat passed out new books.
bureaucrat book new disseminate++ finish

729

technology, technician

The technician arrives in two hours.
technician two-hour arrive will

730
seal, *approve, authorize

The technician approved the plan.
technician himself plan approve

Mind Ticklers

Make the sign _____	and think about . . .
wide, expand, general, broad, width	showing how wide something is
reduce, slim down, lose weight	showing how a person has slimmed down
weigh, pound, weight	a balance scale tipping
shortly, soon, before long, in a little bit	eating soon
no clue, no idea, just don't know	a hole in the head with nothing in it
expert, gifted, can-do	something as easy as eating
major, field, profession, line of work, trade, straight	moving in a specific direction
majority	the people at the top
minority	the people at the bottom
bureaucrat	a person seeking favors
line, string, rope, wire	drawing a line or string in the air
hate, dislike	shooting arrows at a disliked person
expression, make faces	changing the face for different expressions
easy, simple, gentle	one hand sliding easily off the other
break, broken	breaking something into two pieces
appear, seem, apparently	a side-view reflection
appear, show up, come up, emerge	something coming into view
disappear, vanish	something dropping out of sight
ready, all set, prepared	getting ready to move
often, frequent, frequently, habitually	something happening again and again
prepare, plan, ready, in order, organize, arrange, make	placing things in order
profit, benefit, gain, benefits	putting money into your pocket
breakdown, collapse, cave in	something falling apart
give out, pass out, disseminate	handing something to a group of people
technology, technician	being on the cutting edge
seal, approve, authorize	giving a stamp of approval

Practice Sentences

1. The city will widen that street next year.

   next-year street there, city wide will

2. The minority plans to disseminate the flyer beginning tomorrow.

   tomorrow flyer minority plan give-out

3. The expert had no clue what was happening here today.

   today here happen what? expert no-clue

4. How frequently does the technician visit his mother?

   technician, mother his how often (he) visit?

5. Every year it seems she has a new major in college.

   every-year girl her major college seem new

6. When my son broke the lamp on the table, he disappeared.

   son my, lamp table there break, he disappear (finish)

7. I think the boss is ready to approve our raise.

   increase our, think me boss ready approve

8. It seems that the fireman will not show up today or tomorrow.

   today, tomorrow, fireman show-up seem not

9. Dad had an awful breakdown about two years ago.

   approximately two-year-ago, father awful breakdown have

10. The bureaucrat stayed in the minority for almost five years.

    almost five year bureaucrat minority stay

11. The minority became the majority after the last election.

    finish final vote, minority become majority

12. The bureaucrat ignored the people who voted for him.

    people vote for bureaucrat, them he ignore

13. Why did you make faces when Dad cut the rope?

    dad rope cut (you) make-faces why?

14. Dad wanted to slim down, so he started walking every day.

    daily dad walk why? he slim-down want

15. They have no clue how much Mom weighs and she isn't telling.

    weight mom how much?, people no-clue, mom tell refuse

Class Activities

1. In small groups, talk about the answers each student put down for the student activities in Lesson 24.

2. In small groups, sign your nursery rhyme. Select the best nursery rhyme to share in front of the class.

Student Activities

1. Write initialized signs that can be derived from each gloss below.

   a. GROUP OF PEOPLE

   _____

   _____

   b. BOX

   _____

   _____

c. STREET

_____

_____

d. LAND

_____

_____

e. LUNCH

_____

_____

f. SHOW

_____

_____

g. MONEY

_____

_____

h. LAW

_____

_____

2. Write ten directional signs in the lessons covered thus far.

a. _____

b. _____

c. _____

d. _____

e. _____

f. _____

g. _____

h. _____

i. _____

j. _____

3. Write the glosses in this lesson that are signed with both hands using the same handshape.

_____

_____

_____

_____

_____

Lesson 26

Vocabulary

731 stingy, miserly, cherish, precious, treasure
732 revenge, get back at
733 country, county, *foreign
734 stamp, postage stamp
735 letter, note
736 mail, letters, mailman
737 depend, rely, count on
738 offer, *propose, present, *recommend, suggest, *motion, raise, move
739 introduce, present
740 present, gift
741 immediately, right now, quickly
742 culture, *situation, *environment
743 dead, die, death, expire, gone
744 system, technique, procedure, method
745 behind, at the back, in the rear, avoid
746 bother, annoy, disturb, hinder
747 interrupt, butt in, intrude
748 socialize, associate, mingle, each other, interact
749 tolerate, bear, patience, put up with, stand, take, endure, patient
750 suffer, anguish, endure
751 secret, private, confidential, close, password
752 defend, protect, guard, save
753 between, amid
754 decide, decision, figure out, judgment, make up one's mind, determined
755 think for yourself, you decide
756 short time, brief
757 tent, camping
758 garbage, waste, trash, refuse

731
stingy, miserly, cherish, precious, treasure

The stingy old man is staying.
now man old stingy stay

732
revenge, get back at

The police want revenge for the murder.
police revenge want why? murder

733
country, county, *foreign

The country people seem to disappear.
people country, seem disappear

734
stamp, postage stamp

The man bought two old stamps.
man finish two old stamp buy

Deaf Culture Facts and Information

Alexander Graham Bell, who is popularly known as the inventor of the telephone, was a coda, and he married a deaf woman. As a teacher of deaf children, he strongly supported the oral method of teaching and advocated for the removal of sign language and deaf teachers from the classroom. He also opposed the idea of residential schools, which he believed encouraged "intermarriages among the deaf and dumb" and the creation of a "deaf race."

735
letter, note

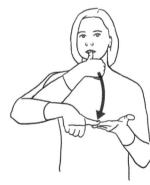

Who got the letter yesterday?
yesterday letter obtain who?

736
mail, letters, mailman

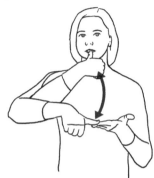

The mail comes early on Saturday.
early Saturday, mail arrive

737
depend, rely, count on

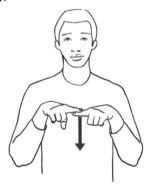

We often depend on her expert knowledge.
expert knowledge hers, we often depend

738
offer, *propose, present, *recommend, suggest, *motion, raise, move

They offered to leave tomorrow.
they offer tomorrow leave

739
introduce, present

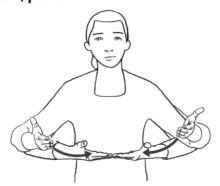

Grandma introduced her family.
finish grandmother family hers, introduce

740
present, gift

That is a very nice present.
gift there very nice

741
immediately, right now, quickly

You must do that immediately.
immediately you must do

742
culture, *situation, *environment

Deaf culture is very interesting.
deaf culture very interest

743
dead, die, death, expire, gone

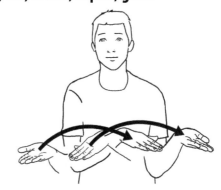

The letter said that he was dead.
letter say what? man dead

744
system, technique, procedure, method

Our system is working fine.
system our fine work

745

behind, at-the-back, in-the-rear, avoid

Sit behind the slim woman.
woman slim, you behind sit

746

bother, annoy, disturb, hinder

Don't bother father; he is sleeping.
father sleep, bother (he) don't

747

interrupt, butt in, intrude

Mother interrupted our phone conversation.
our phone conversation mother interrupt

748

socialize, associate, mingle, each other, interact

They enjoy socializing with deaf people.
socialize with deaf people they enjoy

ASL Grammar Notes

Possessive pronouns (*his, her/hers, your/yours, my/mine*) are formed by moving an Open B handshape in the direction of the possessor.

749

tolerate, bear, patience, put up with, stand, take, endure, patient

Mom cannot tolerate her stepchild.
next child mother hers tolerate cannot

750
suffer, anguish, endure

The man never suffered before dying.
man suffer prior-to dying not

751
secret, private, confidential, close, password

I cannot tell you my secret.
secret my, tell you cannot

752
defend, protect, guard, save

He offered to protect your letters.
letter your, man offer protect

753
between, amid

My uncle found the stamp between the boxes.
uncle my stamp find box-box between

754
decide, decision, figure out, judgment, make up one's mind, determined

You decide which country to visit.
country visit, you decide which

755
think for yourself, you decide

I won't tell you, think for yourself.
me tell-you refuse, think-for-yourself

756
short time, brief

The police interrupted us briefly.
police interrupt us brief

757
tent, camping

My family goes to a secret place to camp.
family my secret place camp go

758
garbage, waste, trash, refuse

After camping, take your garbage with you.
camp finish, garbage you take

Mind Ticklers

Make the sign _____	and think about . . .
stingy, miserly, cherish, precious	holding on to your every word
revenge, get back at	picking on someone
country, county, foreign	farmers wearing shirts thin at the elbows
stamp, postage stamp	what you lick and put on a letter
letter, note	where you put the stamp on a letter
mail, letters, mailman	having many letters
depend, rely, count on	putting the burden on another's shoulders
offer, propose, present, recommend, suggest, motion, raise, move	offering what is in your hands to someone
introduce, present	bringing two people together to meet
present, gift	what you give to someone
immediately, right now, quickly	now, now, now
culture, situation, environment	what surrounds a person
dead, die, death	the act of rolling over and dying
system, technique, procedure	the structure of a system
behind, at the back, in the rear	not with, but behind someone
bother, annoy, disturb, hinder	constantly tapping someone for attention
interrupt, butt in, intrude	coming between two people
socialize, associate, mingle, each other	people milling around
tolerate, bear, patience, put up with, stand, take, endure	the idea of taping your lips shut
suffer, anguish	not saying a word
secret, private, confidential, close, password	your lips being sealed
defend, protect, guard, save	putting your hands up in self-defense
between, amid	something between your fingers
decide, decision, figure out, judgment, make up one's mind, determined	what you think is decided
think for yourself	the signs **think** and **yourself**
short time, brief	the small movement showing briefness
tent, camping	the shape of a tent
garbage, waste, trash, refuse	a basket where trash is thrown

Practice Sentences

1. The family wanted revenge against an unfair system.

   system unfair family revenge want

2. The miserly old mailman retired with a lot of money.

   mail man old miserly, a-lot money he retire have

3. It is more expensive to send letters to foreign countries than to send mail in the U.S.

   letter more expensive send-to foreign country than U.S. mail

4. Can I depend on you to introduce your sister to my brother?

   sister your introduce brother my, me depend you, able?

5. The deaf culture is different than the hearing culture in many ways.

   deaf culture, public culture many way different

6. Don't bother those people, they are socializing with their boss.

   people there bother don't, they socialize with boss their now

7. Don't interrupt Dad, he is talking about camping next week.

   next week camp, dad talk concerning, interrupt don't

8. Family and friends suffered when the boss died.

   boss die, family, friend suffer

9. The doctor told Dad to decide for himself when to lose weight.

   dad slim-down when? doctor finish tell dad, you-decide

10. The team decided to camp between the woods and the road.

    woods, road between, team camp there decide

11. Take the garbage out right now, it smells awful.

    immediately garbage take outside, awful smell

12. The student made a motion to vote.

    student propose vote

13. When did you get the gift from your aunt in the mail?

    gift mail you get from aunt, when?

14. The gifted writer stayed only a short time; he is very busy.

    gifted writer stay short-time, why? he very busy now

15. The policeman stood behind the tree briefly then left.

    policeman behind tree stand short-time, depart

Class Activities

1. In small groups, talk about the answers each student wrote for the student activities in Lesson 25.

2. Students work in groups of three. The instructor says two glosses. The students take turns signing an ASL sentence using the two glosses. The two nonsigners assist the signer.

Student Activities

1. Write glosses for signs that you have learned from your instructor or another person that are different from the signs in this text. Create a mnemonic for each gloss.

   a. _____
   _____

   b. _____
   _____

   c. _____
   _____

   d. _____
   _____

   e. _____
   _____

   f. _____
   _____

   g. _____
   _____

2. Put a piece of paper over the *Think of* section of the Mind Ticklers. Reading only the mnemonic, see if you can guess the gloss correctly.

3. What is the gloss in this lesson that uses double signs? _____

4. List the glosses of the three signs in this lesson that have the same location, handshape, and orientation, but different movements.

   a. _____

   b. _____

   c. _____

Lesson 27

Vocabulary

759 cute, sweet, attractive
760 handsome, good-looking, gorgeous
761 skill, expertise, proficient, ability, talent, exp<u>er</u>t
762 list, itemize
763 advice, influence, advise, counsel
764 background, personal history, qualifications
765 lose, lost, mislay, misplace
766 lose, defeat, defeated, beaten, lost, fail, failure, stop working
767 win, victory, triumph, winn<u>er</u>
768 accept, acceptable, adopt, approve, follow, take on
769 quality, trait, attribute
770 reputation, standing
771 accent
772 encourage, persuade, urge
773 miss, long for, disappoint
774 miss, didn't get, failed to see
775 follow, by, take, trail
776 alone, by one's self, lon<u>er</u>, isolated
777 study, examine
778 afraid, frighten, fear, scare
779 farm, country, farm<u>er</u>
780 sign (ASL), signing
781 sign, poster, notice, put-up, square
782 sign, signature
783 fingerspell, spell
784 save, keep, put aside, put away, preserve, save money
785 suppose, if
786 draw the line, put a stop to, stop, boundary
787 concerned, worried, alarmed

759
cute, sweet, attractive

The cute little girl wrote a letter.
girl short cute letter write finish

760

handsome, good-looking, gorgeous

That handsome man is my husband.
man handsome there my husband

761
skill, expertise, proficient, ability, talent, exp<u>er</u>t

My cousin has a secret skill.
cousin my secret skill have

762

list, itemize

List all the presents you got.
all present you obtain, list

763

advice, influence, advise, counsel

The minister always gave good advice.
preacher advice his good always

764

background, personal history, qualifications

Can we talk about your background?
concerning background your two-of-us talk can?

765

lose, lost, mislay, misplace

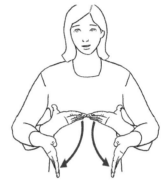

The cute boy lost his hat.
boy cute hat his mislay

Deaf Culture Facts and Information

Immigration to the United States by deaf adults was almost nonexistent toward the end of the 19th century. This was a result of restrictive immigration laws that excluded certain ethnic groups and people with disabilities from entering the country.

766

lose, defeat, defeated, beaten, lost, fail, failure, stop working

Our team lost again yesterday.
yesterday team ours again fail

767
win, victory, triumph, win<u>er</u>

Who do you think will win tomorrow?
tomorrow win you think who?

768
accept, acceptable, adopt, approve, follow, take on

The boys didn't accept losing well.
boy fail, good accept not

769
quality, trait, attribute

Dad's quality of work is acceptable.
work father his, quality accept

770
reputation, standing

Her reputation in church is excellent.
reputation woman hers church there wonderful

ASL Grammar Notes

To emphasize that something will happen, is certain, is affirmative, is positive, or is assured requires the use of nonmanual signals of assertion. A signer may use all or some of the following: head nod, firm expression (brow or eye squint), pursed lips, raised upper lip, or widened lips. Depending on the situation, head nodding may last throughout the entire sentence.

771
accent

Grandma thinks you have an accent.
accent grandmother think you have

772
encourage, persuade, urge

The coach needs to encourage the team.
team, coach encourage need

773
miss, long for, disappoint

They miss seeing the handsome man.
man handsome they disappoint see not

774
miss, didn't get, failed to see

When did they miss the bus?
bus they didn't-get when?

775
follow, by, take, trail

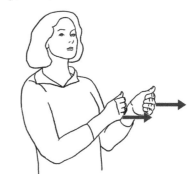

The dog followed the cat's scent.
cat its smell, dog follow

776
alone, by one's self, loner, isolated

The bachelor always worked alone.
bachelor alone work always

777
study, examine

The student forgot to study last night,
ago night student study forget

778
afraid, frighten, fear, scare

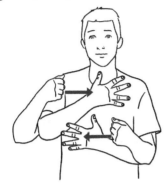

The team is afraid they might lose.
team fail, they afraid maybe will

779
farm, country, farm<u>er</u>

That person grew up on a farm.
person there, farm grow-up

780
sign (ASL), signing

She started signing three months ago.
three-month-ago girl sign start

781
sign, poster, notice, put-up, square

Who put the sign near the farmhouse?
poster near farm house put who?

782
sign, signature

The doctor forgot to sign the papers.
paper doctor signature forget

783
fingerspell, spell

Fingerspell your name now.
now name your fingerspell

784

save, keep, put aside, put away, preserve, save money

I will save the sign for you.
poster me put-away for you will

785

suppose, if

I suppose that will happen regardless.
suppose me that happen regardless will

786

draw the line, put a stop to, stop, boundary

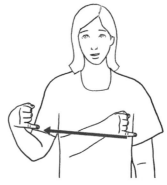

My sister draws the line at getting drunk.
sister my become drunk, draw-the-line

787

concerned, worried, alarmed

Don't be concerned about losing.
fail worried don't

Mind Ticklers

Make the sign _____	and think about . . .
cute, sweet	someone sweet as candy
handsome, good-looking, gorgeous, attractive	outlining an attractive face
skill, expertise, proficient, ability, talent	a person who is very handy
list, itemize	listing things on a piece of paper
advise, influence, advice, counsel	having influence over another person
background, personal history, qualifications	putting your background on paper
lose, lost, mislay, misplace	releasing what was in your hands
lose, defeated, beat, beaten, lost, fail	falling flat on your face
win, victory, triumph, winner	grabbing the winner's flag
accept, adopt, follow, take on, approve	pulling something toward you to accept it
quality, trait, attribute, reputation, standing	your reputation and attributes depend on what kind of heart you have
accent	sounds coming from the voice box
miss, skip, absent, not attend	missing one of the five work days
miss, long for, disappoint	being bitter about missing someone
miss, didn't get, failed to see	not being able to grab what you see
follow, by, take, trail	one hand following the other hand
alone, by one's self, isolated, loner	one person standing all alone
study, examine	your eyes intent on a page
afraid, frighten, fear, scare	every bone in your body shaking
farm, country, farmer	the stereotypical farmer with a beard
sign (ASL), signing	moving your hands quickly
sign, poster, square, put up, notice	the shape of a sign or poster
sign, signature	putting your name on a page
fingerspell, spell	moving your fingers when spelling
save, keep, put aside, put away	protecting what is in your hand
suppose, if	tapping your head as you wonder
draw a line, put a stop to, boundary	drawing a line in the dirt
concerned, worried, alarmed	your heart and feelings going out to someone

Practice Sentences

1. Those cute children are not from the same family.

   children those cute, from same family not

2. I missed sign class three times this month.

   now month me three time sign class skip

3. Suppose the team wins tomorrow, will you make a big sign?

   tomorrow suppose team win, you big poster prepare will?

4. When Dad signs the paper he is responsible for keeping it.

   paper dad sign finish, he responsible hold

5. I lost the stamp, now I cannot mail that letter.

   stamp me misplace now, letter there send cannot

6. Her background and reputation helped her win all the votes.

   woman win all vote why? her background, reputation

7. The farmer had qualities that other farmers wanted.

   farmer himself quality have, other farmer want alike

8. The farmer had to draw the line when people began taking his land.

   land, farmer his, people start take, he draw-the-line must

9. Save your money for a rainy day is always good advice.

   money your save-money for future, good advice always

10. After his defeat, the player wanted to be alone.

    player finish fail, alone he want

11. Father signed for the letter from his long-lost brother.

    letter father sign, from who? brother long-time nothing see

12. I think the boss missed several things in the person's background.

    person girl background hers, boss didn't-get several thing, me think

13. I'm afraid to go with him because he has a bad reputation.

    go with man, me afraid, why? he bad reputation have

14. The group encouraged the dogs out of the house with skill.

    dog+ outside house, group skill encourage

15. We cannot accept the list of people whom you want to advise.

    people list you want advise, we accept cannot

Class Activities

1. As a class, go over student activity 1 from Lesson 26 to discover new sign variations.

2. With a partner, go over student activities 2, 3, and 4 in Lesson 26.

Student Activities

1. Change the following sentences into ASL sentences.

   a. The dump was so full that it had to refuse more refuse.

   _____

   _____

   _____

   b. The soldier decided to desert his dessert in the desert.

   _____

   _____

   _____

   c. Since there is no time like the present, he thought it was time to present the present.

   _____

   _____

   _____

   d. They were too close to the door to close it.

   _____

   _____

   _____

   e. The buck does funny things when the does are present.

   _____

   _____

   _____

   f. The wind was too strong to wind the sail.

   _____

   _____

   _____

   g. Upon seeing the tear in the painting I shed a tear.

   _____

   _____

   _____

2. How are the three signs for the English word *miss* similar and different?

   _____

   _____

   _____

   _____

   _____

   _____

Lesson 28

Vocabulary

788 exact, precise, *perfect, specific, just,
exactly, direct

789 experience, done before

790 safe, *free, *liberty, *independent, release,
save, salvation, turn loose, freedom

791 exchange, trade, substitute, in place of,
instead, replace

792 knock, tap, rap

793 pride, proud, self esteem

794 remember, recall, recollect

795 remind, jog your memory

796 remind me, jog my memory

797 arithmetic, multiply, *math, *algebra,
*geometry, *calculus, figure, figure out,
*mathematics

798 social studies, social security

799 history, in the past, historian

800 psychology, psychologist

801 science, scientist

802 chemistry, chemical, chemist

803 biology, biologist

804 earth, geography

805 world, *universe, *international

806 island, isle

807 quiet, still, calm, be quiet

808 trip, travel, tour

809 fall, trip, fall down, drop, knock down

810 announce, announcement, word, declare,
proclaim

811 famous, outstanding, well known

812 inform, let know, information

813 building, *structure, facility

814 build, *construction, *construct, make,
builder

815 basic, *elementary, basis, grounds,
*inferior

816 drugs, illegal substances

788
**exact, precise, *perfect, specific, just, exactly,
direct**

That sign is exactly what I wanted.
poster there exact itemize me want

789
experience, done before

He has a lot of experience signing.
man experience signing a-lot have

790
**safe, *free, *liberty, *independent, release,
save, salvation, turn loose, freedom**

It is not safe to be alone at night.
night alone safe not

791

**exchange, trade, substitute, in place of,
instead, replace**

The farmers agreed to exchange trucks.
truck exchange, farmer+ agree

Deaf Culture Facts and Information

Hearing adults immigrating to the United States with a deaf child had to post bonds of $500 to $1000 to guarantee that the child would not become dependent on public assistance.

792

knock, tap, rap

A policeman is knocking on the door.
door, policeman knock now

793

pride, proud, self esteem

Father was proud that he won.
father win, proud

794

remember, recall, recollect

Remember to exchange letters tomorrow.
tomorrow letter exchange remember

795

remind, jog your memory

Remind Dad to sign the papers.
paper, father sign, (you) remind-him

796
remind me, jog my memory

Remind me to introduce my mom.
mother my, (you) remind-me introduce

797
arithmetic, multiply, *math, *algebra,
   *geometry, *calculus, figure, figure out,
   *mathematics

Arithmetic is easy to study with friends.
arithmetic with friend, easy study

798
social studies, social security

Social Studies is my favorite class.
class favorite my, social-studies

799
history, in the past, histor<u>ian</u>

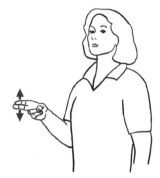

There is a lot to remember in history.
history a-lot remember must

ASL Grammar Notes

Nonmanual signals of negation are commonly used to indicate that something will not happen, something did not happen, has not happened, was not true, or was not one's fault. Negative sentences usually start with either NOT, negative verbs, or negative signals. Negative signals include a headshake from side to side, a frown expression (brow or eye squint), or pursed or loose lips.

800
psychology, psycholog<u>ist</u>

My uncle missed his psychology class.
uncle my, class psychology skip

801
science, scientist

I tolerate my science teacher.
teacher science, me tolerate

802
chemistry, chemical, chem<u>ist</u>

Chemistry is an interesting class.
class chemistry interesting

803
biology, biolog<u>ist</u>

Can you fingerspell biology for me?
biology, fingerspell for me can (you)

804
earth, geography

People say to save the earth.
earth, people say protect

805
world, *universe, *international

The world is not a small place.
world tiny not

806
island, isle

My friend lives on a small island.
friend my, there island tiny live

807
quiet, still, calm, be quiet

The history class became very quiet.
class history become very quiet

808
trip, travel, tour

Let's take a trip around the world.
trip around world we take-up

809
fall, trip, fall down, drop, knock down

Don't fall on the wet snow.
snow wet, fall don't

810
**announce, announcement, word, declare,
   proclaim**

The winner was announced this morning.
now morning winner announce finish

811
famous, outstanding, well known

Do you know any famous people?
people famous, any you know

812
inform, let know, information

Let me know what happened.
itemize happen, (you) inform-me

813
building, *structure, facility

The old building is not safe.
building old safe not

814
build, *construction, *construct, make, build<u>er</u>

In science we built a boat.
class science, boat we build

815
basic, *elementary, basis, grounds, *inferior

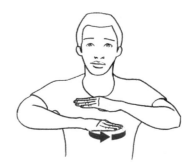

I understand basic arithmetic.
arithmetic basic me understand

816
drugs, illegal substances

Drugs are not allowed in schools.
illegal-drug, school allow not

Mind Ticklers

Make the sign _____	and think about . . .
exact, precise, perfect, specific, just	wanting to hit the nail on the head
experience, done before	gray hair at the temples indicating experience with age
safe, free, liberty, independent, release, save, salvation, turn loose, freedom	breaking the chains that bind you
exchange, trade, substitute, in place of, instead, replace	giving something and getting something in return
knock, tap, rap	knocking on a door
pride, proud, self-esteem	your chest swelling up with pride
remember, recall, recollect	putting what is in your mind on a bulletin board
remind, jog your memory	tapping someone to remind her of something
remind me, jog my memory	asking someone to tap you on your shoulder
arithmetic, multiply, math, algebra, geometry, calculus, figure out, figure	making the multiplication symbol X
social studies, social security	the context in which the S-S is being used
history, in the past	the H handshape for *history*
psychology, psycholog*ist*	the Greek symbol *psi*
science, scient*ist*	pouring liquids between test tubes
chemistry, chemical, chem*ist*	**science** with C handshapes
biology, biolog*ist*	**science** with B handshapes
earth, geography	the rotation of the earth
world, universe, international	the world revolving around the sun
island, isle	an island alone in the ocean
quiet, still, calm, be quiet	making the "shh" gesture with a calming motion
trip, travel, tour	moving from one place to another
fall, trip, fall down, drop, knock down	the act of falling down
announce, announcement, word, declare, proclaim	telling everyone what you have to say
famous, outstanding, well known	everyone talking about something famous
inform, let know, information	sharing the knowledge that you have
building, structure, facility	the floors of a building
build, construction, construct, make, build*er*	putting one block on top of another block
basic, elementary, basis, grounds, inferior	a foundation or base
drugs, illegal substances	shooting up drugs

Practice Sentences

1. No one remembered the exact time people were leaving for their trip.

   people depart trip, exact time none one remember

2. People on drugs do strange things.

   people use drugs, strange things do

3. The student decided to exchange his history class for a social studies class.

   student history class his, he decide social-studies class exchange

4. Don't forget to announce the outstanding player for the day.

   today famous player (you) announce, forget don't

5. The builder had a history of building excellent houses around town.

   builder he history have, wonderful house+ around town he build

6. To me, science and biology are boring, and psychology is a fun class.

   science, biology, bored, psychology class fun, me think

7. You have to remind me which islands we are going to see.

   island we see will, you again must remind-me

8. All the people were proud of the fact that they saved themselves.

   people all proud why? they themselves salvation finish

9. Please don't fall down the steps, you worry us.

   steps you fall-down please don't, we worry concerning you

10. Be quiet and you can hear the tapping on the glass.

    quiet, hear tap window-glass able

11. Long ago people thought that the sun went around the earth.

    long-time ago sun around earth people think

12. Some people have a hard time with basic arithmetic.

    arithmetic basic some people difficult time have

13. The young boy experienced loneliness when his parents left.

    boy young, parents depart, he lonely experience

14. When signing out or signing in please put down the exact time.

    signature in, signature out exact time put-down please

15. He announced that he would stay on the island for six months.

    six months, man stay island, announce (he) will

Class Activity

1. In small groups go over student activities 1 and 2 in Lesson 27.

Student Activities

1. Prosody is frequently used in ASL conversations. Do the following exercise.

   a. Pretend you are holding a ball. Toss it into the air. Catch it, drop it.

   b. Make the ball become three times bigger. Toss it into the air. Catch it.

c. Make the ball become six times smaller. Toss it into the air. Let it drop.

d. Make a ball the size of a golf ball, a baseball, a soft ball, a soccer ball, a basketball, and a medicine ball.

e. Throw a basketball to someone. Catch a basketball thrown to you.

f. Lob a softball to someone. Hit the ball with a bat. Run to first base.

g. Pick up a penny.

h. Pick up a shoe.

i. Pick up a big rock.

j. Pick up a huge rock.

2. Use the correct sign and facial expression to show the differences between the meanings of the following word pairs (look at yourself in a mirror when signing these).

a. happy—joyous

b. knock—pound

c. announce—proclaim

d. famous—outstanding

e. tired—exhausted

f. excited—enthusiastic

g. afraid—terrified

g. angry—furious

h. difficult—nothing to it

i. silly—ridiculous

3. Select four glosses from Lesson 28 that represent classes you have taken and write something about each of them in an ASL sentence.

a. _____

_____

_____

b. _____

_____

_____

c. _____

_____

_____

d. _____

_____

_____

Lesson 29

Vocabulary

817 know that, aware of
818 immature, childish
819 serve, service, wait, wait on, wait<u>er</u>
820 block, stuck, jam, caught
821 block, prevent, bar, obstruct
822 animal
823 insect, bug
824 deer
825 cow, cattle, steer
826 donkey, mule
827 horse, pony
828 snake
829 whale, *dolphin
830 duck
831 rat
832 mouse, mice
833 pig, hog, pork
834 fox
835 elephant
836 turkey, Thanksgiving
837 monkey
838 lion
839 worm
840 turtle, tortoise
841 spider
842 squirrel
843 rabbit, bunny, hare
844 sheep, lamb
845 fish
846 bear
847 wolf

817
know that, aware of

You know that chemistry is easy.
chemistry easy, (you) know-that

818
immature, childish

That child is very immature.
child there very immature

819
serve, service, wait, wait on, wait<u>er</u>

The service in that store is awful.
store there service awful

820
block, stuck, jam, caught

The farmer's car is stuck.
car, farmer his, stuck

821
block, prevent, bar, obstruct

He blocked us from entering.
man prevent us enter

822
animal

No animals live on the island.
animal, island there live none

823
insect, bug

Here you are safe from insects.
insect those, here you safe

824
deer

We followed the deer to the woods.
deer to woods we follow

825
cow, cattle, steer

The man has black and white cows.
cow black white, man have

826
donkey, mule

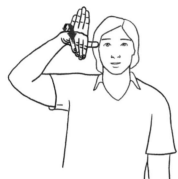

What color is a mule?
mule color what?

Deaf Culture Facts and Information

In the 1920s, Maryland required that deaf individuals be accompanied by a hearing adult when driving an automobile. Four other states simply refused to issue driver's licenses to deaf adults.

827
horse, pony

The horse stood quietly.
horse quiet stand

828
snake

Black snakes have bad reputations.
snakes black bad reputation have

829
whale, *dolphin

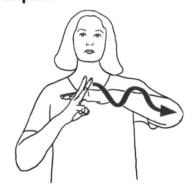

Whales are not small animals.
whale tiny animal, not

830
duck

Two ducks went into the building.
building, two duck into

831
rat

My aunt is afraid of rats.
aunt my, (she) rat afraid

832
mouse, mice

My son lost his little mouse.
mouse tiny, son my mislay

833
pig, hog, pork

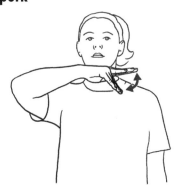

A big pig is exactly what you need.
pig big exact itemize you need

834
fox

Was the fox gray or red?
fox color gray red which?

835
elephant

I think elephants are not small.
elephant tiny me think not

836
turkey, Thanksgiving

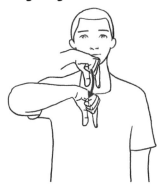

Where will you go this Thanksgiving?
now Thanksgiving you go where?

837
monkey

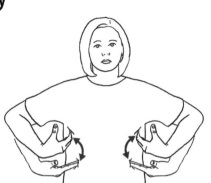

No one saw the monkey in the tree.
monkey there tree, none one see

ASL Grammar Notes

In English, *do*, *does*, and *did* are used for emphatic statements. In ASL emphatic statements are produced by using a more intense facial expression and an exaggerated head nod.

838
lion

What do you think lions eat?
lion, you think eat what?

839
worm

We studied worms in biology class.
class biology, worm we study finish

840
turtle, tortoise

Turtles live a very long time.
turtle, themselves very long-time live

841
spider

We study spiders in science class.
class science, spider we study

842
squirrel

Where did the squirrel hide his food?
squirrel food his hide, where?

843
rabbit, bunny, hare

Bunnies have long ears.
rabbit, ear long-measure have

844
sheep, lamb

Mary has a little lamb.
lamb tiny, Mary have

845
fish

We have three fish in our fish bowl.
fish bowl there, three fish (we) have

846
bear

Black bears like eating fish.
bear black like eat what? fish

847
wolf

The gray wolf had two babies.
wolf gray two baby have

Mind Ticklers

Make the sign _____	and think about . . .
know that, aware of	**know** plus an abbreviation of **that**
immature, childish	a child rubbing his nose
serve, service, wait, wait on	a waiter carrying a tray
block, stuck, jam, caught	something caught in the throat
block, prevent, bar, obstruct	throwing up your hands to protect yourself
animal	the rib cage moving when an animal breathes
insect, bug	the antennae of an insect
deer	the antlers of a deer
cow, cattle	the horns of a cow
donkey, mule	the big ears of a donkey or mule
horse, pony	the small ears of a horse
snake	the forked tongue of a snake
whale, dolphin	a whale's tail diving and submerging in water
duck	the wide bill of a duck
rat	the twitching nose of a rat
mouse, mice	the twitching nose of a mouse
pig, hog, pork	a pig up to its neck in dirt or mud
fox	a fox putting its nose down a rabbit hole
elephant	the trunk of an elephant
turkey, Thanksgiving	the turkey's waddle
monkey	how a monkey scratches itself
lion	the mane of a lion
worm	a worm slowly crawling along
turtle, tortoise	the head of the turtle sticking out its shell
spider	the eight legs of a spider crawling
squirrel	a squirrel holding a nut in its paws
rabbit, bunny, hare	the long ears of a rabbit
sheep, lamb	the shearing of a sheep
fish	a fish swimming through water
bear	a bear marking a tree to indicate its territory
wolf	the pointed snout of a wolf

Practice Sentences

1. You know that your second son is very immature.

   son your second very immature (you) know-that

2. The waiter suggested we eat squirrel; we declined.

   squirrel, waiter suggest we eat, two-of-us reject

3. The farmer had cows, sheep, and pigs, but no horses.

   cow sheep pig farmer have, horse none

4. Two people in our family enjoy eating fish.

   family our, two people fish enjoy eat

5. It was funny seeing the mules pull the car stuck on the road.

   car there stuck, mule pull, funny see there

6. During the fall Mom and Dad hunt bears, deer, and foxes.

   during fall bear, deer, fox, mom dad hunt

7. The spider quietly sat next to the little girl.

   spider next-to girl short quiet sit

8. The monkey escaped and remained free for two weeks.

   monkey escape, continue free two-week

9. A number of different animals live on farms across the U.S.

   animal many different on farm over U-S live

10. The whole family enjoys getting together for Thanksgiving.

    Thanksgiving family all together, enjoy

11. Everyone saw the dolphins from the small island every day.

    daily dolphin from small island every-one see

12. You could see the small insects flying everywhere.

    insect small flutter every place able see

13. We were happy to see the animals free and looking happy.

    animal free, seem happy, we happy see

14. The townspeople built a large animal habitat for the children to enjoy

    people town there house large build for animal, why? children enjoy

15. Before they bought the house, people told them about the snakes nearby.

    snake near, people tell-them prior-to house they buy

Class Activities

1. In groups of three, students take turns saying one of the paired glosses from student activity 2 in Lesson 28. The other two students sign each gloss with appropriate facial expressions. Look at one another and comment.

2. Divide the class into five or six small groups. Each group picks an animal from Lesson 29 and makes the sound of that animal. Have the entire class sing "Old McDonald Had a Farm," with each group singing the animal sound they picked. Go back and repeat each sound as a round.

Student Activities

1. Write four pairs of ASL sentences selecting paired glosses from student activity 2 in Lesson 28.

   a. _____

   _____

   _____

   a. _____

   _____

   _____

   b. _____

   _____

   _____

   b. _____

   _____

   _____

   c. _____

   _____

   _____

   c. _____

   _____

   _____

   d. _____

   _____

   _____

   d. _____

   _____

   _____

2. Use your listing knowledge to write four ASL sentences with the animal signs in this lesson.

   a. _____

   _____

   _____

   b. _____

   _____

   _____

   c. _____

   _____

   _____

   d. _____

   _____

   _____

Lesson 30

Vocabulary

848 crazy, nuts, out of one's mind, weird
849 over, across, cross, after, above
850 above, over
851 reduce, decline, decrease, *lower, *less, downsize, diminish, drop, cut, cut down, make smaller
852 figure, count, add
853 figure, shape, prints, form, image, statue
854 measure, size, inch, ruler, inches, mile
855 height, measure
856 disagree, differ
857 engagement, engaged
858 reservation, appointment, engagement
859 suspect, suspicious
860 exercise, gym, work out
861 number, figure
862 machine, factory, plant, engine
863 special, except, exception, particular, but
864 come here, come over, come back
865 back, come back, go back, take back, give back
866 cut it out, stop it, stop, that's enough, finish it
867 bridge
868 foundation, base, support
869 average, medium, mean
870 practice, *train, *rehearse, *drill
871 answer, reply, respond, *report
872 born, birth, delivery
873 birthday
874 paint, apply, spread, put on
875 imagine, imagination
876 dream, vision

848
crazy, nuts, out of one's mind, weird

I told you my brother is crazy.
brother my, crazy me tell-you

849
over, across, cross, after, above

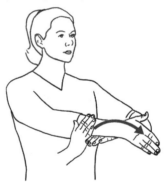

Don't go across the street without me.
street across without me don't

850
above, over

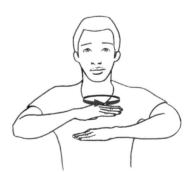

The airplane is over the old building.
building old, airplane above now

851

reduce, decline, decrease, *lower, *less,
    downsize, diminish, drop, cut, cut down,
    make smaller

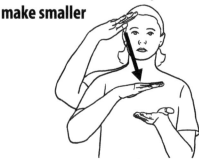

We reduced our time at work.
time work we reduce

Deaf Culture Facts and Information

In 1864, President Abraham Lincoln signed a bill establishing The National Deaf-Mute College, now Gallaudet University, in Washington DC. In 1965, President Lyndon Baines Johnson signed the National Technical Institute for the Deaf (NTID) Act establishing NTID at the Rochester Institute of Technology in New York.

852

figure, count, add

You figure how much we owe.
owe we, how-much you count

853

figure, shape, prints, form, image, statue

The shape of that building is odd.
building there shape strange

854

measure, size, inch, ruler, inches, mile

Measure the width of your house.
house your, wide measure

855

height, measure

The elephant's height is unknown.
elephant height don't-know

856
disagree, differ

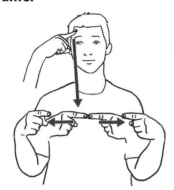

Exactly why do you disagree?
disagree you exact why?

857
engagement, engaged

Our engagement lasted three years.
engagement our, continue three year

858
reservation, appointment, engagement

Where is our reservation tonight?
now-night reservation our where?

859
suspect, suspicious

Grandpa suspected the odd man.
man odd grandfather suspect

860
exercise, gym, work out

The nurse worked out every day.
daily nurse work-out

861
number, figure

What is your favorite number?
number favorite your what?

862

machine, factory, plant, engine

The mules pulled the machine.
machine, mule pull

863

special, except, exception, particular, but

All of our children are special.
children our all special

864

come here, come over, come back

Come here, I want to measure you.
come-here, measure you me want

865

back, come back, go back, take back, give back

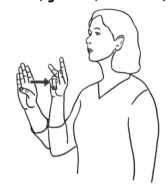

My brother gave back the black snake.
snake black, brother my give-back

866

cut it out, stop it, stop, that's enough, finish it

Stop it, no more talk about rats.
stop-it, rat more talk, stop-it

867

bridge

The bridge is over the road.
bridge above road

868
foundation, base, support

The house's foundation is safe.
foundation house safe

ASL Grammar Notes

Verb phrases in English consist of a verb and a preposition (for example, *sit down*, *hurry up*, *clean up*, *look for*, *make up*, and *pass out*). In ASL, a signer can use just one sign to convey the same meaning as the English concept—SIT, HURRY, CLEAN, SEARCH, INVENT, DISTRIBUTE. The speed and/or intensity of the sign relay additional information to make the meaning clear.

869
average, medium, mean

The boy is average height.
height boy his, average

870
practice, *train, *rehearse, *drill

The team practices every day at 3:00.
daily, time three, team practice

871
answer, reply, respond, *report

We disagree with your answer.
answer your, we disagree

872
born, birth, delivery

She measured 22 inches at birth.
girl born 22 inches

873
birthday

A special birthday is sweet 16.
sweet sixteen birthday special

874
paint, apply, spread, put on

Paint the machine orange and white.
machine, orange white paint

875
imagine, imagination

Imagine you were on an island all alone.
yourself on island alone imagine

876
dream, vision

Don't dream about snakes, rats, and mice.
snake, rat, mice, dream concerning don't

Mind Ticklers

Make the sign _____	and think about . . .
crazy, nuts, out of one's mind	someone being mixed up in the head
over, across, cross, after	going over a barrier
above, over	being above an object
reduce, decline, decrease, lower, less, downsize, diminish, drop, cut back	going from one size to a lesser size
figure, count, add	counting the items in a column
figure, shape, prints, form, image, statue	outlining a shape with your thumbs
measure, size, inch, ruler	measuring something with a ruler
height, measure	measuring how tall something is
disagree, differ	thinking the opposite of another person
engagement, engaged	wearing an engagement ring
reservation, appointment, engagement	locking in a time for someone
suspect, suspicious	scratching your head as if pondering
exercise, gym, workout	lifting weights
number, figures	putting numbers together
machine, factory, plant	the cogs of a machine meshing together
special, except, exception, particular, but	picking one out to be special
come here, come over, come back	gesturing for someone to come to you
back, come back, go back, take back	the handshapes B–K together abbreviating *back*
cut it out, stop it, stop, that's enough, finish it	blocking out any more of something
bridge	making the foundation for a bridge
foundation, base, support	the supports of a building
average, medium, mean	the middle of the hand
practice, train, rehearse, drill	doing something over and over
answer, reply, respond, report	a straight answer from the mouth
born, birth, delivery	a baby coming into the world
birthday	your heart's favorite day
paint, apply, spread, put on	putting paint on with a big brush
imagine, imagination	an imagination is more than an idea
dream, vision	picking ideas from the brain

Practice Sentences

1. Before leaving, the doctor measured the baby's height and weight.

   prior-to depart, baby hers height, weight, doctor measure

2. Several cars made it over the bridge before it collapsed.

   several car success across bridge prior–to bridge collapse

3. The builder suspected that the house's foundation was over 135 years old.

   foundation house more than 135 year old, builder suspect

4. They became engaged, but they disagreed about the wedding date.

   they engage, wedding time they disagree

5. My son's birthday is 11 days after my daughter's birthday.

   birthday son my, 11 day across birthday daughter my

6. Cut it out; you know that it is not safe to play here.

   stop, play here safe not, you know-that

7. Mother is of average height, but Dad's height is more than average.

   mother height average, dad height more than average

8. Who called and made reservations at our favorite eating place?

   reservation, place eat favorite our, telephone who?

9. Please don't forget to give Dad's tan hat back.

   hat tan dad his, (you) give-back forget don't please

10. The police measured the shoeprints hoping to catch the guy.

    shoe prints police measure why? catch man hope

11. Her parents are trying to slim down, so they exercise every day.

    daily parent hers exercise why? try slim-down

12. The factory made special houses for the monkeys to live and play in.

    house special, factory build for monkey live play there

13. If you practice before the test, you will be able to answer all the questions.

    practice prior-to test, all question you answer will

14. The builders disagreed about the height of the bridge.

    bridge height, builder they disagree

15. The hungry birds flew over the dead pig for a long time.

    long-time time bird hungry above pig dead, flutter

Class Activities

1. In small groups go over the student activities in Lesson 28.

2. In small groups have one student turn her back to the other students in the group. The other students agree on a specific animal then quickly share attributes of the animal in sign so the student with her back turned cannot see or hear the conversation. Then have the student join the group as each person shares an attribute until the animal is guessed. Continue until everyone has guessed an animal.

Student Activities

1. Using your listing skills, pick five animals from Lesson 29 and write an ASL sentence, describing three or four things about each animal.

    a. _____
       _____
       _____

    b. _____
       _____
       _____

    c. _____
       _____
       _____

    d. _____
       _____
       _____

    e. _____
       _____
       _____

2. What are the NMS that you could use with the following signs? Practice them in front of a mirror.

    a. That guy is **crazy**.
       _____

    b. Yes, she has a nice **figure**.
       _____

    c. That's enough, **stop-it**.
       _____

    d. I had a great **dream**.
       _____

    e. You are my **special** friend.
       _____

    f. Mom and Dad **disagree**.
       _____

3. What are the directional signs in this lesson?

       _____
       _____
       _____
       _____

Lesson 31

Vocabulary

877 quit, get out, drop out
878 join, take part in, participate, get in, ride
879 pass, by, past, go by, pass by
880 include, involve, everything, inclusive
881 fat, obese
882 thin, skinny
883 thick, heavy, dense
884 thick, width
885 push, shove, knock down, push away
886 honest, truthful
887 serious
888 look at one another, stare at one another
889 notify, warn, alert, notice, probation
890 notice, identify, detect
891 camera
892 picture, photograph, photographer
893 quote, title, subject, topic, theme, motto, issue
894 important, significant, worth, value, count, key, valuable
895 fire, burn, blaze, flame
896 fast, quick, rapid, right away, suddenly
897 worse
898 excited, excite, anxious, eager, excitement
899 dirty, filthy, dirt, mud
900 bite, bite into
901 car accident, accident, collision
902 accident, just happened
903 discuss, debate, discussion
904 jump, jump on, leap
905 value, worth, cost

877
quit, get out, drop out

He quit working on the farm.
man farm there work, quit

878
join, take part in, participate, get in, ride

You can join our history class.
class history our, you join can

879
pass, by, past, go by, pass by

You passed the bridge an hour ago.
one-hour ago you bridge pass

880

include, involve, everything, inclusive

Include my figures with yours.
number my with your include

881

fat, obese

The fat brown cow is my son's.
cow fat brown, my son his

882

thin, skinny

The monkey looks very thin.
monkey himself very thin appearance

883

thick, heavy, dense

The paint on the house is thick.
house, paint there dense

Deaf Culture Facts and Information

The National Registry of Interpreters for the Deaf (RID) was established in 1964 to meet the need for more and better trained sign language interpreters. There are RID chapters in all but two states in the United States, as well as chapters in Puerto Rico and the District of Columbia.

884

thick, width

Look how thick that book is.
book there thick-wide, look-at

885
push, shove, knock down, push away

Everyone tried pushing the elephant.
elephant, every-one try push

886
honest, truthful

I suspect you are an honest person.
you honest person me suspect

887
serious

I am serious about practicing now.
now practice, me serious

888
look at one another, stare at one another

The dog and cat looked at each other.
dog, cat, look-at-one-another

889
notify, warn, alert, notice, probation

They warned him the machine would break.
man, they warn, machine breakdown will

890
notice, identify, detect

He noticed that skinny woman yesterday.
yesterday, skinny woman there man notice

891
camera

The visitor bought a nice camera.
visitor, camera nice buy

892

picture, photograph, photograph<u>er</u>

The fireman's camera takes good pictures.
camera fireman his, picture good

893

quote, title, subject, topic, theme, motto, issue

My son forgot to write the title on his story.
story title son my forget write

894
important, significant, worth, value, count,
key, valuable

It is important that you join us.
important you join (us)

ASL Grammar Notes

Time phrases generally occur at the beginning of a sentence or are established at the beginning of a conversation or story. If a time is not specified, then it is usually assumed that the verb is in the present tense. The sign NOW may be added for clarification.

895
fire, burn, blaze, flame

The church fire was serious.
church fire awful

896
fast, quick, rapid, right away, suddenly

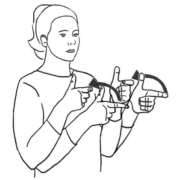

The fire moved through the house fast.
fire through house fast

897
worse

The weather today is worse than yesterday.
today, weather worse than yesterday

898
excited, excite, anxious, eager, excitement

The fat little boy was excited.
boy short fat, excited

899
dirty, filthy, dirt, mud

Why are pigs always dirty?
pig, dirty always, why?

900
bite, bite into

Don't let the snake bite you.
snake bite you let don't

901
car accident, accident, collision

The accident involved a car and truck.
car truck they car-accident

902
accident, just happened

Breaking the camera was an accident.
camera broken accident

903
discuss, debate, discussion

The boss discussed the issue with his employees.
boss, employee+, topic they discuss finish

904
jump, jump on, leap

Don't jump on the bed.
bed jump-on don't

905
value, worth, cost

That picture is worth a lot of money.
picture there a-lot money worth

Mind Ticklers

Make the sign _____	and think about . . .
quit, get out, drop out, give up	removing yourself from the group
join, take part in, participate, get in, ride	becoming part of the group
pass, by, past, go by	one hand moving past the other
include, involve, everything, inclusive	everything around you gathered together
fat, obese	a fat face
thin, skinny	a drawn face
thick, heavy	the cheeks puffed out to show thickness
thick, width	showing the thickness of something
push, shove, knock down, push away	the gesture of pushing something
honest, truthful	putting your honesty on paper
serious	a drawn face to look serious
look at one another, stare at one another	two pair of eyes staring at each other
warn, notify, alert, notice, probation	tapping a person to signal danger
notice, identify	something that attracts your eye
camera	taking a picture with a camera
picture, photograph, photographer	putting what the eye sees onto paper
quote, title, subject, topic, theme, motto	the quotation marks around a title
important, significant, worth, value, count, key, valuable	putting what is important into a bag
fire, burn, blaze	flames shooting upward
fast, quick, rapid, right away, suddenly	moving your hands rapidly to show speed
worse	making a big X with your hands and arms
excited, excite, anxious, eager, excitement	emotions fluttering around in the body
dirty, filthy, dirt, mud	how **pig** and **dirty** are similar signs
bite, bite into	teeth biting into something
accident, car accident	two cars banging into one another
accident, just happened	an accident occurring very quickly
discuss, debate, discussion	trying to make your point
jump, jump on, leap	jumping off of something
value, worth, cost	putting everything together for the cost

Practice Sentences

1. They were crazy to discuss the car accident all night.

   all-night car-accident they discuss, they crazy

2. The value of my camera has increased over the past five years.

   up-to-now five year, camera my value increase

3. They built a small fire to keep warm while camping.

   while camp, fire small they build warm continue

4. The paint on that picture is thick, and I don't like it much.

   picture there, paint dense, me don't-like

5. The skinny girl told me her fat duck would not bite me.

   duck fat bite me, girl skinny tell-me bite not

6. The fire went through the garage in a matter of minutes.

   minute, fire garage finish

7. They identified the honest person and asked her to stay.

   person honest they notice, ask her stay

8. The old man shared the important motto with the entire group.

   motto important, man old with full group share

9. We all agree, we have not seen a dirtier dog.

   dog dirty most, we agree up-to-now see never

10. My family quit their old church and joined a new church.

    church old, family my go, quit, church new join

11. The team practiced for two months and became very serious.

    two-month team practice, they very serious become

12. I noticed that the book my aunt was reading was thick.

    book aunt my read, notice me thick

13. It was an accident; don't worry, Grandma will clean it up.

    that accident, grandma clean-up will, worry don't

14. We passed the store and saw people pushing each other.

    store we pass see what? people push++

15. When my brother gets excited, he goes outside to relax.

    brother my when excited, (he) go outside relax

Class Activities

1. In small groups, go over the student activities in Lesson 30.

2. Students work in pairs. One student thinks of a number from 1 to 500 (for example, 225). Her partner tries to guess the number by asking questions. (NUMBER YOUR BETWEEN 100, 300? YES. NUMBER YOUR BETWEEN 100, 200? NO.) Continue until the number is identified, and then switch roles.

Student Activities

1. Using the vocabulary in this lesson, write five questions in ASL to ask your classmates. Make the questions open-ended.

   a. _____

   _____

   _____

   b. _____

   _____

   _____

   c. _____

   _____

   _____

   d. _____

   _____

   _____

   e. _____

   _____

   _____

2. Select three conceptual sign/words from the Conceptual Sign/Word Appendix and write an ASL sentence for each using the correct conceptual sign.

   a. _____

   _____

   _____

   a. _____

   _____

   _____

   a. _____

   _____

   _____

   b. _____

   _____

   b. _____

   _____

   _____

   b. _____

   _____

   _____

   c. _____

   _____

   _____

   c. _____

   _____

   _____

   c. _____

   _____

   _____

Lesson 32

Vocabulary

906 attempt, *try, *effort
907 park, parking
908 parking lot
909 center, *middle
910 supervise, take care of, watch, look after, keep, house, supervis<u>or</u>
911 graduate
912 freeze, frozen, numb
913 careful, be careful, look out, watch out
914 flag
915 make up, make believe, *fantasy, fiction, invent, *hypothesis, fable, create, pretend
916 exaggerate, drag out, waste time
917 advertise, advertisement, promote, word, publicize, ad, commercial
918 dictionary, *encyclopedia
919 kind, gentle, gracious
920 kind, type, make
921 promote, promotion, high, advance, advancement
922 progress, process, procedure, advance, getting along
923 beside, next to, neighb<u>or</u>
924 spoil, ruin, rotten
925 damage, destroy, demolish
926 kiss, buss
927 gone, all gone, out of, cleaned out, expired, run out of
928 vacant, bare, space, empty, available, nude, naked
929 flexible, adaptable, supple
930 goal, objective, aim
931 point, meaning, aim
932 explain, *directions, describe, tell, direct
933 celebrate, victory, anniversary
934 solve, solution, disappear, go away, melt, dissolve, resolve, work out
935 withdraw, pull out

906
attempt, *try, *effort

My uncle's crazy to attempt that.
uncle my try that, (he) crazy

907
park, parking

Try to park the truck near here.
truck near here park try

908
parking lot

The parking lot looks full.
parking-lot full seem

909
center, *middle

Show me the middle of the room.
room middle, you-show-me

Deaf Culture Facts and Information

A major conflict exists between people who view deafness as a physical impairment (medical model) and those people who see deafness as an important part of cultural identity (cultural model).

910
supervise, take care of, watch, look after, keep, house, supervisor

Mom always looks after our cats.
cat, mother our always look-after

911
graduate

Father never graduated from college.
college, father graduate never

912
freeze, frozen, numb

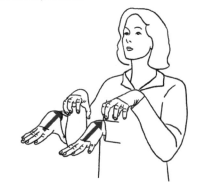

It is freezing outside.
now outside freeze

913
careful, be careful, look out, watch out

Careful, don't cross the bridge.
careful, bridge across don't

914
flag

Our flag is above the building.
building, flag our up-there

915
make up, make believe, *fantasy, fiction, invent, *hypothesis, fable, create, pretend

Grandpa makes up the best stories.
story best, grandfather invent

916
exaggerate, drag out, waste time

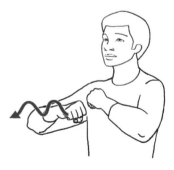

The teacher is exaggerating now.
now teacher exaggerate

917
advertise, advertisement, promote, word, publicize, ad, commercial

They advertised their engagement.
engagement their, (they) advertise

918
dictionary, *encyclopedia

I have a special dictionary.
dictionary special me have

919
kind, gentle, gracious

The kind old lady loves children.
woman kind, old, children she love

920
kind, type, make

What kind of car do you have?
car your, type what?

921
promote, promotion, high, advance, advancement

Mother was promoted last week.
last week mother promote

922
progress, process, procedure, advance, getting along

My boss thinks I am progressing.
boss my think me progress

923
beside, next to, neighbor

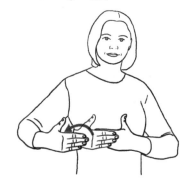

A girl sat next to a spider.
girl next-to spider sit, finish

924
spoil, ruin, rotten

The squirrel ruined our flowers.
flower our, squirrel ruin

925
damage, destroy, demolish

The freeze damaged the apples.
apple damage how? freeze

926
kiss, buss

Count the number of kisses you get.
kiss+ you obtain, how-many count

927
gone, all gone, out of, cleaned out, expired, run out of

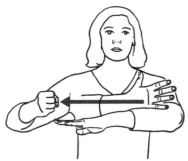

The beer and wine are all gone.
beer, wine, all-gone

928
vacant, bare, space, empty, available, nude, naked

The parking lot is empty now.
now parking-lot empty

929
flexible, adaptable, supple

Dad advises you to be flexible.
you flexible, father advise

ASL Grammar Notes

In addition to time phrases, ASL has other signs that also indicate tense, including WILL, JUST/RECENTLY, NOT-YET, and FINISH.

930
goal, objective, aim

The boss failed to meet his goal.
boss, goal his meet fail

931
point, meaning, aim

I think you understand the point.
point, me think you understand

932
explain, *directions, describe, tell, direct

Carefully explain the policy to the kind man.
man kind, policy you explain carefully

933
celebrate, victory, anniversary

The family celebrated Dad's promotion.
promotion father his, family celebrate

934
solve, solution, disappear, go away, melt, dissolve, resolve, work out

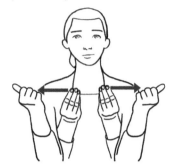

Get the dictionary to solve that question.
dictionary (you) obtain, question solve

935
withdraw, pull out

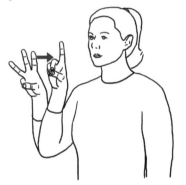

The team tried to withdraw yesterday.
yesterday team withdraw try

Mind Ticklers

Make the sign _____	and think about . . .
attempt, try, effort	putting forth your best effort
park, parking	the vehicle classifier standing still
parking lot	several vehicle classifiers side by side
center, middle	pointing out the middle of your palm
supervise, take care of, watch, look after, house, supervis<u>or</u>	someone's eyes watching everything
graduate	putting a diploma in a student's hand
freeze, frozen, numb	water suddenly becoming hard
careful, be careful, look out, watch out	your eyes looking around for danger
flag	a flag waving in a breeze
make up, make believe, fantasy, fiction, invent	ideas flowing from the head
exaggerate, drag out, waste time	stretching the truth from the mouth
advertise, advertisement, promote, publicize	stretching the truth
dictionary, encyclopedia	turning the pages of a dictionary
kind, gentle, gracious	kindness overflowing from the heart
kind, type, make	the sign **world** with K handshapes
promote, promotion, high, advance	moving up in the world
progress, procedure, advance	moving forward in the world
beside, next to, neighb<u>or</u>	something that is beside you
spoil, ruin, rotten	changing the shape of someone or something
damage, destroy, demolish	tearing something apart
kiss, buss	putting your lips on someone else's lips
gone, all gone, out of, cleaned out	nothing being left on the table or any place
vacant, bare, empty, nude, naked	wiping off something
flexible, adaptable, supple	being able to bend something back and forth
goal, objective, aim, cause	a goal for which you are aiming
point, aim	the point of your finger
explain, directions, describe, tell, direct	conversing with someone
celebrate, victory, anniversary	waving flags in celebration
solve, solution, disappear, go away, melt, dissolve, resolve, vanish	having something dissolve in your hands
withdraw, pull out	pulling back the letters W-D

Practice Sentences

1. He tried to kiss the little girl, but she pushed him away.

   kiss girl short boy try, girl push-away

2. The supervisor froze outside drawing winter pictures.

   outside supervisor freeze why? picture winter he draw

3. The policeman told the best stories, but he dragged them out.

   policeman story his best, except (he) exaggerate

4. The team decided to withdraw when the girls ridiculed it.

   team decide withdraw why? girl+ ridicule

5. Grandma advertised my parent's 40th wedding anniversary.

   wedding anniversary parent my 40, grandma advertise

6. Please explain to me how the food was gone in two hours.

   two-hour food all-gone how? explain please

7. Look in the dictionary to solve the spelling of words.

   word spell (you) look-at dictionary solve

8. The parking lot was empty about two hours after the event.

   event finish, later two-hour parking-lot empty

9. Since graduating two years ago, our son has received three promotions.

   two year ago, son our graduate, up-to-now three promotion finish

10. We understand the seriousness of the point you are making.

    point your, we understand serious

11. The man said that he was flexible but would not change.

    flexible himself man say, regardless, change refuse

12. The white flag next to the parking lot is where I will meet you.

    parking-lot flag white next-to, place there me meet you will

13. Let me explain our progress first, then you can speak.

    first, me explain progress, then speak you able

14. The supervisor wants to put the TV in the middle of the room.

    T-V, supervisor want put room there middle

15. Be careful when you walk through the parking lot. People drive crazy.

    you through parking-lot walk careful, people crazy drive

Class Activities

1. In small groups, go over the student activities in Lesson 31.

2. Each student gets a partner and picks an object in the environment. The other partner asks yes/no questions in ASL with appropriate NMS, trying to guess the object through elimination (BIG? PEOPLE SIT-ON? ROOM BACK?). Switch roles when the object is guessed.

Student Activities

1. Draw a line between the sign glosses that have something in common. Then write what their similarities are.

   a. BE CAREFUL   TYPE

   b. POINT   WASTE TIME

   c. GENTLE   VACANT

   d. ADVERTISE   INCLUDE

   e. WITHDRAW   SUPERVISE

   f. ALL GONE   COME BACK

   g. PARTICIPATE   GOAL

   a. _____

   _____

   b. _____

   _____

   c. _____

   _____

   d. _____

   _____

   e. _____

   _____

   f. _____

   _____

   g. _____

   _____

2. How are the signs for the glosses below similar and different?

   SUPERVISE, BE CAREFUL, KEEP

   _____

   _____

   _____

   _____

   _____

Lesson 33

Vocabulary

936 game, match, contest, sports
937 baseball
938 basketball
939 football
940 ball, softball
941 volleyball
942 tennis
943 table tennis, ping pong
944 bowl, bowling, bowler
945 hockey
946 soccer, kick, kicker
947 boat, boating
948 swim, swimming, swimmer
949 bike, bicycle, cycling, biking, biker
950 golf, golfer
951 wrestle, wrestling, wrestler
952 fishing, fish, fisherman
953 cards, playing cards, shuffle
954 deal, dealer
955 throw
956 rich, wealthy, wealth
957 audience, hoard, crowd, group, house
958 swear, cuss, vulgar, curse, talk dirty
959 promise, swear, oath, vow, word
960 low, lower, less
961 jail, prison, prisoner
962 workshop
963 up and down, not stable, erratic

936
game, match, contest, sports

We enjoy playing different games.
game+ different+ we enjoy play

937
baseball

The baseball game seemed to drag out.
baseball game seem drag-out

938
basketball

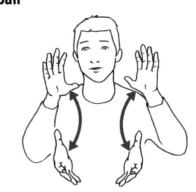

I never played basketball in college.
ago me college, basketball play never

939
football

College football is great to watch.
football college wonderful look-at

940
ball, softball

We can play ball later today.
today later, ball we play

941
volleyball

Everyone can play volleyball.
volleyball, every-one play can

942
tennis

Where do you play tennis?
tennis, you play where?

943
table tennis, ping pong

We play table tennis at home.
table-tennis home we play

944
bowl, bowling, bowler

We go bowling on Tuesday night.
night Tuesday, bowling we go

945
hockey

Hockey is played a lot in the North.
hockey north vicinity a-lot play

Deaf Culture Facts and Information

In 1990, President George H. W. Bush signed into law the Americans with Disabilities Act (ADA). This law made discrimination based on disability illegal. It also required accommodations for people with disabilities to be made in public transportation, employment, public programs, telecommunications, and many other public venues.

946
soccer, kick, kicker

The whole world enjoys soccer.
soccer, all world enjoy

947
boat, boating

No one I know has a boat.
boat, none me know have

948
swim, swimming, swimmer

Be careful when you go swimming.
swim you go, be-careful

949
bike, bicycle, cycling, biking, biker

You can bike in the parking lot, not on the street.
bike there parking-lot can, street don't

950
golf, golfer

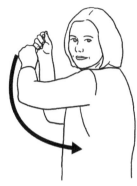

Explain how to play golf.
golf how play, explain

951
wrestle, wrestling, wrestler

The policeman wrestled in college.
ago policeman college there wrestle

952
fishing, fish, fisherman

My grandpa taught me to fish.
grandfather my fishing teach-me

953
cards, playing cards, shuffle

What card games do you like to play?
cards, you enjoy game play which?

954
deal, dealer

Whose turn is it to deal the cards?
deal-card next-turn who?

955
throw

Throw the ball to your sister.
ball, sister your, you throw

956
rich, wealthy, wealth

Basketball players are very rich.
player basketball very rich

ASL Grammar Notes

Conditional sentences have two parts—a condition and a result. A pause and a change of nonmanual signals occurs between the two parts. A conditional sentence may start with IF, IMAGINE/SUPPOSE, and HAPPEN. Nonmanual signals in the conditional part are raised brows, head and body tilt, and the pause.

957
audience, hoard, crowd, group, house

The crowd loved the baseball game.
baseball game, audience love

958
swear, cuss, vulgar, curse, talk dirty

Don't swear when you play games.
game play, (you) swear don't

959
promise, swear, oath, vow, word

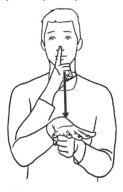

Promise you will let me go boating.
boat me go, you allow, promise will

960
low, lower, less

We need to sit lower with little children.
children short, we sit low must

961
jail, prison, prison<u>er</u>

The jail is in the country.
jail place where? country

962
workshop

Yesterday, we went to a training workshop.
yesterday, workshop training we go

963
up and down, not stable, erratic

Dad's playing is erratic.
play, father his, up-and-down

Mind Ticklers

Make the sign _____	and think about . . .
game, match	two people butting heads in a game
baseball	swinging a baseball bat
basketball	making a two-handed shot
football	two lines of players clashing
ball	the shape of a ball
volleyball	hitting the volleyball with both hands
tennis	swinging a racket back and forth
table tennis, ping pong	serving and hitting the ball
bowl, bowling, bowler	throwing the ball with three fingers in the holes
hockey	a hockey stick scraping the ice
soccer, kick, kicker	kicking a soccer ball
boat, boating	the hull of a boat
swim, swimming, swimmer	the gesture of swimming
biking, bicycle, cycling, bike	pedaling a bicycle
golf, golfer	hitting a golf ball
wrestle, wrestling, wrestler	grabbing an opponent's hands
fishing, fish, fisherman	the act of throwing a fishing line
cards, playing cards, shuffle	shuffling cards
deal, dealer	dealing cards to each player
throw	the act of throwing a ball
rich, wealthy, wealth	a pile of money in your hand
audience, hoard, crowd, group, house	all the people sitting in a theater
swear, cuss, vulgar, curse, talk dirty	biting your tongue for cursing
promise, swear, oath, vow, word	sealing the truth coming from your lips
low, lower, less	indicating how low something is
jail, prison, prisoner	the bars in a jail cell
workshop	the W and S handshapes indicating people sitting in a circle
up and down, not stable, erratic	going from high points to low points

Practice Sentences

1. Both the football and baseball games were canceled because of the rain.

   football, baseball game both cancel why? rain

2. The basketball and volleyball games were played indoors.

   basketball, volleyball game inside play

3. The prisoners are trying to learn how to play soccer.

   soccer, prisoner try learn play

4. They promised the workshop on table tennis would be next Tuesday.

   next-week Tuesday, table-tennis workshop will people promise

5. My bowling game is up and down. I wish I could bowl better.

   bowling my up-and-down, me wish bowling my better possible

6. The card dealer became rich working for wealthy people.

   card dealer himself rich how? for wealthy people work

7. After playing golf the men decided to go fishing in the afternoon.

   finish golf play, man++ decide go fishing afternoon

8. Throw me the orange and green ball and I will take it home.

   ball orange, green, (you) throw-me, me take home will

9. How long has your brother been swimming competitively?

   brother your swim compete how long?

10. If anyone in the audience started swearing, the game would stop.

    suppose any person audience there start swear, game stop will

11. My sister already graduated, but she still plays basketball when she can.

    sister my graduate finish, basketball when possible, she play still

12. The tennis player had established several goals for the year.

    year now tennis player several goal for himself establish+

13. Explain how college wrestling is different from professional wrestling.

    wrestle college, wrestle professional, different how? explain

14. What kind of swimming do you enjoy the most?

    swimming, kind you enjoy most, what?

15. The kind man took me boating with his family on Sunday.

    Sunday man gentle, me with family his, boat take-me

Class Activities

1. In small groups, go over the student activities in Lesson 32.

2. Divide the class into small groups. The instructor writes five incomplete sentences on the board (for example, I'm looking for a spouse who . . ., The first time I met a deaf person . . ., My best friend is really . . .). Each student in each group will finish two of the incomplete sentences by signing them with three or four different endings.

Student Activities

1. Without looking at the Mind Ticklers for this lesson, write a mnemonic for the following glosses.

   a. WRESTLING

   _____

   _____

   b. SOCCER

   _____

   _____

   c. GAME

   _____

   _____

   d. BASKETBALL

   _____

   _____

   e. FOOTBALL

   _____

   _____

   f. BALL

   _____

   _____

2. Which signs in this lesson would be considered iconic?

   _____

   _____

   _____

   _____

   _____

3. From the list of glosses for sports in this lesson, pick one that you enjoy playing and one that you enjoy watching. Then write ASL sentences explaining why.

   a. _____

   _____

   _____

   b. _____

   _____

   _____

Lesson 34

Vocabulary

964 river, stream
965 ocean, sea
966 lake, pond
967 beach, seashore, coast
968 rock, stone
969 mountain, peak
970 hill, mound
971 ground, soil, sand, dirt
972 land
973 interpret, interpreting, interpret<u>er</u>
974 translate, transliterate, transformation
975 wise, wisdom, *philosophy, *philosop<u>her</u>
976 among, amongst, amid
977 grass, hay
978 wait, pass the time
979 charge, cost, price, fine, tax, bill
980 blame, charge, fault, accuse
981 something, someone, somebody
982 schedule, matrix, chart, calendar
983 print, publish, newspaper
984 oh, I see; I see; that's it; I agree
985 relationship, association, cooperation, teamwork
986 regular, regularly, all along
987 same, similar, same as
988 same, alike, like, too, also
989 same, standard, in common, common, similar
990 same, no change, like before, consistent
991 memorize

964
river, stream

We used to swim in the river.
ago river there we swim

965
ocean, sea

I prefer swimming in the ocean.
ocean swim me favorite

966
lake, pond

Fishing in a lake is fun.
fishing lake there fun

967
beach, seashore, coast

We stay at the beach for two weeks.
two-week we beach stay

Deaf Culture Facts and Information

In 1958, President Dwight D. Eisenhower signed the law establishing the Captioned Films for the Deaf program. In 1990, the Television Decoder Circuitry Act became law, requiring all television sets with a screen of 13 inches or larger to incorporate closed-caption technology.

968
rock, stone

The old house is made of stone.
house old, build stone

969
mountain, peak

I know of a beautiful lake in the mountains.
lake beautiful, mountain there me know

970
hill, mound

Grandma lives on a small hill.
hill tiny grandmother live there

971
ground, soil, sand, dirt

The soil here is good for growing.
for grow, soil here good

972
land

The minister bought land near the ocean.
land near ocean, minister buy finish

973
interpret, interpreting, interpreter

Interpreting is what I enjoy doing.
interpret me enjoy

974
translate, transliterate, transformation

The girl translates very well.
girl herself very good translate

975
wise, wisdom, *philosophy, *philosopher

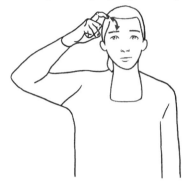

It is wise to be careful in water.
in water wise be-careful

976
among, amongst, amid

The players walked among the audience.
player+ among audience walk

977
grass, hay

No grass is on the mountain.
mountain, grass there, none

978
wait, pass the time

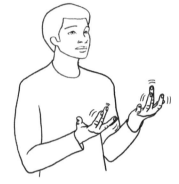

Wait for me near the river.
river near (you) for me wait

979
charge, cost, price, fine, tax, bill

Do they charge for you to bowl?
bowling place charge (you)

980
blame, charge, fault, accuse

Don't blame the team for losing.
team fail, (you) blame team don't

981
something, someone, somebody

Somebody built a house here.
house here somebody build finish

982
schedule, matrix, chart, calendar

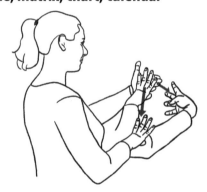

Do you have a soccer schedule?
schedule soccer (you) have

983
print, publish, newspaper

Print the fall schedule now.
now, schedule fall print

984

oh, I see; I see; that's it; I agree

Oh, I see; you finally went swimming.
oh-I-see, finally you swim go

ASL Grammar Notes

The infinitive is the base form of a verb that comes after the word *to*. In sentences, infinitives act as nouns, adjectives, or adverbs. In ASL, the word *to* is not signed with infinitives; for example, *I like to eat at 6:00* is signed as TIME 6 ME LIKE EAT.

985

relationship, association, cooperation, teamwork

Our relationship has been damaged.
relationship our damage finish

986

regular, regularly, all along

We take regular trips to the beach.
travel beach we go regular

987

same, similar, same as

We have the same interpreter for math.
interpreter math, same-as two-of-us have

988

same, alike, like, too, also

My brother looks like me.
brother my, appearance same me

989
same, standard, in common, common, similar

Students in college are the same.
student there college, common

990
same, no change, like before, consistent

The big lake looks the same.
lake big, seem no-change

991
memorize

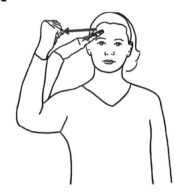

She memorized all our names.
name+ our, girl all memorize

Mind Ticklers

Make the sign _____	and think about . . .
river, stream	the width and movement of a river
ocean, sea	the waves in the ocean
lake, pond	indicating the size of a lake
beach, seashore	the downward slope of sand on the beach
rock, stone	the hardness of rocks
mountain, peak	a lot of rocks forming a mountain
hill, mound	drawing a hill in the air
ground, soil, sand	feeling soil in your hand
land	soil making up the land
interpret, interpreting, interpreter	signing what someone else says
translate, transliterate, transformation	changing one language to another
wise, wisdom, philosophy, philosopher	the depth of knowledge in the brain
among, amongst, amid	going in and out of several objects
grass, hay	a cow or horse eating hay
wait, pass the time	twiddling your fingers while waiting
charge, cost, fine, tax, bill	the amount of money being deducted
blame, charge, fault, accuse	pushing the responsibility onto someone else
something, someone, somebody	the classifier for a person
schedule, matrix, chart	the grid of a planning sheet
print, publish, newspaper	putting words on paper
oh, I see; I see; I agree; that's it	a backchannel response showing you agree
relationship, association, cooperation	being connected to someone or something
regular, all along	repeating the sign **right**
same, similar, same as	two things exactly alike
same, alike, like, too, also	the Y handshape showing similarity
same, standard, in common, common, similar	everything around you being the same
same, no change, like before	repeating the sign **stay**
memorize	holding onto something you know

Practice Sentences

1. Dad prefers fishing in that river more than any other.

   river there dad fishing favorite than other

2. How long do the two of us need to wait for something to happen?

   for something happen, two-of-us need wait, how long-time?

3. Where we live now, the newspaper comes on a regular basis.

   place we now live, newspaper regular arrive

4. Try to memorize the way to the beach when we go this afternoon.

   now afternoon we go beach, path (you) try memorize

5. Dad told the doctor there was no change in the way that he felt.

   feel change, dad tell doctor, change none

6. My relationship with my family is the same.

   relationship (my), with family my no-change

7. The workshop in two weeks will be in the mountains.

   next-two-week workshop, mountain there happen will

8. There is a standard charge for fishing in the mountain lake.

   fishing, mountain lake charge standard have

9. Please schedule five hours for interpreting next week on Monday.

   next-week Monday, five-hour interpret schedule please

10. Something happened at home and my father blamed his father for it.

    home something happen, father my blame father his

11. The hill behind our house is a good place to sit and relax.

    hill behind house our, good place sit relax

12. Do the deaf college students prefer interpreting or transliterating?

    college students deaf, they favorite interpret, transliterate, which?

13. All the people in the audience enjoyed hearing the philosopher.

    audience people all, philosopher lecture they enjoy

14. That land has rich black soil for raising plants.

    land there soil black wonderful for grow-plants

15. I don't like our beach; it has too many rocks and no grass.

    beach our, me don't-like, why? rock many, grass none

Class Activities

1. In small groups, go over the student activities in Lesson 33.

2. Ten minutes before the end of class, the instructor fingerspells a state. The first student to fingerspell the capital of the state correctly may leave class. Continue the activity until all the students are excused or time runs out.

Student Activities

1. There are two conceptual sign/words in this lesson, _____ and _____. Write an English sentence for each of the conceptual sign/words. Then write an ASL sentence for each English meaning, using the correct conceptual sign/gloss (one without multiple meanings). **Be original.**

    a. _____

    _____

    _____

    a. _____

    _____

    _____

    b. _____

    _____

    _____

    b. _____

    _____

    _____

    c. _____

    _____

    _____

    c. _____

    _____

    _____

    d. _____

    _____

    _____

    d. _____

    _____

    _____

    e. _____

    _____

    _____

    e. _____

    _____

    _____

    f. _____

    _____

    _____

    f. _____

    _____

    _____

2. Which signs in this lesson can be initialized?

    _____

    _____

3. List the signs in this lesson that can be directional.

    _____

    _____

Lesson 35

Vocabulary

992 fight, battle, fighter
993 war, engagement, battle
994 bomb, explosion, blow up
995 army, soldier, military
996 navy
997 marijuana, pot
998 selfish, stingy
999 honor, *respect
1000 hurry, quick, fast
1001 invent, devise, make up, original, create
1002 invention
1003 danger, dangerous, hazard, threat
1004 argue, quarrel, debate, dispute
1005 program
1006 project
1007 sick, ill, *disease, sickness
1008 hurt, pain, sore, painful, ache
1009 examination, medical exam, physical
1010 mumps
1011 measles
1012 cough
1013 developmentally delayed
1014 psychiatry, psychiatrist
1015 patient
1016 dentist
1017 hospital, *infirmary
1018 operation, surgery, surgeon
1019 medicine, medical, drugs
1020 pills, take medicine
1021 not that, just wait, not what I mean

992
fight, battle, fighter

The hockey player liked fighting.
fight hockey player like

993
war, engagement, battle

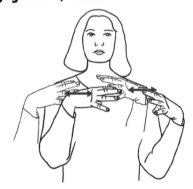

The war lasted five years.
five year war continue

994
bomb, explosion, blow up

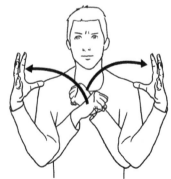

I heard the explosion last night.
ago night explosion me hear

995
army, soldier, military

The army has several interpreters.
army several interpreter have

996
navy

My brother joined the navy.
brother my, navy he join

997
marijuana, pot

Dad knows marijuana is bad.
marijuana bad, father know

998
selfish, stingy

He is stingy like his dad.
boy selfish father same-as

Deaf Culture Facts and Information

Deaf clubs, which were at one time located in every major city in the United States, originally served as information, socialization, and entertainment centers for Deaf people. The advent of technologies such as instant messaging, videophones, and closed captioning has caused a decline in the importance of clubs for Deaf people.

999
honor, *respect

Honor thy mother and father.
mother father your, honor

1000
hurry, quick, fast

Hurry, the fight is about to begin.
hurry, fight ready start

1001
invent, devise, make up, original, create

The wise man invented something.
man wise, something invent

1002
invention

Her invention will help everyone.
invention girl hers, help every-one will

1003
danger, dangerous, hazard, threat

The ocean can be dangerous.
ocean danger can

1004
argue, quarrel, debate, dispute

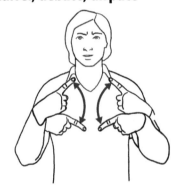

The interpreter argued with the teacher.
interpreter, teacher argue

1005
program

When will the program begin?
program start when?

1006
project

Our project is among the best.
project our among best

1007
sick, ill, *disease, sickness

Dad went home sick today.
today father go home sick

1008
hurt, pain, sore, painful, ache

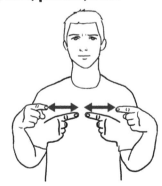

How did you hurt yourself?
yourself hurt how?

1009
examination, medical exam, physical

I have a yearly physical exam.
yearly me medical-exam have

ASL Grammar Notes

The signing space is where the majority of signs are made. In ASL, the signing space is the rectangular area from the top of the head to the waistline and between the shoulders.

1010
mumps

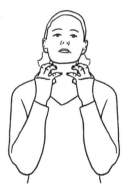

My three children had mumps.
mumps three children my have finish

1011
measles

Mom never had measles.
measles, mother have, never

1012
cough

You have a bad cough.
cough your bad

1013
developmentally delayed

My dog acts developmentally delayed.
dog my behave same-as what? D-D

1014
psychiatry, psychiatrist

A psychiatrist is also a doctor.
psychiatrist alike doctor

1015
patient

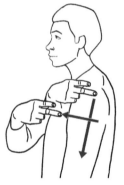

Mom is not a good patient.
mother good patient, not

1016
dentist

The dentist is sick today.
today dentist sick

1017

hospital, *infirmary

The hospital has many patients.
patient++ hospital there many have

1018

operation, surgery, surge<u>on</u>

The operation lasted five hours.
operation five-hour continue

1019

medicine, medical, drugs

My medicine has not changed.
medicine my no-change

1020

pills, take medicine

Don't forget, take two pills every day.
daily two pill+, forget don't

1021

not that, just wait, not what I mean

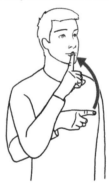

Just wait, Grandpa will tell you later.
just-wait, later grandfather tell-you will

Mind Ticklers

Make the sign _____	and think about . . .
fight, battle, fighter	the gesture of fighting with someone
war, engagement, battle	battle lines going back and forth
bomb, explosion, blow up, fireworks	a bomb exploding
army, soldier, military	soldiers carrying rifles
navy	the two rows of buttons on navy pants
marijuana, pot, joint	puffing on a joint
selfish, stingy	pulling everything to yourself
honor, respect	respect coming from the mind
hurry, quick, fast	moving ahead quickly
invent, devise, make up, original	ideas coming from the head
invention	an idea that takes form
danger, dangerous	warning yourself of danger
argue, quarrel, debate, dispute	two people shaking their fingers at one another
program	reading the front and back of a program
project	abbreviating *project* by signing **program** with P-J
sick, ill, disease, sickness	your head and stomach hurting
hurt, pain, sore, painful, ache	nerves throbbing in pain
examination, medical exam, physical	the doctor searching to find something wrong
mumps	the place mumps occur
measles	spots on your face
cough	the chest heaving up and down
developmentally delayed	D–D handshapes
psychiatry, psychiatrist	**doctor** with a P handshape
patient	signing **hospital** with a P handshape
dentist	a dentist working on your teeth
hospital, infirmary	a red cross on the shoulder
operation, surgery, surgeon	making a surgical cut
medicine, medical	counting the pills in your hand
pills, take medicine	putting a pill in your mouth
not that, just wait, not what I mean	a forceful "shh" sign and head shake

Practice Sentences

1. The fight started because the two girls were arguing over the boy.

   fight start why? girl two-of-them concerning boy argue

2. The dentist lost a lot of patients because he didn't respect them.

   patient+ dentist lose many why?, he respect them not

3. The medical school at my university sees a lot of very sick people.

   people a-lot very sick, medical school university my examination

4. I know that your project is dangerous. Be careful, we don't want an explosion.

   project your me know-that dangerous, careful, explosion (we) don't-want

5. The dentist will present his new invention at the hospital next Thursday.

   next-week Thursday, in hospital, new invention dentist his introduce will

6. You need to take your medicine morning and night, not noon.

   take-medicine yours must morning night, noon not

7. The operation lasted about five hours, and the doctor was successful.

   approximately five-hours, operation continue, doctor success finish

8. The army was in the war, but not the navy.

   war, army join, but navy join not

9. The little boy became very sick with either the measles or mumps.

   either measles, mumps boy short very sick become

10. Every time she coughed, her chest and abdomen hurt.

    every time girl cough, chest abdomen hers hurt

11. The stingy old man refused to buy medicine for his illness.

    man old stingy, medicine buy for illness his, refuse

12. Who said that Dad wanted to hurry back from the war?

    war, dad want hurry back say who?

13. Take the white pill in the morning, the red one at noon, and none at night.

    morning pill white, noon pill red, night pill none

14. We always hear a lot of explosions on the Fourth of July.

    fourth July a-lot explosion we always hear

15. All the navy ships were far far out in the ocean.

    ship navy, all out ocean, far++

Class Activity

1. In small groups, go over the student activities in Lesson 34.

Student Activities

1. Write five ASL rhetorical sentences using signs from this lesson.

   a. _____
   _____
   _____

   b. _____
   _____
   _____
   _____

   c. _____
   _____
   _____
   _____

   d. _____
   _____
   _____
   _____

   e. _____
   _____
   _____

2. Sign the following sentences using directional signs.

   a. Don't blame me. He is blaming you. We are blaming them.

   b. Respect your parents and they will respect you.

   c. I argued with Dad. Mom and my sister argued. Everyone was arguing.

   d. Help me first, then I will help you. Help all those people. Dad helps Mom.

   e. Give me the paper. I will give you the money. Give everyone money.

   f. I am moving next week. Move the table over there. Move that close to me.

   g. You and I disagree. Mom and Dad disagree. Why do the two of them disagree?

   h. Are you teasing me? He teases everyone. I enjoy teasing Mom.

3. Circle the correct response.

   a. A positive comment is usually accompanied by the head shaking / nodding.

   b. A negative comment is usually accompanied by the head shaking / nodding.

Lesson 36

Vocabulary

1022 pregnant
1023 well, healthy, brave, courage, strong
1024 upset, disturb, disturbed
1025 thing, article, object, *material, product, *equipment
1026 column, article
1027 key
1028 lock
1029 mean, rough, harsh, unkind, cruel
1030 rough, crude, rude, not smooth
1031 smooth, flat
1032 queen
1033 king
1034 ghost, spirit, soul
1035 flower
1036 join, put together, connect, connecting, fasten, unite
1037 let go, release, disconnect, unfasten, break off
1038 change, alter, adapt, correct, turn
1039 time, period, era
1040 full, satisfied, sated
1041 choice, choose, select, pick, prefer
1042 beat, defeat, conquer, overcome
1043 beat, punch, hit, abuse, strike, impact
1044 only, just
1045 recently, a while ago, just, a little bit ago
1046 debt, owe, afford, due
1047 but, however
1048 poor, poorly, impoverished, inadequate
1049 almost, nearly, about
1050 pick up

1022
pregnant

My sister is four months pregnant.
sister my, pregnant four-month

1023
well, healthy, brave, courage, strong

Are you well now?
now, you healthy?

1024
upset, disturb, disturbed

You look a little upset.
upset little-bit (you) seem

1025
thing, article, object, *material, product, *equipment

That thing is dangerous.
thing there danger

Deaf Culture Facts and Information

The Americans with Disabilities Act (ADA) has several provisions that affect deaf people. Among them is the requirement for "auxiliary aids and services," such as qualified interpreters or other effective methods of making aurally delivered materials available to individuals with hearing loss.

1026
column, article

The newspaper printed my article.
column my, newspaper print

1027
key

The pregnant lady has my key.
key my, lady pregnant have

1028
lock

She was wise to lock the house.
woman wise, house lock

1029
mean, rough, harsh, unkind, cruel

He is a mean fighter.
man, he cruel fighter

1030
rough, crude, rude, not smooth

The ground is very rough.
now ground rough very

1031
smooth, flat

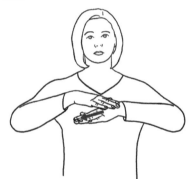

I think the new road feels smooth.
road new, think me smooth

1032
queen

The queen is pregnant again.
again queen pregnant

1033
king

The king loves the queen.
king he queen love

1034
ghost, spirit, soul

We don't believe in ghosts.
ghost we believe not

1035
flower

The young queen loves flowers.
queen young, flower she love

1036
join, put together, connect, connecting, fasten, unite

The two houses were joined.
house two join finish

1037
let go, release, disconnect, unfasten, break off

Don't let go of the mean dog.
dog cruel release don't

1038
change, alter, adapt, correct, turn

Change is upsetting to some people.
change, people some upset

1039
time, period, era

Your sister did that six times.
sister your six time that do

1040
full, satisfied, sated

Eat until you are full.
(you) eat until sated

1041
choice, choose, select, pick, prefer

What choice do I have now?
now choice have me what?

1042
beat, defeat, conquer, overcome

We cannot beat that team.
team there we defeat cannot

1043
beat, punch, hit, abuse, strike, impact

The king never abused the queen.
queen, king abuse never

1044
only, just

Only the queen has the key.
key, only queen have

1045
recently, a while ago, just, a little bit ago

They went to the beach recently.
recently they beach go

ASL Grammar Notes

The version of a sign shown in most ASL books is called the citation form. For example, books show the sign RIGHT (*correct*) made with two hands, index fingers pointing out, with the right hand coming down on the left hand. The conversation form of RIGHT (*correct*) may be made with the dominant hand hitting the body, hitting a table, or forcefully moving down in front of the body.

1046
debt, owe, afford, due

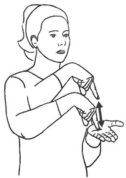

The psychiatrist is always in debt.
psychiatrist, herself, debt always have

1047
but, however

You can go, but I cannot.
you go can, but me go cannot

1048
poor, poorly, impoverished, inadequate

The boy was always poor.
boy poor always

1049
almost, nearly, about

We almost bought a beach house.
house beach we almost buy

1050
pick up

Pick up the keys and give them to me.
key, you pick-up, give-me

Mind Ticklers

Make the sign _____	and think about . . .
pregnant	the abdomen being round
well, healthy, brave, courage	puffing out your chest
upset, disturb, disturbed	your stomach turning upside down
thing, article, object, material, product, equipment	showing something in your hand
column, article	the width of a column on a page
key	turning a key in a lock
lock	turning a deadbolt on a door
mean, rough, harsh, unkind, rude	bumping your knuckles together is rough
rough, crude, rude, not smooth	the palm of your hand being rough
smooth, flat, clean	a surface that is smooth
queen, king	the sash worn by royalty
ghost spirit, soul	a spirit coming from the ground
flower	smelling a flower
join, put together, connect, connecting, fasten, unite	two objects being joined
let go, release, disconnect, unfasten, break off	two objects separating
change, alter, adapt, correct, turn	turning something upside down to change it
period, time, era	an indefinite number of hours on a clock
full, satisfied, sated	food coming all the way up to the chin
choice, choose, select, pick, prefer	having several items to choose from
beat, defeat, conquer, overcome	overcoming what was in your way
beat, punch, hit, abuse, strike, impact	striking someone with your fist
just, only	a single item
recently, a while ago, just, a little bit ago	something that just happened in time
debt, owe, afford, due	pointing to the amount you owe on a bill
but, however	opening an issue for further discussion
poor, poorly, impoverished, inadequate	poor people with holes in their shirts
almost, nearly	almost catching your other hand
pick up	the act of picking something up

Practice Sentences

1. The queen was not upset that she was pregnant.

   queen pregnant, she upset not

2. The king was excited because his army defeated their enemy again.

   king excited why? army his enemy their again defeat

3. Only five brave soldiers came to save the king and queen.

   only five brave soldier come for king queen salvation

4. Dad just took his medicine before you and Mom arrived.

   prior-to mom you arrive, dad recently take-medicine his

5. After paying off all of his debts, the sick man was almost poor.

   man sick, debt his all cancel finish, now (he) almost poor

6. The queen becomes upset when she sees animals being abused.

   animal abuse queen see, (she) become upset

7. Pick up your brother and give him the house keys.

   brother yours pick-up, house keys give (him)

8. There are several things on the table, but I cannot see them.

   several things table there, me see them cannot

9. You have two choices; you can join the Army or Navy.

   two choice (you) have, army navy join which?

10. They just don't believe all the cats and dogs will be released.

    cat dog all release, people doubt will

11. My uncle enjoyed reading your recent article in the magazine.

    uncle my read, enjoy recent article your, magazine there

12. If you change your behavior now, only a few people will know it.

    behavior your, suppose change, only few people know will

13. It is almost time to release the birds the queen wants freed.

    bird+, queen want free, now almost time release

14. What you said in the teacher's class was mean and crude.

    teacher class hers, itemize you say, unkind crude

15. We had a choice—we could take the rough road or the smooth road.

    choice we have, rough road, smooth road, take-up which?

Class Activities

1. In small groups, take turns signing one of the directional phrases in student activity 2 in Lesson 35.

2. The class divides in half. The instructor assigns a gloss from Lesson 36 to a student in each group. The students write down a simple sentence using their gloss and then they exchange sentences within their group. Then the students walk around the room signing the sentence on the paper until they find the matching gloss.

Student Activities

1. Look at the signs in this lesson and group them based on their handshape similarity.

    <u>most similar</u>   <u>similar</u>   <u>less similar</u>

    _____   _____   _____

    _____   _____   _____

    _____   _____   _____

    _____   _____   _____

    _____   _____   _____

2. Which gloss is a time indicator? _____ Go back to Lesson 17 and put this gloss in the proper place on your time drawing.

3. Practice signing the backchannel feedback responses you might use when reinforcing a signer's comments.

    a. OH, I SEE   b. NO, NO, NO

    c. RIGHT   d. SURE, NO PROBLEM

    e. DISGUST   f. NO!

    g. SURE/TRUE   h. YES, OF COURSE

    i. SICK   j. REALLY

    k. OH, ALL RIGHT   l. DON'T KNOW

    m. YES   n. NEAT

    o. YEAH   p. NONE

    q. FINE   r. I KNOW THAT

    s. HAVEN'T   t. I KNOW

Lesson 37

Vocabulary

1051 fruit
1052 pineapple
1053 apple
1054 peach
1055 pear
1056 banana
1057 strawberry
1058 *lemon, sour, bitter
1059 grapes
1060 pumpkin, melon
1061 watermelon
1062 tomato
1063 vegetables
1064 corn on the cob
1065 peas
1066 cheese
1067 potato
1068 onion
1069 dessert, date
1070 sandwich
1071 meat
1072 hamburger
1073 sausage, bologna
1074 hot dog, wiener
1075 bacon
1076 spaghetti
1077 egg
1078 milk
1079 butter
1080 ice cream
1081 popcorn
1082 crackers, biscuit
1083 salad
1084 juice

**1051
fruit**

Pick up all the fruit.
fruit all, pick-up

**1052
pineapple**

The pineapples are very small.
pineapple, very small

**1053
apple**

Dad recently ate the apples.
recently father apple eat

1054
peach

The peach pie made me full.
pie peach cause me sated

1055
pear

The hospital gave out pears.
pear+, hospital disseminate

1056
banana

Are bananas always yellow?
banana yellow always

1057
strawberry

We pick strawberries every year.
every-year strawberry we pick

Deaf Culture Facts and Information

State Vocational Rehabilitation (VR) agencies furnish a wide variety of services to deaf individuals and others with disabilities. These services are designed to provide clients with the skills and knowledge to return to work, to enter a new line of work, or to enter the workforce for the first time.

1058
***lemon, sour, bitter**

The lemon tree has a disease.
tree lemon disease have

1059
grapes

Grapes are red or green.
grape, red, green

1060
pumpkin, melon

The farmer grew big pumpkins.
pumpkin big, farmer grow-plant

1061
watermelon

The dentist bought watermelons at the market.
watermelon+, store there, dentist buy

1062
tomato

The soldier raised tomatoes.
soldier, tomato grow-plant

1063
vegetables

Don't forget to eat your vegetables.
vegetable your, forget eat don't

1064
corn on the cob

I love corn on the cob.
corn-on-the-cob, me love

1065
peas

Put butter on the peas.
peas, butter put

1066
cheese

The farmer makes the best cheese.
cheese best, farmer himself create

1067
potato

How do you like your potato?
potato your, you favor?

1068
onion

Onions make me cry.
onion cause cry me

1069
dessert, date

Everyone likes good dessert.
dessert good, every-one enjoy

1070
sandwich

What is in the sandwich?
sandwich, inside, what?

1071
meat, content, substance

The king doesn't eat meat.
meat, king eat not

ASL Grammar Notes

Iconic signs look like what they represent. For example, the sign BABY resembles the motion of rocking a baby, FISHING represents throwing out a fishing line, CRYING imitates tears rolling down the face, and LISTENING pantomimes cupping the hand over the ear.

1072
hamburger

Who has the best hamburgers?
hamburger best, have who?

1073
sausage, bologna

Where is the sausage you bought?
sausage you buy, now where?

1074
hot dog, wiener

The pregnant lady ate two hot dogs.
lady pregnant two hot-dog eat

1075
bacon

Bacon comes from pigs.
bacon from pig

1076
spaghetti

Where is the spaghetti?
spaghetti, where?

1077
egg

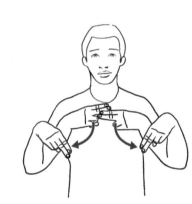

Eat sausage with your eggs.
egg with sausage you eat

1078
milk

Milk is good for you.
milk for you healthy good

1079
butter

Put butter on your bread.
bread you butter

1080
ice cream

Who doesn't like ice cream?
ice-cream, don't-like who?

1081
popcorn

The popcorn smells great.
popcorn marvelous smell

1082
crackers, biscuit

The biscuits are buttery and soft.
biscuit+ butter have, soft

1083
salad

The salad needs more tomato.
tomato, salad more need

1084
juice

The baby likes orange juice.
orange juice, baby like

Mind Ticklers

Make the sign _____	and think about . . .
fruit	an F handshape near the mouth
pineapple	a P handshape near the mouth
apple	an apple being red like your cheek
peach	the fuzz on a peach being similar to face fuzz
pear	the shape of a pear
banana	peeling a banana
strawberry	pulling the stem off while eating a strawberry
lemon, sour, bitter	your face twisting up when you eat something sour
grapes	a cluster of grapes
pumpkin, melon	thumping a melon to see if it is good
watermelon	signing **water** plus **melon**
tomato	slicing a tomato
vegetables	a V handshape near your mouth
corn on the cob	eating corn on the cob
peas	pulling the peas from a pod
cheese	pressing milk to make cheese
potato	sticking a fork into a potato
onion	onions making your eyes water
dessert, date	two people coming together
sandwich	putting two slices of bread into your mouth
meat	meat hanging from a hook
hamburger	making a hamburger patty
sausage, bologna	links of sausage
hot dog	a hot dog in a bun
bacon	bacon curling when cooked
spaghetti	the thin strands of spaghetti pasta
egg	breaking open an egg
milk	milking a cow
butter	buttering a piece of bread
ice cream	licking an ice cream cone
popcorn	kernels of popcorn popping
crackers, biscuit	determining if the biscuit is soft
salad	tossing a salad with forks
juice	the J handshape near the mouth

Practice Sentences

1. Mom makes a great fruit salad with oranges, watermelon, and apples.

   fruit salad, mom create wonderful, orange watermelon apple have

2. You know that tomatoes are a fruit and not a vegetable.

   tomato, you know-that fruit, vegetable not

3. The pregnant lady craved corn on the cob and popcorn at the same time.

   lady pregnant, corn-on-the-cob, popcorn same time hungry

4. Tell me which kind of juice you like—orange, tomato, or grape?

   juice, type you like, orange tomato grape which?

5. When I was a kid I tried freezing milk to make ice cream.

   ago kid me freeze milk, create ice cream me try

6. After eating all the vegetables, meat, and fruit, I am sated.

   finish sated me, vegetable meat fruit all me eat

7. When you make a salad, please put onions and bacon in it for me.

   salad you make, onion bacon put for me, please

8. Mom had to lock the dessert in the closet so we would not eat it all.

   dessert mom lock closet there must, if not, we all eat

9. My good friend never puts meat on his sandwich.

   friend my good, sandwich his, meat put never

10. We order biscuits with egg and sausage every Wednesday morning.

    every-Wednesday morning biscuit egg sausage we order

11. I don't like butter in my popcorn, but my sister and brother do.

    popcorn my, butter don't-like, sister brother my like

12. Tell me again what each of you wants on your hot dogs.

    hot-dog each you want what? again tell-me

13. You have two choices for dessert tomorrow, fruit or ice cream.

    tomorrow dessert, two choice (you) have, fruit ice-cream

14. It is strange, but a person can buy pink, yellow, or red tomatoes.

    tomato person able pink yellow red buy, that strange

15. Who wants me to put bacon and onions on their hamburgers?

    hamburger yours, bacon onion me put, want who?

Class Activities

1. In small groups, go over the student activities in Lesson 36. Then practice the backchannel feedback signs together.

2. Students get into pairs. One student in each pair turns his back to the instructor. The instructor signs an open-ended question using recently learned vocabulary, such as WOMEN PREGNANT YOU KNOW HOW-MANY? The student facing the instructor signs the sentence to his partner who responds appropriately. After five sentences, partners change places and the instructor signs five more questions.

Student Activities

1. Write three of your favorite foods included in this lesson for each category below.

   <u>vegetables</u>   <u>fruits</u>   <u>meats</u>

   _____   _____   _____

   _____   _____   _____

   _____   _____   _____

2. For each sign listed below, find another sign that has the same parameters for handshape, movement, and location.

	same handshape	same movement	same location
Example:			
FEEL	*sick*	*happy*	*my*
RESPONSIBILITY			
FORGET			
CUTE			
ENJOY			
BICYCLE			
UGLY			
BEST			
WORSE			
MONKEY			
DISCUSS			

3. Write a short paragraph using the signs from Lesson 37, and then write four questions about your paragraph.

   _____

   _____

   _____

   _____

   _____

   _____

   _____

   _____

   _____

   _____

Lesson 38

Vocabulary

1085 jelly, jam, preserves
1086 toast
1087 taco
1088 french fries
1089 donuts
1090 gravy, grease, oil
1091 bread
1092 soup
1093 rice
1094 cake
1095 cookie
1096 pizza
1097 salt
1098 pepper
1099 sugar, sweet, diabetic
1100 vinegar
1101 candy
1102 nuts, peanuts
1103 lettuce, cabbage
1104 pie
1105 shrimp
1106 cook (n.), cook (v.), kitchen, chef
1107 chips
1108 potato chips
1109 thirsty
1110 breakfast
1111 lunch
1112 dinner, dining
1113 plant, seeds, sow
1114 McDonald's
1115 Walmart
1116 Wendy's
1117 Hardee's
1118 Starbucks
1119 Burger King
1120 Target

1085
jelly, jam, preserves

Peach jelly is my favorite.
jelly peach my prefer

1086
toast

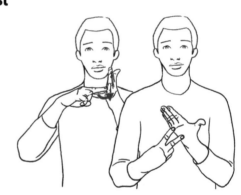

Put grape jelly on your toast.
jelly grape, toast (you) put

1087
taco

I like a good taco.
taco good, me enjoy

1088
french fries

Do you like french fries?
french-fries you like

1089
donuts

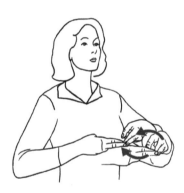

What kind of donut is that?
donut there, type what?

1090
gravy, grease, oil

I like turkey gravy on my potatoes.
potato, turkey gravy on, me prefer

1091
bread

My aunt doesn't like white bread.
bread white, aunt my don't like

Deaf Culture Facts and Information

Title V of the Rehabilitation Act of 1973 prohibits discrimination against people with disabilities and requires accessibility in employment, education, health, welfare, and social services. This discrimination resulted from negative attitudes and physical and communication barriers. The Act requires employers to make reasonable accommodations for disabled employees.

1092
soup

My favorite lunch is chicken soup and crackers.
lunch prefer my what? chicken soup, crackers

1093
rice

Mom bought both brown and white rice.
rice brown, white mother buy finish

1094
cake

The chocolate cake is finished.
cake chocolate now finish

1095
cookie

The dog ate all the chocolate cookies.
cookie chocolate, dog eat all

1096
pizza

The hospital gave pizza to the patients.
patient them, hospital pizza disseminate

1097
salt

I like tomatoes with salt.
tomato with salt, me prefer

1098
pepper

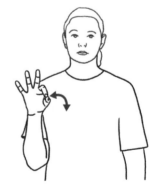

You forgot to pepper the vegetables.
vegetable, pepper you forget

1099
sugar, sweet, diabetic

I don't want sugar in my coffee.
sugar, in coffee my, don't-want

1100
vinegar

Mom makes a vinegar cake.
cake with vinegar, mother create

1101
candy

Lemon candy is on the table.
candy lemon, there table now

1102
nuts, peanuts

Who ate all the nuts?
nut, eat all, who?

1103
lettuce, cabbage

Please, no lettuce for me.
lettuce, for me none please

1104
pie

Who made the apple pie?
pie apple create who?

1105
shrimp

The shrimp at the market were huge.
shrimp, market there big

ASL Grammar Notes

Changing the movement of some verbs to a repetitive circular motion indicates that the action is continuing for a long period or that it is done frequently. For example, the circular motion can be added to the sign WORK to indicate working often or for a long time.

1106
cook (n.), cook (v.), kitchen, chef

Who is the best cook here.
cook here, best who?

1107
chips

Chips are on the floor.
chip, there floor now

1108
potato chips

The patient asked for potato chips.
potato chip patient request

1109
thirsty

Dad is thirsty for milk.
milk, father thirsty now

1110
breakfast

What time is breakfast?
breakfast time what?

1111
lunch

Lunch today is at 1:15.
today lunch time 1:15

1112
dinner, dining

Dinner tonight is at my house.
tonight, dinner my house

1113
plant, seeds, sow

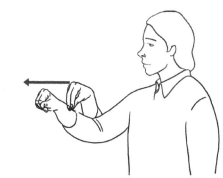

Next year we will plant onions.
next-year onion we sow will

1114
McDonald's

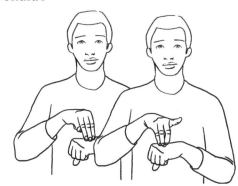

McDonald's has good french fries.
french-fries good, McDonald's have

1115
Walmart

Walmart is not far from here.
Walmart from here, far not

1116
Wendy's

Wendy's has good hamburgers.
hamburger good, Wendy's have

1117
Hardee's

Hardee's is my favorite place.
Hardee's, favorite place my

1118
Starbucks

Starbuck's coffee is very good.
coffee Starbuck's very good

1119
Burger King

Burger King is near my house.
house my near Burger King

1120
Target

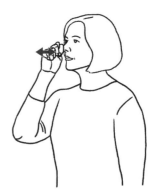

Target is where Mom goes to shop.
mother shopping where? Target

Mind Ticklers

Make the sign _____	and think about . . .
jelly, jam, preserves	spreading jelly on bread
toast	sticking a fork in hot toast to turn it
taco	the filling in a taco
french fries	dipping potatoes in oil
donuts	the shape of a donut
gravy, grease, oil	the drippings from meat
bread	slicing a loaf of bread
soup	spooning soup to your mouth
rice	eating rice with chopsticks
cake	a cake rising while baking
cookie	cutting cookies with a cookie cutter
pizza	drawing a Z and ending in an A
salt	tapping salt off a salt knife
pepper	shaking the pepper shaker
sugar, sweet, diabetic	licking something sweet
vinegar	the sour taste of vinegar
candy	licking a piece of candy
nuts, peanuts	peanut butter sticking to the roof of your mouth
lettuce, cabbage	a head of lettuce or cabbage
pie	cutting a wedge of pie
shrimp	how shrimp swim
kitchen, cook, chef	turning food over in a skillet
chips	putting a chip into your mouth
potato chips	signing **potato** then **chip**
thirsty	wanting water to trickle down your throat
breakfast, lunch, dinner	eating with the handshape of the first letter of each word
plant, seeds, sow	spreading seeds with your hands
McDonald's	showing the golden arches
Walmart	signing **cheap** with a W
Wendy's	the freckles on Wendy's face
Hardee's	another sign for *hard*
Burger King	signing **king** with B and K handshapes
Target	a T handshape on the nose

Practice Sentences

1. Tell me where you like to buy hamburgers, Wendy's or Burger King?

   place hamburger buy prefer you tell-me, Wendy's, Burger King, which?

2. Butter my bread and put strawberry jelly on it, please.

   bread my, butter, strawberry jelly put-on please

3. The team decided to have lunch at Hardee's and dinner at McDonald's.

   lunch Hardee's, dinner McDonald's, team decide

4. Mom agreed to make pies and cake for the meeting tomorrow.

   tomorrow meeting pie cake, mom agree prepare

5. At Thanksgiving, my family has a number of different desserts.

   dessert different+ family my, Thanksgiving have

6. Dad likes eating peanuts and drinking beer while watching football.

   during football dad look-at, eat peanuts, drink beer he like

7. Things not to eat on a diet are bread, rice, and potatoes.

   bread rice potato, if diet, eat don't

8. Will you join me for a coffee at Starbucks later today?

   later today, you join me coffee there Starbucks will

9. I don't eat a lot at lunch, I prefer waiting until dinner to eat a lot.

   lunch me eat a-lot not, me prefer wait dinner eat a-lot

10. Grandma buys most of our clothes at her favorite store, Target.

    grandma store her favorite Target, most clothes our, there she buy

11. Dad likes planting tomatoes and Mom likes planting flowers.

    tomato dad sow like, flower mom sow like

12. No one ate many cookies. They had too much sugar in them.

    cookie many, none one eat, why? cookie a-lot sugar have

13. Just bring me a hamburger, french fries, and a Coke for lunch.

    lunch my only hamburger french-fries Coke (you) bring me

14. When the king awakes in the morning he is always thirsty.

    morning when king awake he thirsty always

15. Don't forget to put butter and jelly on my toast every day.

    daily butter jelly toast my put, forget not

Class Activities

1. In small groups, go over the student activities in Lesson 37.

2. In small groups, each student signs his paragraph from Lesson 37. He then asks his questions about the paragraph, and the others in the group respond in sign.

Student Activities

1. Using the foods from Lessons 37 and 38, create three meals for someone you know. These meals are for_____.

    breakfast   lunch   dinner

    _____   _____   _____

    _____   _____   _____

    _____   _____   _____

    _____   _____   _____

    _____   _____   _____

2. List the signs for foods that you know can be purchased at McDonald's.

    _____

    _____

    _____

3. Your rich aunt just gave you $1,000 for a new wardrobe. List the clothing you would purchase at Walmart or Target, and estimate the costs. Add up the total for how much you spend.

    clothing   cost

    _____   _____

    _____   _____

    _____   _____

    _____   _____

    _____   _____

    _____   _____

    _____   _____

    _____   _____

Lesson 39

Vocabulary

1121 board
1122 board of trustees
1123 member, membership
1124 committee
1125 staff
1126 president, superintendent
1127 government, *federal, *politics
1128 law, lawyer, attorney
1129 illegal, against the law, forbidden
1130 Senate, Senator
1131 legislature, legislator
1132 legislation
1133 meeting, convention, session
1134 Democrat
1135 Republican
1136 delegate
1137 smile, grin
1138 laugh, giggle
1139 friendly, pleasant, cheerful
1140 personality, *attitude, *character
1141 beard, Santa Claus
1142 thick, dense
1143 develop, development, *mature
1144 attention, pay attention, concentrate
1145 school for the deaf, institution
1146 ship, cruise
1147 rubber
1148 concept, *theory
1149 apply, reserve, put to use
1150 apply, volunteer (n.), volunteer (v.), applicant

1121
board

The board ordered donuts.
donut, board order finish

1122
board of trustees

The board of trustees ate breakfast.
breakfast, board-of-trustees eat finish

1123
member, membership

Each member had french fries.
french-fries each member have finish

1124
committee

The coffee committee chose Starbucks.
Starbucks coffee committee choose

1125
staff

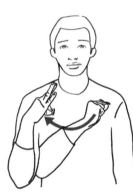

The staff passed out apples.
apple, staff disseminate

1126
president, superintendent

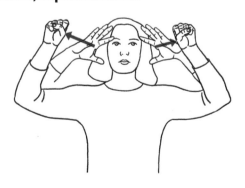

Which president is in the White House?
now white house president, which?

1127
government, *federal, *politics

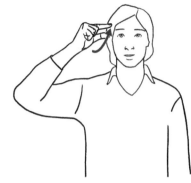

The government upset a lot of people.
people a-lot, government upset

1128
law, lawyer, attorney

The new law is acceptable.
law new acceptable

1129
illegal, against the law, forbidden

It is illegal to abuse people.
people abuse illegal

1130
Senate, Senator

The Senate has 100 members.
senate, 100 member have

Deaf Culture Facts and Information

The first school for the deaf opened in 1817 in Hartford, Connecticut as the Connecticut Asylum for the Education and Instruction of Deaf and Dumb Persons. Later, it was renamed the American School for the Deaf. The school was founded by a deaf Frenchman named Laurent Clerc and two hearing men, Thomas Hopkins Gallaudet and Mason Fitch Cogswell. The school is still open today.

1131
legislature, legislator

The legislators go home tomorrow.
tomorrow, legislator they home go

1132
legislation

That is bad legislation.
legislation that bad

1133
meeting, convention, session

When is the committee meeting?
meeting committee when?

1134
Democrat

Mom and Dad are Democrats.
mother father, Democrat

1135
Republican

Your sister is a Republican.
sister your, Republican

1136
delegate

The delegate got sick and went home.
delegate sick become, home go finish

1137
smile, grin

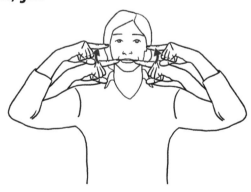

The president never smiles.
president smile, never

1138
laugh, giggle

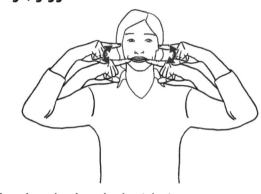

They laughed at the legislation.
legislation they see, laugh

ASL Grammar Notes

Adverbs that tell about the intensity of an action, adjective, or other adverb are called *adverbs of degree*. Some examples of adverbs of degree are *very*, *extremely*, *rather*, *somewhat*, *quite*, *pretty*, and *really*.

1139
friendly, pleasant, cheerful

I like the friendly lawyer.
lawyer friendly, me like

1140
personality, *attitude, *character

Her personality is great.
personality girl hers marvelous

1141
beard, Santa Claus

Dad looks friendly with a white beard.
beard white, father have appearance friendly

1142
thick, dense

The baby has thick hair.
baby, hair thick have

1143
develop, development, *mature

The project developed overnight.
overnight project develop

1144
attention, pay attention, concentrate

Visitors must pay attention in the Senate.
senate, visitor there pay-attention must

1145
school for the deaf, institution

The school for the deaf closed.
ago school-for-the-deaf close

1146
ship, cruise

The big ship stopped at an island.
ship big island there stop

1147
rubber

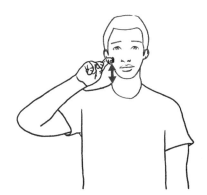

The boys practiced with a rubber ball.
boy+ use ball rubber practice

1148
concept, *theory

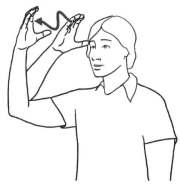

The lawyer's concept was wrong.
concept, lawyer his, wrong

1149
apply, reserve, put to use

Apply your present knowledge to solve the problem.
knowledge your apply for problem solve

1150
apply, volunteer (n.), volunteer (v.), applica<u>nt</u>

The volunteers arrive today.
today volunteer arrive

Mind Ticklers

Make the sign _____	and think about . . .
board	board members wearing nice clothes
board of trustees	B and T handshapes moving across the chest
member	an M handshape moving across the chest
committee	people on committees wearing name tags
staff	S and F handshapes moving across the chest
president, superintendent	George Washington's tricornered hat
government, federal, politics	the head of government
law, lawyer, attorney	writing laws on paper
illegal, against the law, forbidden, not allowed	emphasizing that something is illegal
Senate, Senator	an S handshape moving across the chest
legislature, legislator	an L handshape moving across the chest
legislation	legislation written on paper
meeting, convention, session	everyone coming together to talk
Democrat	shaking a D handshape
Republican	shaking an R handshape
delegate	a D handshape moving across the chest
smile, grin	the act of smiling
laugh, giggle	more than a smile
friendly, pleasant, cheerful	a cheerful look on your face
personality, reputation, attitude, character	all these traits that come from the heart
beard, Santa Claus	outlining a bushy beard
thick, dense	puffing out the cheek to indicate thickness
develop, development, mature	something rising from the ground
attention, pay attention, concentrate	a horse's blinders
school for the deaf, institution	the I handshapes for *institution*
ship, cruise	the vehicle classifier on water
rubber	chewing gum
concept, theory	a concept coming from the head
apply, reserve, put to use, assignment	putting paper on a spindle for later action
apply, volunteer, applicant	pulling yourself forward for action

Practice Sentences

1. The board members were angry there was no coffee or donuts.

   board member angry why? coffee donuts none

2. The lawyer forgot to shave this morning and he looked awful.

   now morning lawyer shave forget, (he) appearance awful

3. The committee decided to work through lunch and leave early.

   committee decide through lunch work, then early depart

4. The Democrats and Republicans had a very friendly dinner recently.

   recent democrat republican friendly dinner have

5. The school for the deaf brought Santa Claus in and the children giggled.

   Santa Claus go school-for-the-deaf, children laugh

6. Your brother has a wonderful personality and a friendly smile.

   brother your personality wonderful, smile friendly have

7. Pay attention, we need to discuss the cruise's departure time and place.

   pay-attention cruise time depart, place depart, we need discuss

8. The volunteer forgot how to apply what she learned at camp.

   camp itemize learn volunteer, (she) finish forget how apply

9. It is illegal for the board of trustees to select a president.

   board-of-trustees president select, illegal

10. We agree that the government developed a strange concept.

    government, strange concept develop, we agree

11. Your theory is good, and the staff will act on it soon.

    theory your good, soon staff do something will

12. What are the names of the two senators running for president?

    two senator compete for president, name their what?

13. The delegate applied for membership on the last committee.

    final committee delegate for membership volunteer

14. The legislature is responsible for passing legislation.

    legislation pass, responsible who? legislature

15. The senator always ate pizza and drank beer on Tuesdays.

    every-Tuesday senator pizza eat beer drink always

Class Activities

1. In small groups, go over the student activities in Lesson 38.

2. The instructor makes a list of ten items found in each of the following categories: farm, city, house, school, stadium, park, and restaurant. The students get into small groups. The instructor tells the students the category and fingerspells one of the items. The first student to identify the item gets a point for her team, and the first team to get ten points wins.

Student Activities

1. Turn to the practice sentences for Lesson 39. Put a piece of paper over each English sentence. Look at the corresponding ASL sentence and read it aloud in English.

2. What is the difference between the signs in each pair?

    a. SUMMER/DRY

    _____

    _____

    b. RED/CUTE

    _____

    _____

    c. SHORT/TRAIN

    _____

    _____

    d. SIT/CHAIR

    _____

    _____

3. Think of four additional pairs of similar signs and explain their differences.

    a. _____

    _____

    _____

    _____

    b. _____

    _____

    _____

    _____

    c. _____

    _____

    _____

    _____

    d. _____

    _____

    _____

    _____

4. This lesson contains glosses for the signs LEGISLATION, ILLEGAL, and LAW. Several other signs are made the same way but with different handshapes, and still other glosses have the same handshape but the context determines the gloss. How many glosses can you find that fit these descriptions?

    _____

    _____

    _____

    _____

    _____

    _____

Lesson 40

Vocabulary

1151 common sense

1152 music, sing, song, *poem, musician

1153 discouraged, *depressed, blue, let down

1154 match, light

1155 match, go together, combine, merge, similar, fit

1156 match, compare, comparison

1157 pressure, stress

1158 lonely, lonesome

1159 circle, round

1160 rub, erase, scrub

1161 ignorant, stupid, dumb

1162 careless, reckless, negligent

1163 cigarette

1164 smoke, smoker

1165 vacation, holiday, *retire, break, leave, stop working

1166 lazy

1167 march, parade

1168 funeral

1169 habit, custom, *used to, *tradition

1170 evil, sin, wicked

1171 brag, boast, show off

1172 subscribe, welfare

1173 deep, detail, in depth

1174 drown

1175 drunk, intoxicated

1176 look up, find, page

1177 reason, realize, rationale

1178 paragraph

1179 decline, deteriorate, get worse, loss

1180 clock

1151
common sense

That job requires common sense.
common-sense, that job require

1152
music, sing, song, *poem, musician

Music is everywhere.
music every place

1153
discouraged, *depressed, blue, let down

The members were discouraged.
member they discourage

1154
match, light

I need a match for the fire.
fire, match-light me need

Deaf Culture Facts and Information

After the opening of the American School for the Deaf in Hartford, CT, deaf individuals helped to establish 23 additional schools for deaf children in the United States between 1817 and 1911.

1155
match, go together, combine, merge, similar, fit

Your clothes match well.
clothes your good go-together

1156
match, compare, comparison

They compared their beards.
beard+ men theirs they compare

1157
pressure, stress

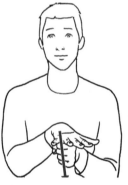

The lawyer worked under pressure.
pressure, lawyer continue work

1158
lonely, lonesome

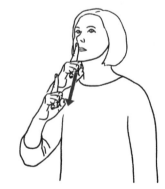

The delegate felt lonely.
delegate lonely feel

1159
circle, round

The old building was a circle.
building old shape circle

1160
rub, erase, scrub

Don't forget to scrub your shoes.
shoe your, forget scrub don't

1161
ignorant, stupid, dumb

He is just ignorant.
man, ignorant

1162
careless, reckless, negligent

The fireman drove carelessly.
fireman careless drive

1163
cigarette

I need a match for my cigarette.
cigarette my, match-light me need

1164
smoke, smoker

He started smoking long ago.
ago, man smoke start

1165
vacation, holiday, *retire, break, leave, stop working

When is our next vacation?
vacation our next, when?

1166
lazy

Who is that lazy person?
there person lazy, who?

1167
march, parade

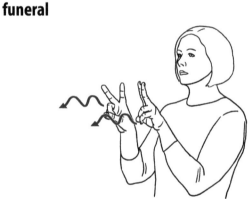

The parade is coming to town.
parade town here come

1168
funeral

The senator's funeral is tomorrow.
tomorrow funeral senator his

1169
habit, custom, *used to, *tradition

That is a great family tradition.
that family tradition marvelous

1170
evil, sin, wicked

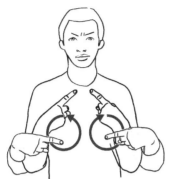

No evil person lives here.
person evil live here none

1171
brag, boast, show off

The senator was always bragging.
senator brag always

1172
subscribe, welfare

I heard your aunt is on welfare.
aunt your obtain welfare me hear

1173
deep, detail, in depth

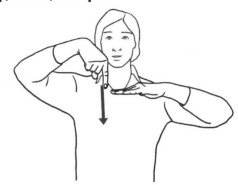

I'll tell you that in depth later.
later that in-depth, me tell-you

1174
drown

No one can drown in that lake.
lake there can drown, not

1175
drunk, intoxicated

No one I know was drunk.
person drunk, me know, none

1176
look up, find, page

Look up the time of the parade.
parade time look-up

1177
reason, realize, rationale

There is no good reason for smoking.
smoking, good reason, none

1178
paragraph

Read paragraph number two.
paragraph number two, read

1179
decline, deteriorate, get worse, loss

Father's health is getting worse.
health, father his decline

1180
clock

The bedroom clock is broken.
clock bedroom there broken

Mind Ticklers

Make the sign _____	and think about . . .
common sense	C–S handshapes at the head
music, sing, song, poem	conducting music
discourage, depressed, blue, let down	having a sinking feeling
match, light	striking a match
match, go together, combine, merge, similar, fit	two objects fitting together
compare, comparison, match	seeing if two things in your hands match
pressure, stress	things weighing on your mind
lonely, lonesome	a person who is silent
circle, round	drawing a circle in the air
rub, erase, scrub	the act of scrubbing in your hand
ignorant, stupid, dumb	preventing things from going into your head
careless, reckless, negligent	not allowing thoughts into your head
cigarette	showing the length of a cigarette
smoke, smoker	puffing on a cigarette
vacation, holiday, retire, break, leave	sitting back and relaxing
lazy	an L handshape lying on the shoulder
march, parade	legs of marchers moving in unison
funeral	pallbearers carrying a coffin
habit, custom, used to	being locked into something in your head
evil, sin, wicked	something evil that can hurt you
brag, boast, show off	pointing only to yourself
welfare, subscribe	pulling money from the air
deep, detail, in depth	showing how deep something is
drown	going under water head first
drunk, intoxicated	not being able to find your mouth with a drink
look up, find, page	thumbing through the pages of a book
reason, realize, rationale	an R handshape at your head
paragraph	the size of a paragraph on a page
decline, deteriorate, get worse, loss	going down from "good" to not so good
clock	the sign for *time* and the outline of a clock

Practice Sentences

1. The senator smoked a lot because he was under a lot of pressure.

   senator a-lot smoke why? he a-lot pressure have

2. Father complained about two lazy men who worked for him.

   two men lazy, for father work, father complain++

3. Smoking in bed is a stupid and careless thing to do.

   smoke in bed stupid, careless

4. When the legislator becomes depressed, he drives around for hours.

   legislator become depressed, he hour+ drive++

5. Use common sense and you will be happy with the results.

   common-sense you use, result, you happy

6. Where can I get a match for my cigarette?

   cigarette my, match-light me get where?

7. Your sister sings beautifully and you should brag about her.

   sister your sing beautiful, brag concerning her (you) should

8. After we march in the parade we plan to vacation for two weeks.

   finish we march, vacation for two-week we plan

9. Very few people went to the funeral for the wicked man.

   man wicked funeral have, people very few go

10. The teacher was able to match the words to the music.

    word+ music go-together teacher able

11. You know that it is impossible to compare apples and oranges.

    apple orange compare, (you) know-that impossible

12. I want you to look up the kind of clock we have in the bedroom.

    clock itemize type bedroom there have, me want you look-up

13. Everyone has bad habits they wish they could stop.

    habit bad every-one have, wish able stop

14. Erase the previous time of the meeting and put down seven o'clock.

    meeting time ago erase, now time seven put-down

15. The lonely man misses his son who drowned.

    man lonely why? son his drown

Class Activities

1. In small groups share your answers to student activities 2–4 in Lesson 39. Discuss the differences within your group.

2. Students get into pairs and sign sentences with inflective verbs to one another as they are voiced by the instructor. Here are some examples: *My mother is sick. My mother is really sick. My mother is always sick.* Additional verbs could be *cry, work, tease, sit down,* and *study.*

Student Activities

1. Write the location where each sign is made. For example, know—*forehead*

   a. pressure _____

   b. erase _____

   c. vacation _____

   d. page _____

   e. brag _____

   f. hospital _____

   g. match-light _____

   h. lazy _____

   i. stupid _____

   j. smoker _____

2. What are the nonmanual signals used with the following? (It helps to look in a mirror when signing them.)

   a. who? _____

   _____

   b. yes _____

   _____

   c. no _____

   _____

   d. yes/no questions _____

   _____

   e. heavy _____

   _____

   f. cannot _____

   _____

   g. hot _____

   _____

   h. very cold _____

   _____

Lesson 41

Vocabulary

1181 copy, imitate, follow
1182 copy, duplicate
1183 earn, collect, make, raise, income, salary, wages, gather, collector
1184 basement, cellar
1185 discriminate, discrimination, victimize
1186 agenda, *policy, *principle, *rules, *constitution, *code of *ethics, *regulations, account
1187 principal
1188 purpose, mean, intent, intention, meaning
1189 misunderstand, misinterpret
1190 puzzled, mystery, perplexed
1191 because, since
1192 embarrass, ashamed, shame
1193 shy, bashful, timid
1194 satisfied, pleased, contented, satisfactory, satisfy
1195 content, relieved, relief
1196 punish, penalty, correct, discipline
1197 throw out, discard, eject
1198 ride (animal)
1199 ride (vehicle)
1200 electric, electricity
1201 evaluate, evaluation
1202 diploma, degree
1203 bring, deliver
1204 carry, transport
1205 research, researcher
1206 dash, leave, take off, split, hurry off
1207 strong, *energy, *power, *authority, pull
1208 put off, postpone, delay
1209 front
1210 emphasis, stress, emphasize, impress
1211 require, demand, call for, insist

1181
copy, imitate, follow

He imitates his best friend.
boy best friend his, (he) imitate

1182
copy, duplicate

The volunteer made 60 copies.
volunteer 60 copy++ produce finish

1183
earn, collect, make, raise, income, salary, wages, gather, collector

How much do you earn monthly?
monthly you earn how-much?

1184
basement, cellar

The basement is dark and wet.
basement dark, wet

1185
discriminate, discrimination, victimize

Discrimination any time is bad.
discriminate any time bad

1186
agenda, *policy, *principle, *rules,
   ***constitution, *code of *ethics,**
   ***regulations, account**

What is the school's policy?
policy school their, what?

1187
principal

The principal is sick again.
principal again sick

1188
mean, purpose, intent, intention, meaning

What is the meaning of that chapter?
chapter that, purpose what?

1189
misunderstand, misinterpret

They misunderstood the principle.
principle, they misunderstand

1190
puzzled, mystery, perplexed

No one solved the mystery.
mystery, person none solve

Deaf Culture Facts and Information

In the 1960s, Dr. William Stokoe proclaimed that ASL has all the components necessary to be considered a language. Schools for deaf children began using ASL in their classes in the 1970s.

1191
because, since

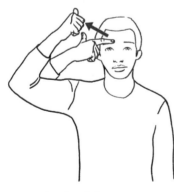

He left because he is sick.
man depart why? because (he) sick

1192
embarrass, ashamed, shame

The principal was embarrassed.
principal himself embarrass

1193
shy, bashful, timid

The little girl is very shy.
girl short very shy

1194
satisfied, pleased, contented, satisfactory, satisfy

We are satisfied with the policy.
policy, we satisfy

1195
content, relieved, relief

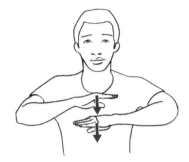

I'm relieved the copies are finished.
copies finish, me relieved

1196
punish, penalty, correct, discipline

The principal had to punish the boys.
boy+ punish, principal must

1197
throw out, discard, eject

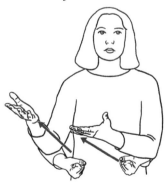

Throw out all the dirty copies.
copies dirty, throw-out

1198
ride (animal)

Our friends rode an elephant.
elephant, friend our, they ride-animal

1199
ride (vehicle)

The children enjoy riding in the car.
children ride-vehicle, enjoy

1200
electric, electricity

The electric clock is not running.
clock electric, operate not

1201
evaluate, evaluation

We need to discuss your evaluation.
evaluation your, two-of-us need discuss

ASL Grammar Notes

Adverbs that tell how something happens are called *adverbs of manner*. They may be incorporated into the verb or signed separately depending on the word or phrase they modify. Adverbs of manner include words like *quickly, slowly, sadly*, and *nicely*.

My friend walks slowly.   Mom sat down quickly.
FRIEND MY WALK (sign   MOM FAST (big sign
    WALK in slow motion)   quickly) SIT

1202
diploma, degree

The young man has three degrees.
man young degree+ three have

1203
bring, deliver

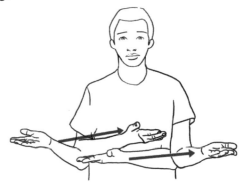

Deliver the copies to the principal's office.
office principal his, you copies bring

1204
carry, transport

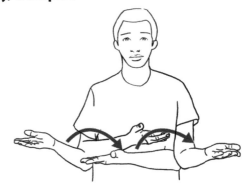

The volunteer carried the cigarettes.
cigarette, volunteer carry finish

1205
research, researcher

My uncle loves doing research.
uncle my, research love

1206
dash, leave, take off, split, hurry off

We have to leave now for our appointment.
now, for appointment we dash must

1207
strong, *energy, *power, *authority, pull

That little boy is strong.
boy short there strong

1208
put off, postpone, delay

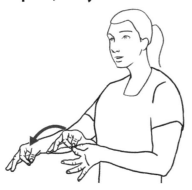

The parade was postponed.
parade postpone finish

1209
front

Stand in front of the store.
store front there (you) stand

1210
emphasis, stress, emphasize, impress

Our teacher emphasized the need to review the lesson.
review lesson must, teacher our emphasize

1211
require, demand, call for, insist

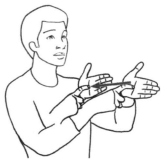

The strikers posted their demands on the factory door.
require strik_er_ their put-up where? door factory

Mind Ticklers

Make the sign _____	and think about . . .
copy, imitate, follow	taking something and putting it on paper
copy, duplicate	a copy machine taking a picture
earn, collect, make, raise, income, salary	collecting wages in your hand
basement, cellar	the area under the house
discriminate, discrimination, victimize	discrimination being worse than criticism
agenda, *policy, *principle, *rules	a policy written on a page
principal	the person overseeing a school
purpose, mean, intent, intention	pointing to a paragraph on a piece of paper to explain its meaning
misunderstand, misinterpret	reversing what is in your head
puzzle, mystery, perplexed	a big question in your head
because, since	a reason for everything in your mind
embarrass, ashamed, shame	your face becoming red
shy, bashful, timid	not wanting to show your face
satisfied, pleased, contented, satisfy	your emotions being just right
content, relieved, relief	your emotions calming down
punish, penalty, correct, discipline	pain running down the arm
throw out, discard	the act of throwing something out
ride (animal)	throwing both legs over an animal
ride (vehicle)	jumping in with both feet
electric, electricity	electricity jumping from one pole to another
evaluate, evaluation	judging someone or thing
diploma, degree	the rolled piece of paper you receive at graduation
bring, deliver	bringing what is in your hands
carry, transport	something that takes more effort to bring
research, researcher	a person who investigates something
dash, leave, take off, split, hurry off	getting out of a situation quickly
strong, energy, power, authority, pull	showing your muscles
put off, postpone, delay	extending something into the future
front	putting something in front of yourself
emphasis, stress, emphasize, impress	showing something to someone with force
require, demand, call for, insist	pulling something you want toward you

Practice Sentences

1. Watch the little boy; he enjoys imitating his father.

   boy short look-at, imitate father his (he) enjoy

2. The principal's health was slowly getting worse every day.

   daily, health principal his seem decline

3. The electrician misunderstood what we meant about the electric clock.

   clock electric itemize we intend, electrician misunderstand

4. We were all puzzled about why Dad looked embarrassed when he got home.

   dad arrive home, we puzzled he embarrass seem

5. Sorry, I have to take off because I have another interpreting job now.

   sorry me dash now must, other work interpret have

6. Are all the members satisfied with the new policy we passed?

   policy new we approve, member all satisfy

7. We were relieved that the secretary finished making the copies.

   copy+ secretary finish, we all relieved

8. Who was responsible for evaluating the match last night?

   last night game evaluate, responsible who?

9. All the copies made yesterday have to be thrown out and new ones have to be made.

   yesterday copy+ all, throw-out must, new copy+ now prepare

10. Your little sister looks shy whenever boys come to the house.

    sister short your seem shy, why? boy+ house come

11. Please carry all the old newspapers downstairs to the basement.

    newspaper old all, basement downstairs carry please

12. The speaker tried to emphasize the importance of putting off the meeting.

    meeting postpone important, speaker try emphasize

13. The punishment was required to establish an example for everyone.

    punishment require why? establish example for every-one

14. Children were riding horses in front of the closed store.

    store close, children front there horse ride

15. The family is relieved that their oldest son finally got a degree.

    son oldest, finally degree get, family relieved

Class Activities

1. In small groups, go over the student activities from Lesson 40.

2. In small groups, the students take turns building a story. The first student starts by signing, "I'm going on a trip and I'm taking a hat." The next student signs the same sentence adding a new item, such as a book. Students continue adding to the list, repeating each previous item taken on the trip.

Student Activities

1. Time phrases usually go in front of an ASL sentence. Write some common time phrases used in ASL.

<u>present</u>   <u>past</u>   <u>future</u>

_____   _____   _____

_____   _____   _____

_____   _____   _____

_____   _____   _____

_____   _____   _____

2. Write the conceptual sign/words in Lesson 41.

a. _____

_____

b. _____

_____

c. _____

_____

d. _____

_____

e. _____

Lesson 42

Vocabulary

1212 insurance
1213 library, librarian
1214 establish, set up, found, form, set
1215 guilty
1216 innocent, not guilty, naïve
1217 touch, reach, been there
1218 various, variety
1219 weak, weakness, fragile, feeble
1220 nation, national
1221 normal, usual, naturally, of course, nature
1222 tired, exhausted, worn out
1223 pet, spoiled, favorite
1224 steal, stole
1225 jealous, envy, envious
1226 mainstream
1227 polite, manners, courteous
1228 formal, fancy, sophisticated, elaborate, class
1229 support, back, in favor of, *reinforce, stand behind, pull for, advocate, sponsor
1230 loan, lend
1231 borrow
1232 worn out, not working, give out
1233 fail, unsuccessful, flop, defeat, lose, lost
1234 line, line up
1235 laptop
1236 taste
1237 spoon
1238 fork
1239 napkin
1240 restaurant

1212
insurance

My car insurance was cancelled.
insurance, car my cancel finish

1213
library, librarian

The library is in the basement.
library, down-there basement

1214
establish, set up, found, form, set

The principal established a new policy.
policy new, principal establish

1215
guilty

He is guilty of concealing evidence.
man guilty what? evidence hide

Deaf Culture Facts and Information

The oral method of teaching deaf children to speak and speechread with limited or no use of sign language is strongly opposed by the Deaf community. The use of American Sign Language is central to being Deaf, and attempts to limit its use are viewed as attacks on Deaf culture.

1216
innocent, not guilty, naïve

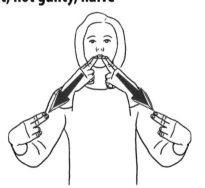

The innocent firefighter stayed on the job.
firefighter innocent, work continue

1217
touch, reach, been there

I can't reach the books.
book those, me touch, cannot

1218
various, variety

She likes various boys.
girl, various boy+ she like

1219
weak, weakness, fragile, feeble

His weakness embarrassed us.
boy weak his, us embarrass

1220
nation, national

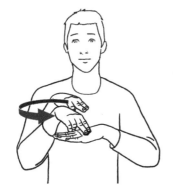

The nation is not at war.
now nation, war, not

1221
normal, usual, naturally, of course, nature

She acts normal for her age.
girl age her, normal behave

1222
tired, exhausted, worn out

Grandpa looks very tired today.
today grandfather very tired seem

1223
pet, spoiled, favorite

Your daughter is spoiled.
daughter your spoiled

1224
steal, stole

He stole because he is poor.
boy steal why? poor

1225
jealous, envy, envious

Mom is jealous of her sister.
sister, mother hers, mother jealous

1226
mainstream

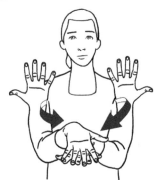

Many deaf children are mainstreamed.
children deaf many mainstream

1227
polite, manners, courteous

Be polite, don't embarrass me.
you polite behave, embarrass me don't

1228
formal, fancy, sophisticated, elaborate, class

Where is the formal dance?
dance formal where?

1229
support, back, in favor of, *reinforce, stand behind, pull for, advocate, sponsor

The family supported the guilty man.
man guilty, family support

1230
loan, lend

Don't loan him any money.
money, loan man don't

1231
borrow

The police officer borrowed my car.
car my, police borrow

1232
worn out, not working, give out

The electric clock is worn out.
clock electric, worn-out

1233
fail, unsuccessful, flop, defeat, lose, lost

My aunt failed math in college.
aunt my, college math fail

1234
line, line up

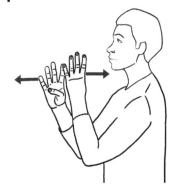

Line up to go to the library.
library, line-up go

1235
laptop

Where did you put my new laptop?
laptop new my, (you) put where?

ASL Grammar Notes

Yes-no questions require a yes or no response. Yes-no questions in ASL have no particular word order. The nonmanual signals that accompany yes-no questions are raised eyebrows, widened eyes, and tilting the head and/or body forward. Sometimes the shoulders are raised and sometimes the last sign is held. The signer usually maintains direct eye gaze with the addressee.

1236
taste

What does that taste like?
that taste alike what?

1237
spoon

The spoon is on the floor.
spoon there floor

1238
fork

Why do we have two forks?
fork two why?

1239
napkin

My napkin is yellow.
napkin my yellow

1240
restaurant

That restaurant has the best food.
restaurant there food best

Mind Ticklers

Make the sign _____	and think about . . .
insurance	the I handshape shaking
library	the L handshape circling
establish, set up, founded, form, set	putting something up on firm ground
guilty	how your heart beats fast when you feel guilty
innocent, not guilty, naive	saying the truth to show innocence
touch, reach, been there	landing someplace
various, variety	how things change by going up and down
weak, weakness, fragile, feeble	not being able to stand
nation, national	an N handshape showing large nations
normal, usual, naturally, of course, nature	skin being natural
tired, exhausted	shoulders slumping over in exhaustion
pet, spoiled, favorite	the natural gesture of petting an animal
steal, stole	taking something underhandedly
jealous, envy, envious	biting your finger not to say something
mainstream	everyone coming together as one
polite, manners, courteous	acting in a fine way
formal, fancy, sophisticated, elaborate, class	someone more than polite
support, back, in favor of, reinforce, stand behind, pull for	providing support for something
loan, lend	giving something you have to someone
borrow	taking something you are borrowing
worn out, not working, give up	the pieces of something spilling out of your hands
fail, unsuccessful, flop	not being able to stand any longer
line, line up	people standing in a line
laptop	raising the top of a laptop
taste	tasting with your tongue
spoon	spooning up soup
fork	stabbing a piece of bread
napkin	wiping your mouth
restaurant	wiping your mouth at a restaurant

Practice Sentences

1. Mom always puts our fork and spoon on the napkin.

   napkin, fork spoon mom put there always

2. The best restaurant in town is between the library and insurance building.

   restaurant here town, best, between library building, insurance building

3. We won't know if the man is guilty or innocent until he goes to court.

   man guilty innocent we don't-know, first he court go

4. Various people were lined up to use the man's laptop.

   laptop man his, people various line-up use want

5. The engine failed to start because it is worn out.

   engine start fail why? because worn-out

6. The insurance company would not lend him any more money.

   money more, insurance company lend man not

7. The brother stole the show and the sisters were jealous.

   sister+ jealous why? brother best perform

8. A national committee talked about mainstreaming deaf children.

   deaf children mainstream, national committee discuss

9. They lined up to support him, but he failed again.

   people line-up support boy, but boy again fail

10. Everyone laughed because the teacher's pet failed to show up.

    pet teacher hers show-up fail, every-one laugh

11. The student senate members are going to a formal dance and need to be polite.

    formal dance, member student senate go, now polite behave must

12. Of course we like the principal, he is our father.

    principal of-course we like, he father our

13. The ending of his wonderful story was weak.

    story man his wonderful, but end (story) weak

14. I loaned my new laptop to my roommate and never saw it again.

    laptop new my, roommate my me loan, me see again never

15. Of course the whole family is exhausted, they work hard.

    all family tired of-course, they hard work

Class Activities

1. In small groups, go over the student activities in Lesson 41.

2. In small groups, one student fingerspells a common word. The next student fingerspells a word that rhymes with the first word. Students continue taking turns fingerspelling rhyming words until they can think of no more. Then they start with a new word.

Student Activities

1. The compound interrogatives in ASL include WHAT'S-UP? HOW-OLD? and HOW-MANY? Use each sign in an ASL sentence.

   a. _____

   _____

   _____

   b. _____

   _____

   _____

   _____

   c. _____

   _____

   _____

2. Write an ASL sentence for each pair of glosses below.

   a. INNOCENT/GUILTY

   _____

   _____

   _____

   b. NAPKIN/RESTAURANT

   _____

   _____

   _____

   c. LIBRARY/INSURANCE

   _____

   _____

   _____

   d. STEAL/LAPTOP

   _____

   _____

   _____

   e. FORK/SPOON

   _____

   _____

   _____

   f. TRUE/LUCKY

   _____

   _____

   _____

3. The word *and* in ASL is generally shown by a slight upper body shift or shoulder shift. Sign the following pairs of words in the phrases below by turning the body slightly.

   a. GRANDMA/GRANDPA ME LOVE

   b. GUILTY/INNOCENT TELL-ME

   c. LOAN/BORROW MONEY WRONG

   d. BROTHER/SISTER GO FINISH

   e. FORK/SPOON WHERE?

   f. DEAF/HARD-OF-HEARING MAN WHICH?

   g. LIE-DOWN/STAND DOG WHICH?

   h. POLITE/IMPOLITE WHO?

   i. DEMOCRAT/REPUBLICAN YOU WHICH?

   j. KING/QUEEN WE SEE WILL

Lesson 43

Vocabulary

1241 dish, plate, saucer
1242 cup
1243 bottle
1244 glass (drinking)
1245 glass (window)
1246 delicious, tasty
1247 coax, urge
1248 limit, *restrict, *minimum
1249 awkward, clumsy
1250 stubborn
1251 narrow
1252 lucky, good luck
1253 curious, inquisitive
1254 summary, condense, abbreviate, brief
1255 calm down, settle down
1256 temperature, fever, degrees, thermometer
1257 metal
1258 sex
1259 true, truth, sure, real, really, original
1260 lie, fib, untruth
1261 lie, lie down, recline, lay
1262 lecture, talk, speech, speaker
1263 express, expression, let it out
1264 fair, so-so, mediocre
1265 butterfly
1266 brilliant, really smart
1267 complex, complicated
1268 poor, pity, unfortunate, sympathy
1269 worship, adore, really love
1270 dwell on, think about, perseverate, obsess
1271 hearing (person), public, hearing person
1272 wow, unbelievable, fantastic, crazy

1241
dish, plate, saucer

That dish is dirty.
dish there dirty

1242
cup

We have several coffee cups.
cup coffee several we have

1243
bottle

Please don't drink from the bottle.
bottle itself use drink don't, please

1244
glass (drinking)

Put four glasses on the table.
glass four, table there put

1245
glass (window)

The basement glass is colored.
glass there basement color have

1246
delicious, tasty

That restaurant has delicious food.
restaurant there food delicious

1247
coax, urge

Dad coaxed the dog out of the house.
dog inside house, father outside house coax

Deaf Culture Facts and Information

Strong opposition to the use of cochlear implants—and hearing aids to a lesser degree—exists among some members of the Deaf community. This is often justified in terms of a rejection of the view that deafness is something that needs to be "fixed" (medical model) rather than a natural condition (cultural model).

1248
limit, *restrict, *minimum

We are limited to working four days a week.
work four-day weekly, we limit have

1249
awkward, clumsy

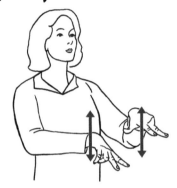

Using a fork is awkward for him.
fork, boy awkward use

1250
stubborn

She is embarrassed about being stubborn.
girl herself stubborn, she embarrass

1251
narrow

The road becomes very narrow.
road very narrow become

1252
lucky, good luck

You are lucky the glass didn't break.
lucky you, glass-drinking break not

1253
curious, inquisitive

I'm curious about your punishment.
punishment your, me curious

1254
summary, condense, abbreviate, brief

You can summarize the chapter.
chapter summarize you can

1255

calm down, settle down

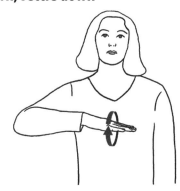

Calm down, it is time for bed.
time bed, calm-down

1256

temperature, fever, degrees, thermometer

My uncle has a high temperature.
uncle my temperature high have

1257

metal

The cup is made of metal.
cup, itself metal

1258

sex

Children are curious about sex.
sex, children curious

ASL Grammar Notes

Some yes-no questions begin with a wiggling question mark (informal) or a simple question mark (formal). The nonmanual signals that accompany these sentences are the same as for other yes-no questions: raised eyebrows, widened eyes, and tilting the head and/or body forward. These questions are often asked when the signer is surprised by the information he or she is being given, or when the signer wants to check what the other person is saying. For example,

DIVORCE PLAN YOU TRUE (wiggling question mark) (ASL)
Are you really planning to get a divorce? (English)

1259

true, truth, sure, real, really, original

It's true; I will go fishing on Sunday.
true, Sunday me fishing will

1260
lie, fib, untruth

You're lucky he doesn't lie.
lucky you, boy lie not

1261
lie, lie down, recline, lay

Lie here with all of us.
join us, here lay

1262
lecture, talk, speech, speaker

The stubborn man refused to lecture.
man stubborn, lecture he refuse

1263
express, expression, let it out

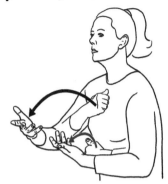

You can express yourself with me.
with me, express yourself can

1264
fair, so-so, mediocre

The restaurant food is so-so.
food restaurant so-so

1265
butterfly

The butterfly is yellow and black.
butterfly there, yellow black

1266
brilliant, really smart

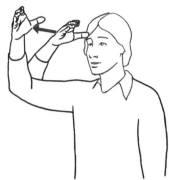

People tell me your son is brilliant.
son your brilliant, people tell-me

1267
complex, complicated

Tell us about some complex issues.
issue some complex, tell us

1268
poor, pity, unfortunate, sympathy

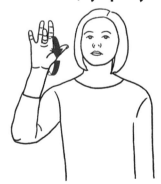

That poor woman fell and broke her leg.
woman there pity, fall leg break

1269
worship, adore, really love

My aunt adores anything red.
aunt my any thing red adore

Deaf Culture Facts and Information

When a Deaf person uses a sign language interpreter, hearing people should speak directly to the Deaf person rather than the interpreter. Hearing people may feel awkward because the Deaf person is looking at the interpreter, but this is the preferred arrangement.

1270
dwell on, think about, perseverate, obsess

The farmer seems to dwell on the temperature.
temperature, seem farmer dwell-on

1271
hearing (person), public, hearing person

That hearing person makes glass bottles.
hearing-person there glass bottle make

1272
wow, unbelievable, fantastic, crazy

Wow, you really saw that happen!
wow, that happen you really see

Mind Ticklers

Make the sign _____	and think about . . .
dish, plate, saucer	the size of a plate or saucer
cup	the size of a cup
bottle	the neck of a bottle
glass (drinking)	a glass being taller than a cup
glass (window)	glass being like the enamel on your teeth
delicious, tasty	something being very tasty
coax, urge	pulling someone to your way of thinking
limit, restrict, minimum	showing the acceptable amount
awkward, clumsy	not walking very well
stubborn	a mule being stubborn
narrow	a path becoming more narrow
lucky, good luck	what you have as being your favorite
curious, inquisitive	sticking your neck out to see what happened
summary, condense, abbreviate, brief	squeezing everything into one place
calm down, settle down	pushing down your feelings or anger
temperature, fever, degrees	showing the range of degrees on a thermometer
metal	something hard like your jaw
sex	both female and male sexes
true, truth, sure, real, really, original	words coming straight from the mouth
lie, fib, untruth	words not coming straight from the mouth
lie, lie down, recline, lay	the natural position of lying down
lecture, talk, speech	gesturing with your hands while lecturing
express, expression, let it out	releasing everything bottled up inside
fair, so-so, mediocre	the opposite of things on an even keel
butterfly	the wings of a butterfly in flight
brilliant, really smart	your brains protruding from your head
complex, complicated	question marks before your eyes
poor, pity, unfortunate, sympathy	heartfelt sorrow for someone
worship, adore, really love	kissing the hand of something loved
dwell on, think about, perseverate, obsess	going over and over something in your mind
hearing person, public	a person talking
wow, unbelievable, fantastic	something amazing passing before your eyes

Practice Sentences

1. The dishes, cups, glasses, and napkins are on the table now.

   now on table dish+ cup+ glass-drinking+ napkin+

2. Don't tell him what happened or he will dwell on it for days.

   happen what? tell man don't, he dwell-on-it long-time will

3. The young girl was really brilliant but too stubborn to do well.

   girl young brilliant really, but do good not, she stubborn

4. The poor kid worshipped his grandfather who was mean to him.

   kid pity, grandfather his he adore, grandfather himself unkind

5. The writer was curious how you summarized the chapter.

   chapter you summarize, writer he curious how

6. You can express your feelings to the psychiatrist any time.

   any time feeling your express for psychiatrist able

7. The librarian lay down for a minute and fell asleep.

   librarian, one-minute lay-down sleep finish

8. You have to taste this peach, it is delicious.

   peach you taste must, delicious

9. The man said that he would rather be lucky than good.

   man prefer lucky than good he say

10. We encouraged him to remove the restrictions immediately.

    immediately man subtract limit, we encourage (him)

11. The silver bridge was made of steel but still collapsed.

    bridge silver itself steel, regardless collapse

12. The little boy's temperature went up, so he went to the hospital.

    temperature boy short his up, hospital he go

13. Don't lie to your father or he will restrict your activities.

    activity your father your restrict will, lie don't

14. Everyone liked the movie except me; I thought it was so-so.

    movie every-one like except me, me think so-so

15. Describe the different colors you see on the butterfly.

    butterfly different+ color you see, describe

Class Activities

1. In small groups, go over the student activities in Lesson 42.

2. Students take turns signing a sentence that has three signs with the same handshape. For example, My **aunt** carries a **purse every day**; I was **satisfied** to get a **B** in **biology**; I **looked for** my **strange cousin**. Go through the alphabet, changing the handshape every five minutes.

Student Activities

1. Write four ASL sentences about things that your family does during Christmas.

   a. _____

   _____

   b. _____

   _____

   c. _____

   _____

   d. _____

   _____

2. Write an ASL response to the following:

   a. FATHER STUBBORN WHY?

   _____

   _____

   b. MOVIE VERY COMPLEX

   _____

   _____

   c. UNCLE MY BRILLIANT NOT

   _____

   _____

   d. SISTER MY CURIOUS ALWAYS

   _____

   _____

   e. FRIEND YOURS LUCKY ALWAYS WHO?

   _____

   _____

3. Write four costumes that you wore during Halloween when you were young.

   a. _____

   b. _____

   c. _____

   d. _____

4. Which signs in this lesson are made near the head?

   a. _____

   b. _____

   c. _____

   d. _____

   e. _____

   f. _____

Lesson 44

Vocabulary

1273 Christmas, Xmas
1274 Easter
1275 Halloween
1276 Valentine's Day
1277 Thanksgiving
1278 Africa, African
1279 America, American
1280 Asia, Asian
1281 Australia, Australian
1282 Canada, Canadian
1283 China, Chinese
1284 Egypt, Egyptian
1285 England, English
1286 Europe, European
1287 France, French
1288 Germany, German
1289 Holland, The Netherlands, Dutch
1290 India, Indian
1291 Iran, Iranian
1292 Ireland, Irish
1293 Israel, Israeli
1294 Italy, Italian
1295 Japan, Japanese
1296 Korea, Korean
1297 Mexico, Mexican
1298 Philippines, Philippine
1299 Russia, Russian
1300 Spain, Spanish
1301 USA
1302 Vietnam, Vietnamese

**1273
Christmas, Xmas**

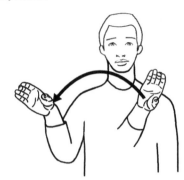

Christmas is a happy time of year.
Christmas yearly happy time

**1274
Easter**

The minister lectured all day Easter.
all-day Easter minister lecture++

**1275
Halloween**

Children really love to get candy on Halloween.
Halloween children receive candy adore

1276
Valentine's Day

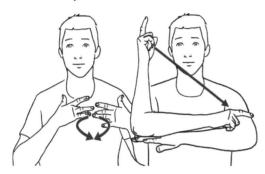

Don't forget to get flowers for Valentine's Day.

Valentine's Day, flowers buy forget not

Deaf Culture Facts and Information

Technology has provided deaf people with a number of devices to assist them at work and other activities: videophones (VP), telecommunications devices for the Deaf (TDDs or TTYs), fire and smoke alarms with strobe lights, doorbells with lights, baby alert lights, and electronic notetakers.

1277
Thanksgiving

Thanksgiving dinner is at our house this year.

now year, Thanksgiving dinner house our have

1278
Africa, African

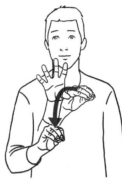

How long will she lecture about Africa?

Africa how long-time woman lecture will

1279
America, American

America is the land of the free.

America, country for people free

1280
Asia, Asian

We eat Asian food every Saturday.

each Saturday, Asian food we eat

1281
Australia, Australian

The flight to Australia lasted 22 hours.
Australia, airplane fly-soar there 22 hours continue

1282
Canada, Canadian (ASL)

A lot of wolves and bears are in Canada.
Canada, wolves bears a-lot have

1283
China, Chinese

The Chinese government restricts where visitors go.
visitors travel, government China limit

1284
Egypt, Egyptian (ASL)

Do you think Egypt is a complex country?
Egypt complex think you

1285
England, English (ASL)

Afternoon tea is a tradition in England.
England there tea afternoon custom

1286
Europe, European (ASL)

Our son traveled all over Europe.
Europe son our travel vicinity

1287
France, French (ASL)

France is famous for its wines.
France famous why? wine

1288
Germany, German (ASL)

Do you know anyone who speaks German?
talk German, you know who?

1289
Holland, The Netherlands, Dutch (ASL)

Holland has wonderful cheese.
Holland cheese wonderful there

1290
India, Indian (ASL)

My best friend lives in India.
India, best friend my there live

1291
Iran, Iranian

Iran and America do not get along.
Iran, America get-along not

1292
Ireland, Irish (ASL)

Long ago Ireland was famous for its potatoes.
ago Ireland famous what? potato

1293
Israel, Israeli (ASL)

My laptop was made in Israel.
laptop my Israel produce

1294
Italy, Italian (ASL)

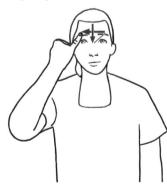

When is the best time to go to Italy?
Italy, best time travel there when?

1295
Japan, Japanese

Our teacher encouraged us to see Japan.
Japan, teacher encourage us visit there

1296
Korea, Korean

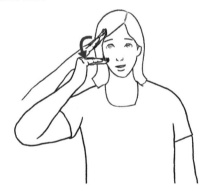

I hear that Korean people are nice.
people Korea nice me hear

1297
Mexico, Mexican

Mexico is not a safe country.
country Mexico safe not

1298
Philippines, Philippine (ASL)

The Philippines is made up of many islands.
Philippines many-many island have

1299
Russia, Russian (ASL)

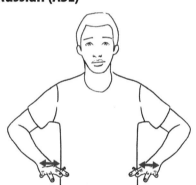

The Russian restaurant closed last week.
restaurant Russia, last-week close

1300
Spain, Spanish (ASL)

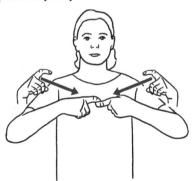

My wife wants to go to Spain.
wife my Spain want go

1301
USA

Team USA won the international basketball
competition.
**basketball competition international, USA team
win finish**

1302
Vietnam, Vietnamese

Vietnam and the USA cooperated to find
missing soldiers.
Vietnam, USA cooperate find soldier disappear

Mind Ticklers

Make the sign _____	and think about . . .
Christmas	half a Christmas wreath
Easter	throwing your E handshapes up in celebration
Halloween	wearing a mask
Valentine's Day	outlining your heart
Thanksgiving	giving thanks
Africa	the shape of the African continent
America	split-rail fences
Australia	kangaroos hopping
Canada	shaking snow off your coat
China	the buttons on a tunic
Egypt	a snake head on a crown
England	England being a big island
France	pulling a kerchief from a sleeve
Germany	an eagle's wings
Holland	a traditional Dutch hat
India	the forehead decoration worn by Indian women
Ireland	Irish potatoes
Israel	the beards of Orthodox Jewish men
Italy	the Catholic sign of the cross
Japan	the shape of the island of Japan
Mexico	the brim of a large sombrero
Philippines	many islands making up the Philippines
Russia	the Russian dance with hands on hips
Spain	fastening a cape
USA	fingerspelling the initials U-S-A

Conceptual Sign/Word Appendix

Students are encouraged to cover the columns on the page that show the appropriate gloss and reference number. This provides a self-checking system. For another activity, students can change the English sentences into ASL.

ABOUT

It is **about** time to leave.	almost	1049
I saw it **about** here yesterday.	approximately	512
What **about** your friend?	concerning	513

ABOVE

The airplane is **above** the mountain.	above	850
It is **above** my limit.	across	849

ACCIDENT

He **accidentally** came early.	accident	902
His license was suspended after the **accident**.	car-accident	901
Forgetting his mother's birthday was an awful **accident**.	mistake	168

ACT

The first two **acts** were great.	drama	348
Don't **act** like that around my sister.	behave	189

ADD

Show me the **add** sign.	positive	285
Add all these numbers for me.	sum	287
Add up my bill please	count	852
He is always **adding** to my bill.	increase	376
Add the flour to the batter.	add	286

ADMIT

Don't **admit** anyone under ten to the party.	allow	299
He **admitted** everything in court.	confess	300
The plan is to **admit** the first ten people.	welcome	301

ADVANCE

The **advanced** sign class is over.	promote	921
The Indians **advanced** toward the group slowly.	progress	922
His knowledge of sign language has **advanced**.	improve	314

AFTER

See me **after** the second act.	finish	342
My arithmetic class is **after** French.	next	333
Is that dog **after** my cat again?	chase	341
I'll go first; you come **after** me.	turn	114
You can play **after** you eat.	over	849
After tomorrow we all stop eating candy.	from-now-on	330

AGAINST

Are you really **against** that idea?	oppose	642
Put the TV **against** the wall.	near	69
Smoking pot is **against** the law.	illegal	1129

AID

Dad's (hearing) **aid** is broken.	hearing-aid	369
Aid is coming soon.	help	156

AIM

He took careful **aim** and fired.	point	931
Her **aim** is to become a doctor.	goal	930

ANXIOUS

Before a test, she always becomes **anxious**.	worry	453
	or **nervous**	452
Are you **anxious** to start your vacation?	enthusiastic	451
	or **excited**	898

APPEAR

You always **appear** at the wrong time.	show-up	721
You **appear** a little flushed.	look	378
It **appears** that you made a small mistake.	seem	720
He will **appear** in the play.	perform	348

APPLY

No one **applied** for that job.	volunteer	1150
You need to **apply** what you learn.	apply	1149
Apply the glue with care.	spread	874
Dad **applied** his ingenuity to fix the refrigerator.	use	657

APPROVE

Dad **approved** the new contract.	approve	730
The family **approved** the new design.	accept	768

AROUND

Dad walks **around** the block daily.	around	689
They lost their money **around** here.	approximately	512

ARTICLE

Read this funny **article**.	column	1026
He lost four of the five **articles** he brought.	thing	1025

ASSOCIATION

The National **Association** of the Deaf is big.	association	41
My **association** with him is better than ever.	relationship	985

AWFUL

That is an **awful**-looking dress.	ugly	318
It was truly an **awful** accident.	awful	316
My headache is **awful**.	bad	61

BACK

Will you **back** the president?	support	1229
My **back** is aching again.	back	407
When will you be **back** home?	come-back	865
Give that money **back** to me.	give-back	865
The people in **back** of me talked throughout the movie.	behind	745

BEAR

That is either a grizzly or a black **bear**.	**bear**	846
I cannot **bear** the thought of you leaving.	**tolerate**	749

BEAT

Our team **beat** theirs badly.	**defeat**	1042
He **beat** on his dog.	**hit**	1043

BEFORE

I never saw that happen **before**.	**past**	216
He spoke **before** the group **before** lunch.	**in-front-of** **prior-to**	328 329
She looked it over **before** buying it.	**prior-to**	329

BELOW

We put the flower seeds **below** the ground.	**beneath**	374
You told me it was **below** $20.00.	**less-than**	375

BITE

Let's get a **bite** before the play.	**food**	23
Careful, the cat **bites** strangers.	**bite**	900

BLOCK

The car was **blocked** by the truck.	**block**	820
They succeeded in **blocking** the vote.	**prevent**	821

BLOW UP

Dad **blew up** when he heard the news.	**mad**	552
The new building **blew up**.	**explosion**	994

BREAK

Who will **break** the news to them.	**tell**	932
He meant to **break** the pencil.	**fracture**	719
We will now take a 5-minute **break**.	**intermission**	262
A two-week **break** from work is nice.	**vacation**	1165

BRIGHT

Dad gave me a **bright** new penny.	**shiny**	100
That light is too **bright**.	**clear**	395
What a **bright** little girl.	**smart**	396

BUT

No one showed up **but** her.	**except**	863
I saw her, **but** she didn't see me.	**however**	1047
He is **but** a child.	**only**	1044
It never rains, **but** it pours.	**that**	16

BY

Drive **by** my old house.	**pass**	876
Put the broom **by** the door.	**near**	69
He does everything **by** the book.	**follow**	775
Enter **by** the front door.	**through**	349
He studied **by** night for his degree.	**during**	238
They did everything **by** force.	**with**	9

CALL

The teacher always **calls** on me.	**summon**	309
They plan to **call** the baby Jonah.	**name**	308
I **called** my mother in Boston yesterday.	**telephone**	310

Mother always **called** us for dinner at 5:00.	yell	311
The recipe **called** for chocolate chips.	required	1211

CAN

I **can** do that for you.	able	184
You think he **can** still be living?	maybe	188
I think he **can** do that.	possible	186

CARRY

Carry the girl's books.	carry	1204
New York will **carry** the election for him.	win	767
Her decisions always **carry** weight.	have	159
The ball **carried** over 200 yards.	go	8
The crime **carried** a stiff penalty.	require	1211

CATCH

The police cannot **catch** the robber.	apprehend	691
When I throw this, you **catch** it.	catch	690
I always **catch** a cold in the fall.	get	71
My foot was **caught** in the door.	stuck	820

CAUSE

His **cause** was to defeat the enemy.	goal	930
What do you think **caused** the accident?	cause	321

CHARGE

They **charged** $2.00 a person.	bill	979
He was **charged** with child neglect.	blame	980
The children were in her **charge**.	responsibility	771

CHECK

Check my paper for me, please.	correct	487
I need to **check** our food supply.	inspect	486
Write a **check** for $12.00.	check	485
He had no **checks** on his paper.	marks	484
Do the copies **check** with the originals?	agree	231

CLASS

She has no **class**.	polite	1228
class was cancelled for the second time.	class	41

CLEAN

The car had very **clean** lines.	nice	62
Clean up the room before tomorrow.	clean-up	63
Make sure you get a **clean** copy.	good	6
The robbers **cleaned** out the room.	empty	928
It was cut to make a **clean** edge.	smooth	1031

CLOSE

You have to **close** the door when you leave.	close	529
My friend lives very **close** to me.	near	69
We are very **close**.	friend	130
She is very **closed** mouth about her family.	secret	751
It was a very **close** competition.	hot	337
Obviously, we have to **close** this meeting.	stop	866
	or **finish**	343

COLD

Is it **cold** outside?	temperature	153

I have an awful **cold**.	cold	154
He mother is very **cold**.	aloof	155

COME

No one will **come** here today.	come	17
Come over and stay with me.	come-over	17
I am happy nothing like that **came** up.	appear	721
The total bill **came** to $45.00.	sum	287
No one believed it would **come** true.	success	650

COMMAND

The foreign student had a good **command** of English.	understand	158
The general **commands** the army.	controls	491
No one gave the **command** to leave.	order	440

COMPLETE

When can you **complete** this job?	finish	342
When will the **complete** job be done?	whole	553
The party was a **complete** surprise.	total	556

CONTENT

She was very **content** with her work	satisfied	1194
The book's **content** was interesting.	meat	1071
Mom is **content**, her dog lived.	relieved	1195

COPY

Copy what is on the board.	imitate	1181
Make a **copy** for the teacher.	copy	1182
That is not real, it is a **copy**.	fake	115

CORRECT

The teacher will **correct** the papers.	check	487
What is the **correct** time?	right	161
If it is wrong, can I **correct** it later?	change	897
Father **corrected** the boy for breaking the window.	discipline	1196
Mom is always **correcting** me.	criticize	487

COUNT

You can always **count** on his help.	depend	737
Melissa can **count** to 100.	count	852
Of course, everything you say **counts**.	important	894
Count me in, that's probably what I need.	include	880

COURSE

My arithmetic **course** is easy.	course	269
Which **course** will take us to Mexico?	way	697
Of **course**, I agree with you.	naturally	1221

COVER

Be sure to put on some **covers** tonight.	blanket	692
We **covered** all the material in the book	finish	342
The men **covered** up their mistakes.	vague	695
Today we will **cover** chapters 2 and 3.	go-over	693

CROSS

We'll **cross** that bridge when we come to it.	across	849
She is **cross** with her son.	angry	336
Place the **cross** on the altar.	cross	285

CRY

Don't **cry** when everyone leaves.	cry	506
Their **cry** was "Remember the Alamo."	motto	893
The hurt men **cried** for help.	yell	312

CUT

Three boys were **cut** from the team.	terminate	258
I had to take a **cut** in pay.	reduce	851
Don't **cut** the ribbon yet.	scissors	257
Sorry, I can't **cut** class again.	skip	260
You have to **cut** that out.	stop	387
Why do you always **cut** up in class?	silly	427
Who **cut** his finger?	wound	259

DECLINE

There has been a **decline** in the economy.	reduce	851
He **declined** to say anything until tomorrow.	refuse	436
Dad **declined** his promotion.	turn-down	437
Mom's hearing is **declining**.	decline	1179

DIRECT

She **directed** each person to leave immediately.	ordered	440
Who will **direct** the play?	manage	491
I expect **direct** answers from you.	precise	788
Can you **direct** me to the bathroom?	explain or **show**	932 685

DISAPPEAR

He **disappeared** after staying only ten minutes.	vanish	722
The snow seemed to **disappear** overnight.	melt	934

DISAPPOINT

The **disappointed** people left early.	discourage	1153
I was **disappointed** you didn't show up.	disappoint	773

DISTURB

He **disturbed** the papers on my desk.	mix-up	686
Your father is working; don't **disturb** him.	bother	746
Seeing the accident obviously **disturbed** her.	upset	1024

DRAW

After seven rounds the fight was a **draw**.	tie	540
Draw several pictures for me.	draw	515
Will you **draw** the curtains please?	close	529
The first thing to do is to **draw** trump.	pull	653
He **draws** a big salary for his job.	get	71
She **drew** several comparisons for us.	made	725

DRESS

Who volunteered to **dress** the deer?	clean	62
Mother's **dress** is an old one.	dress	659
Hurry **dress** the baby before he becomes cold.	clothe	663

DROP

I had to **drop** playing golf and tennis.	give-up	545
Drop over for some coffee or tea.	come-over	17

She **dropped** out of college during her second year.	**quit**	877
Did you **drop** this pencil?	**drop**	522
My uncle **dropped** dead playing golf.	**fall-down**	809
The plane had to **drop** its speed to land.	**decrease**	851

DRY

The show was **dry**.	**boring**	335
The basement was warm and **dry**.	**dry**	335
I'm **dry**; can you give me some water?	**thirsty**	1109
The first two oil wells were **dry**.	**empty**	928

ENGAGEMENT

Our **engagement** is for 12:00.	**appointment**	858
She decided to return her **engagement** ring.	**engagement**	857
The army was not prepared for any **engagement**.	**battle**	99

EVER

They have done that for **ever**.	**always**	641
Do you **ever** play football?	**sometimes**	216
Have you **ever** played football?	**ago**	216

FACE

He tried to **face** his wife, but couldn't.	**confront**	328
The soldiers were ordered to **face** right.	**look**	18
She had several marks on her **face**.	**face**	378
Face him like a man.	**meet**	332
	or **confront**	328

FAIR

The movie was just **fair**.	**so-so**	1264
It looks like it may be a **fair** day.	**nice**	62
My daughter is very **fair**.	**light**	395
It appeared to be a **fair** fight.	**even**	540

FALL

I enjoy **fall** when the leaves change colors.	**autumn**	461
Don't **fall** from the porch.	**fall**	759
After dinner, several people **fell** sick.	**become**	521

FIGURE

What do you **figure** will happen now?	**feel**	435
I cannot **figure** my scores.	**count**	852
The **figure** of a woman was on the screen.	**figure**	853
Can you **figure** this out for me?	**figure-out**	797
Name a famous **figure** in American history.	**person**	102
I've already **figured** out the best course.	**decide**	754
Think of a **figure** from one to ten.	**number**	561

FILL

The delicious dinner **filled** me.	**sated**	1040
Please **fill** each glass with milk.	**fill**	556

FINAL

The **final** week in December is Christmas vacation.	**last**	557
Finally, you graduated from college.	**success**	650

FIND

Help me **find** my shoes, please.	look-for	377
Did you **find** that on the bed?	find	249

FINE

He was **fined** $20.00 for speeding.	charge	979
You all look **fine** today.	fine	434
This was a very **fine** dinner.	good	6
What a **fine** day for skiing.	beautiful	317

FIRE

The **fire** lasted all night.	fire	895
He was **fired** from his fourth job.	terminate	258
His team was **fired** up and ready to play.	excite	448

FLY

How often do you **fly** to Miami?	fly-soar	178
The bird couldn't **fly** with a broken wing.	flutter	179
The whole family took **flight** from Europe.	escape	490
Our **flight** leaves at noon today.	airplane	177

FOLLOW

Try to **follow** his example.	copy	1181
Do you always **follow** her advice?	accept	768
Follow me out of this place.	follow	775

FORM

The people **formed** a circle.	create	319
She made a **form** from clay.	shape	853
The girls **formed** a new group.	establish	1214

GAIN

His first year in business, he showed little **gain**.	profit	726
Run faster, he is **gaining** on us.	chase	341
After the operation she showed considerable **gains**.	improvement	314
I notice you are **gaining** a little weight.	increase	376

GET

What will you **get** for your birthday?	get	71
She **get**s mad when you leave early.	become	521
I plan to **get** home around 11:30.	arrive	514
Can you **get** her to quit work?	force	320
Mom will **get** you today.	summon	309

GIVE

Please **give** my brother his hat.	hand	197
The army **gave up** after four months.	surrender	393
Why did you have to **give** up tennis?	drop	545

GLASS

Hand me a **glass** of water.	glass	1244
The **glass** table top is broken.	glass	1245
His **glasses** are always falling off.	eyeglasses	678

GONE

All the fruit salad is **gone**.	out of	927
Will you be **gone** a long time?	not-here	261

He was **gone** from class again.	**absent**	260
All of my grandparents are **gone**.	**dead**	743

GRANT

Can you **grant** me several requests?	**give-me**	197
No one can **grant** that except your father.	**allow**	299
I **grant** that what I did was a mistake.	**admit**	300
Granted, that happened before I knew it.	**correct**	161

GROUND

Put the boxes on the **ground**.	**soil**	971
His play**ground** is the world.	**place**	356
What **grounds** do you have for saying that?	**basis**	815

GROW

I have three **grown** children.	**grow-up**	647
Mother **grows** odd-looking flowers.	**grow (plant)**	648
He has **grown** very cautious recently.	**become**	521

HAND

How did you hurt your **hand**?	**hand**	402
Hand that to me, please.	**give**	197
The ranch **hand** quit working.	**person**	102
Give me a **hand** in finishing this, please.	**help**	156
That picture shows the **hand** of a master.	**skill**	761
I want you on **hand** if there is an accident.	**here**	164

HANG

Finally, he is learning to **hang** his clothes.	**closet**	602
His future **hangs** on having a good year.	**depend**	737
We will **hang** around until a decision is made.	**wait**	978

HARD

It was a **hard** problem to solve.	**difficult**	325
The chair was old and **hard**.	**hard**	459
The boss was **hard** on his employees.	**mean**	1029
Try your **hardest** to succeed.	**best**	524

HAVE

They **have** several new cars.	**possess**	159
I **have had** mumps before.	**finish** and **possess**	342 159
Dad **has** been working here 12 years.	**since**	245
Mother and I **have** not left for work.	**not-yet**	246
They **have** to leave before noon.	**must**	362

HEAD

My **head** hurts again.	**head**	402
Who is the **head** of the department?	**boss**	133
I plan to **head** the group into the mountains.	**lead**	649
He is out of his **head**.	**crazy**	848

HIGH

How **high** can you reach?	**high**	35
She recently moved to a **high** position.	**important** or **advance**	894 921

Everything in the store is **high** today.	expensive	579
The young boy acted **high**.	stoned	505

HIT

She never **hits** her dog.	punch	1043
The painting made a big **hit**.	success	650

HOLD

Hold this for me while I'm on vacation.	keep	251
Hold this for a second.	hold	431
The beliefs some people **hold** are controversial.	have	159
He **held** that we never landed on the moon.	believe	334
Hold up, he is not finished.	suspend	298

HOT

The contest was **hot** throughout.	even / or hot	540 / 152
Hot coffee tastes good on cold mornings.	hot	152
She was really **hot** after being fired.	angry	337
He only wants $50.00 for the TV, so it must be **hot**.	steal	1224
They are really **hot** to get this finished.	eager	451

HOUSE

Can you visit grandmother's old **house**?	house	25
They expected a large **house** on opening night.	audience	956
Don't worry, my parents can **house** all ten animals.	take-care-of	910

HUNT

Do you enjoy **hunting** deer?	hunting	652
I was **hunting** for my shoes.	look-for	377

IN FRONT OF

They cut **in front of** us in line.	ahead	645
No one could stand **in front of** that crowd.	before	328

JAM

Put some butter and **jam** on my toast, please.	jelly	1085
Tell me if you are in a **jam**.	trouble	453
My foot was **jammed** in the door.	stuck	820

JOIN

Can you **join** us for lunch next week?	participate	878
Take each end of the pipes and **join** them.	connect	1036

JUDGE

Where is the **judge** going now?	judge+er	150
Who will **judge** the horse show?	judge	150
The **judgment** was made last week.	decision	754

JUMP

Don't **jump** on the chair.	jump	904
He **jumped** bail for the second time.	escape	490
Prices seem to **jump** every day.	increase	376
Everyone **jumped** on him for what he said.	criticize	437

JUST

We **just** saw him leave.	recently	1045

I want **just** one sandwich.	**only**	1044
That was a **just** decision.	**fair**	540
	or **good**	6
The new car cost **just** more than I had.	**little-bit**	433
We thought it was **just** right.	**exactly**	788

KEEP

Keep my watch while I swim.	**hold**	431
Milk will not **keep** for a long time.	**continue**	252
Keep away while I am working.	**go-away**	519
Will you **keep** my dog for several weeks?	**supervise**	910
Keep your money in a bank.	**save-money**	784
She **keeps** her will in the safe.	**keep**	251

KEY

The house **key** is lost again.	**key**	1027
He knew the **key** thing to say.	**important**	894
What is the **key** to your heart?	**way**	696

KICK

Don't **kick** the door again.	**kick**	946
Why **kick** about things you cannot change?	**complain**	386
She always gets a **kick** out of his stories.	**enjoyment**	555

KIND

What a **kind** person you are!	**gentle**	919
What **kind** of person are you?	**type**	204

KNOCK

Knock on the door twice.	**knock**	792

Who saw him **knock** down the woman?	**push**	885
The fighter was **knocked** down several times.	**fall**	809

LAND

Dad **landed** a terrific job.	**get**	71
Illinois is the **land** of Lincoln.	**home**	223
Our **land** is full of trees.	**land**	306
They left the **Land** of Israel.	**country**	733

LAST

This is the **last** apple I have.	**final**	557
Will this **last** a long time?	**continue**	252
What happened **last** night?	**past**	216

LEAVE

Can we **leave** here soon?	**depart**	167
He is on annual **leave** for two weeks.	**vacation**	1165
Don't **leave** your pictures on the desk.	**abandon**	166

LEFT

Go two blocks, then turn **left**.	**left-direction**	165
They **left** everything behind the store.	**abandon**	166
They **left** more than an hour ago.	**depart**	167

LEND

Lend my uncle $10.00 until next week.	**loan**	1230
Lend me a hand with this engine.	**give-me**	197
Doesn't this picture **lend** beauty to the office?	**add**	286

LENGTH

What was the **length** of the first show?	**time**	26

| The **length** of the rope is 23 feet long. | long | 302 |
| What **length** of time did you wish? | long-time | 215 |

LET

The movie was a real **let** down.	discourage	1153
Let him know the second it happens.	inform	812
Let me go so I can pay you.	allow	299

LIE

| That was not a white **lie**. | lie | 1260 |
| **Lie** here and sleep for a little bit. | lay | 1261 |

LIGHT

It is **light** in here now.	bright	395
That old box is **light** now.	not-heavy	391
It looks like the **light** has blown.	light	392
No **light** is coming in the window.	sun	467
Do you have a **light**, please?	match	1154
His punishment was very **light**.	easy	718

LIKE

We all **like** the same thing.	appreciate	233
Is it **like** that all the time?	same	988
I would **like** to finish college.	like	37

LINE

What is your **line** of work?	profession	711
Put a **line** on the floor.	string	215
What a long **line** of people!	line-up	1234

LITTLE

The **little** girl ran away from home.	short	33
Can you lend me a **little** bit of money?	little-bit	433
That happened a **little** bit ago.	recently	1045
That was just a **little** house, but it was comfortable.	tiny	34

LOCATE

When you leave here, where will you **locate**?	live	346
Can you **locate** your hometown on the map?	find	249
The best **location** is near the restaurant.	place	356

LONG

It looks about seven inches **long**.	measure	302
How **long** will you stay with us?	long-time	215
He always **longs** for his sweetheart.	wish	363
They will all leave before **long**.	soon	708

LOOK

Look and tell me what you see.	look	18
My brother **looks** handsome in a suit.	appear	378
Look at me while I do this.	look-at	232
We decided to **look** for gold.	search	377
It **looks** like it might rain.	seem	720
The girls **looked** him over when he entered.	look-over	693
We better **look** over our notes again.	review	694
Look up the new vocabulary right away.	look-up	1176
Look out! The dog is dangerous.	careful	913

Will you **look** after my pet rats?	keep	910

MAKE

You can't **make** him do that!	force	320
I will **make** coffee for us.	make	319
Please **make** the bed for tonight.	prepare	725
That **make** of car is very popular now.	kind	920
You better **make** up your mind now.	decide	754
She is very good at **making** up stories.	invent	915
They decided to **make** a horse barn.	build	814
	or **make**	319
My aunt **make**s it home in an hour.	arrive	514
Father used to **make** $10,000 a year.	earn	1183
I know you will **make** a good doctor.	become	521

MATCH

I need a **match** to start the fire.	match	1154
He lost all four of his tennis **matches**.	game	936
You cannot **match** apples and oranges.	compare	1156
The little girl's shoes **match** her dress.	go-together	1155
The rabbit was no **match** for the turtle.	competition	495

MEAN

He is a **mean** person.	unkind	1029
They didn't **mean** to say that.	intend	1188
Add these numbers for me to get the **mean**.	average	869

MIND

Do you **mind** if I kiss you?	care	386
Children should **mind** their parents.	obey	384
Try to improve your **mind**.	brain	5
I don't **mind** what you say or do.	don't-care	455

MISS

Will we **miss** the train now?	didn't-get	774
My sister really **misses** Mom.	disappoint	773
The children's clothes are **missing**.	gone	261
I decided to **miss** class tomorrow.	skip	260

MOTION

His **motion** was defeated.	propose	738
All this **motion** is making me sick.	move	195

MOVE

I **move** that this meeting be adjourned.	propose	738
Sit there without **moving** for a minute.	move	195
Something **moved** him to say that.	cause	321

NAME

I won't change my **name**.	name	307
He **named** all of his dogs the same.	called	308
I want that, **name** your price.	tell-me	527
The minister wants us to **name** the day.	decide	754

NEED

She has several **needs** that must be fulfilled.	wish	363

What do you **need** now?	**want**	77
Mother **needs** to lose weight.	**need**	361

NEXT

Do you want to go **next**?	**turn**	114
What do you think will happen **next**?	**next**	333
A young girl sat **next** to my brother.	**next to**	923
Uncle John can't go until **next** week	**next-week**	227
Next year will be a very good year.	**next-year**	219

NO

No, she is not here any more.	**exclamation**	74
There are **no** more apples.	**none**	288
He refused to take **no** for an answer.	**exclamation**	74

NOTICE

They never **noticed** my new shoes.	**notice**	890
Put the **notices** on trees and buildings.	**poster**	781
The army moved suddenly without any **notice**.	**warning**	889

NUMBER

Write several **numbers** for me.	**number**	861
His days left in the office are **numbered**.	**limit**	1248
A large **number** of people did not show up.	**many**	347
I have a **number** of things to say.	**several**	323

NUTS

My aunt is a little **nuts**.	**crazy**	848
He always eats **nuts** and drinks beer.	**nuts**	1102

OBJECT

Place all the **objects** on the table.	**thing**	1025
Why must you always **object** to everything?	**complain** or **disagree**	386 856

OFFER

I **offered** to postpone it for several weeks.	**willing**	503
I **offered** to give money.	**promise**	959
What do you plan to **offer** the church?	**give**	197
He **offered** several alternatives.	**propose**	738

OLD

He was an **old** boyfriend.	**former**	239
How **old** are you now?	**old**	458
She is an **old** hand at that.	**experience**	789

ON

Who turned **on** the television?	**turn-on**	587
Place the food **on** the table.	**on**	67
My apartment is **on** the beach.	**near**	69
Go **on**, I will stop you occasionally.	**proceed**	681
Mom refused to take **on** any more responsibility.	**accept**	768

ONCE

They come only **once** in a while.	**occasionally**	254
Mother said things only **once**.	**once**	255
Once upon a time, the good king had a daughter.	**former**	239
Father told her to come home at **once**.	**immediately**	741
Once I see him, I will know for sure.	**when**	200

ONLY

He knocked **only** once.	only	1044
We have **only** three more weeks of school!	exactly	788

ORDER

The boss **ordered** two hamburgers.	order	440
My dad is a member of the Benevolent and Protective **Order** of Elks.	group	41
His life is in good **order**.	plan	725

ORIGINAL

That looks like an **original** picture.	true	1259
The **original** plan was changed again.	first	350
He always brings something **original**.	new	351
She is considered a very **original** thinker.	invent	1001

OUT

They were **out** of onions.	all-gone	927
Leave the dog **outside** tonight.	out	585
Which way do we go **out**?	out	585
The teacher decided not to give **out** the notes.	disseminate	728
They are **out** shopping tonight.	gone	585
It took several hours for the fire to go **out**.	disappear	934
They cried **out** of hunger.	because	1191

OVER

They were fighting **over** money again.	about	513
Run **over** the bridge and wait for us.	across	849
Are the signs **over** the door yet?	above	850
Everyone is glad the work is **over**.	finish	342
My aunt fell **over** when she saw me.	fall	809
The play went **over** the allotted time.	past	879
You made a mistake, so do it **over**.	again	324
His work has improved **over** the years.	during	238

PART

We want you to take **part** in family matters.	join	878
No **part** of the pie is to be cut.	part	256
They argued all night but **parted** as friends.	leave	167
You have to do your **part** to finish this.	duty	76
Can we **part** this in the middle?	separate	142

PAST

Forget about the **past** and move on.	ago	216
They walked **past** the fire station this morning.	pass	879
Now that you are home, my worries are **past**.	finish	343

PATIENT

The **patient** was crying for help.	patient	1015
Be **patient** for just a little longer.	tolerate	749

PERFECT

She always knows the **perfect** thing to say!	perfect	788
To be promoted, you must **perfect** your skills.	improve	314

PERMIT

I can **permit** you to leave early.	allow	299
She just got her driver's **permit**.	license	293

PICK

That dog is the **pick** of the litter.	best	524
Pick the paper that looks the best.	choose	1041
Father **picked** up the dinner bill.	pay	571
Pick up the shoes on the floor.	pick-up	1050

PLACE

No one wanted to go back to that **place**.	location	356
Place the picture on the mantel.	put	196
Your **place** is at the head of the table.	sit	36
What is your **place** in the organization?	position	356
Be quiet! It's not your **place** to comment.	responsible	771
She lives in a high income **place**.	area	356

PLANT

My neighbor **plants** corn every summer.	sow	1113
All my **plants** seem to die overnight.	grow	648
He **planted** the seeds of doubt in her mind.	put	196
The deaf man has worked at that **plant** for 12 years.	factory	862

PLAY

You can **play** with your toys now.	play	24
The **play** was really fantastic.	performance	348
She **played** on his sympathy.	work	76

POINT

He made several good **points**.	meaning	931
It is not polite to **point**.	point	15
What is the **point** of saying that?	purpose	1188
Walk to the **point** that I described.	place	356
I wish that you would **point** that out for me.	show	685
Don't **point** that gun at me.	aim	931

POOR

The **poor** house is on Main Street.	poor	1048
That was a **poor** choice of words.	bad	61
Poor father, the news depressed him.	pity	1268

PREFER

I **prefer** cake to pie anytime.	prefer	432
Do you **prefer** to leave now or later?	want	77
Let me think about which one I **prefer**.	choose	1041

PRESENT

The best **present** was the antique clock.	gift	740
You must be **present** tomorrow at 9:00.	here	164
The **present** time is good enough to begin.	now	7
I want to **present** my sister to you.	introduce	739
Do you wish to **present** your grievances?	propose	738

PRINT

Print your name on the line.	write	266
Printing was a good occupation for deaf people.	print	983
The animal's **footprints** were everywhere.	figure or **steps**	741 580

PROCEDURE

Which **procedure** will you select?	way	697
The medical **procedure** was interesting.	process	922
They followed the established **procedure.**	system	744

PULL

She had a lot of **pull** with the company.	power or **influence**	1207 763
Pull the wagon closer to the barn.	pull	653
Who are you **pulling** for to win?	support	1229

PUT

Put the oranges in the refrigerator.	place	196
Put off leaving until tomorrow.	delay	1208
We **put** up several interesting signs.	put-up	781
I can't **put** up with noisy children.	tolerate	749
How can I **put** it so you will understand.	say	194

QUIZ

Can we **quiz** him about the accident?	question	358
The **quiz** was not difficult.	test	683

RAISE

I **raised** an adopted child.	raise	647
What kind of crops do you **raise**?	grow	648
The church is trying to **raise** funds.	collect	1183
Will they **raise** the rent this year?	increase	376
He **raised** an interesting question.	propose	738

REACH

Can you **reach** the clock above the door?	touch	1217
We will **reach** home about midnight.	arrive	514

REDUCE

They had to **reduce** their energy bill.	reduce	851
Mother needs to **reduce** so she can wear her old clothes.	slim-down	706
We need to **reduce** this picture.	downsize	851

RELEASE

After 18 years at the same store, they **released** her.	laid-off	441
You have to **release** your end of the wire.	disconnect	1037
Release the news bulletin now.	disseminate	728
Everyone was excited when the animals were **released**.	free	790

RESPECT

Always **respect** what your parents tell you.	respect	999
Respect the government; it has a difficult task.	support	1229
Dad was wrong in many **respects**.	way	696

REST

Rest here for a few minutes.	**relax**	547
Sure, I ate the **rest** of it!	**leftovers**	166
Rest the gun against the fence.	**put**	196

RETURN

Will you **return** from your trip soon?	**come-back**	864
Please **return** my picture and ring.	**give-me**	197
They had to **return** all the money immediately.	**give-back**	865
Mom **returned** the hat for a larger size.	**exchange**	791

REVEAL

When will you **reveal** your invention?	**show**	685
The newspaper will **reveal** his identity.	**tell**	526

RIDE

He can **ride** a variety of animals.	**ride**	1198
You can **ride** with me tomorrow.	**ride-in-a-vehicle**	1199
They are always **riding** him for his mistakes.	**tease**	326
I refuse to **ride** the bandwagon.	**join**	878
The neighbors took a **ride** to Disney World.	**trip**	808

RIGHT

His **right** to an interpreter was denied.	**privilege**	160
Turn to the **right** after the second traffic light.	**right-direction**	162
They made the **right** decision.	**correct**	161
Everything is **right** where you left it.	**exact**	788

Do it for me **right** away.	**immediately**	741

ROUGH

She had a **rough** day at work.	**difficult**	325
It was a **rough** road to travel.	**not-smooth**	1030
The dog plays too **rough** with the baby.	**mean**	1029

RULE

I need a straight-edge **rule** to get this exactly right.	**measure**	854
What **rule** did you break this time?	**policy**	1186
The queen **ruled** with an iron hand.	**govern**	491

RUN

Who **runs** the company when the president is away?	**control**	491
You will **run** against the country's best athletes.	**compete**	495
Run around the block with me.	**jog**	492
His nose **runs** all the time.	**runny-nose**	493
I think I hear the water **running**.	**dripping**	494
Will you **run** off 200 copies for me?	**make**	319
She **ran** away from home four times.	**escape**	490
Now my car **runs** fine.	**works**	496

SAFE/SAVE

I will **save** you from that gang of boys.	**protect**	752
Save some of that for me, please.	**keep**	431
Save your money for college.	**save**	251
The soldiers **saved** the people.	**salvation**	790

Is your purse **safe** on the desk?	**all-right**	160
It is a **safe** bet to make.	**good**	6

SAME

All the horses look the **same**.	**standard**	989
She does the **same** thing every day.	**same**	987
The brothers look the **same**.	**alike**	988
My doctor gave me the **same** medicine as last time.	**no-change**	990

SECOND

He is the **second** from the right.	**numerical**	563
Wait a **second** for me to finish.	**time**	236

SEE

See that man in the blue coat?	**see**	2
I **see**! You do it without adding.	**understand**	1583
Can you **see** if the clock is right?	**check**	486
I want you to **see** how this is done.	**watch**	18
Please **see** all the girls home.	**take**	543
Every day, the doctor sees many patients.	**help**	156

SENSE

He had no **sense** of remorse.	**feeling**	435
You look like you have more **sense**.	**brain**	5

SENTENCE

He was **sentenced** to jail for two years.	**send**	263

The first **sentence** of the paragraph is not clear.	**sentence**	191

SHARP

Be careful! That knife is **sharp**.	**shiny**	100
She has a **sharp** car.	**beautiful**	317
She is really **sharp** in arithmetic.	**smart**	397

SHORT

My brother is very **short**.	**short**	33
I only need a **short** piece of string.	**small**	34
The lecture was very **short**.	**brief**	756

SHOW

Let me **show** you what to do.	**show**	685
We are going to the 5:00 **show**.	**film**	684
The first **show** of the season was *Oklahoma*.	**performance**	348
Try not to **show** off for company.	**brag**	1171
Will she **show** up for her appointment?	**appear**	721

SIGN

The circus **sign** is an old one.	**poster**	781
Sign language class starts at 8:00 a.m.	**sign**	780
Can you **sign** my card for me?	**signature**	782

SPEECH

The president's **speech** was really good.	**lecture**	1262
His **speech** is much more intelligible now.	**speech**	368

STAND

Stand closer to me for the picture.	**stand**	446

The deer **stand** he uses is gone.	**place**	356
My sister can't **stand** our cousin.	**tolerate**	749
Will you **stand** behind me on this issue?	**support**	1229
Stand up when she comes in here.	**stand-up**	449

STEP

Take two **steps** and then turn around.	**walk**	114
The porch **step** is broken again.	**flight**	621

STILL

Why is it so **still** in the nursery?	**quiet**	807
I **still** think you are right.	**continue**	253
The book is not perfect, **still** it is good.	**but**	1047

STRIKE

The iron workers' **strike** lasted four months.	**rebel**	535
He promised never to **strike** his dog again.	**hit**	1043
The singer wanted to **strike** the first paragraph of her contract.	**cancel**	487

SUBJECT

My **subject** for tonight is "The History of Deafness."	**topic**	893
English is my best **subject**.	**course**	269
Several **subjects** were required for the experiment.	**people**	103

SUSPECT

The **suspect** escaped during the evening.	**person**	859
Do you **suspect** anything has changed?	**think**	5
I know that he is honest, and I **suspect** that he is right.	**imagine** or **suspect**	875 1131

SWEAR

Do you **swear** to tell the whole truth?	**promise**	959
I heard you **swearing** at the cat last night.	**curse**	958

TAKE

Take this suitcase with you.	**take**	543
I can't **take** this anymore.	**tolerate**	749
Take this road to Philadelphia.	**follow**	775
How did your aunt **take** the news?	**accept**	768
Take away all the wrong words.	**subtract**	283
He is **taking** 18 credits this semester.	**take-up**	544

TALK

We **talked** almost all night.	**chat**	290
I think you need to **talk** more often.	**say**	194
All three **talks** were excellent.	**lecture**	1262

TALL

How **tall** is that building?	**height**	855
My oldest daughter is very **tall**.	**tall**	35

TELL

She was **telling** him how to go.	**explain**	932
Tell me what you are thinking.	**tell-me**	527
Tell everyone who is the boss here.	**announce**	810

THROUGH

Run **through** that again for me.	**say**	194
I'm finally **through** with my book.	**completed**	342
Go **through** the book from front to back.	**read**	198
Through this door walk great people.	**passage**	349

TIE

The first match ended in a **tie** score.	**even**	540
Tie a blue string around the box.	**knot**	569

TIME

What **time** is it now?	**time**	26
I didn't have a job at that **time**.	**period**	1039

TO

Come with me **to** the farm.	**to**	65
They sang and drank **to** the music.	**with**	9
What will Mother say **to** this mistake?	**about**	513
He wants **to** sing, **to** play, and **to** dance.	**fingerspell T-O**	
Father made a toast **to** mother's health.	**for**	70

TOTAL

No one mentioned the **total** number to expect.	**all**	553
Please **total** these numbers for me.	**sum**	287
Our vacation was a **total** failure.	**complete**	556

TRADE

My uncle is **trading** cars again.	**exchange**	791
The tinker **trade** is almost extinct.	**work** or **profession**	76 711

TRAIL

The hunters **trailed** the animal for almost a mile.	**follow**	775
Which **trail** takes us to the forest?	**path**	696
The dogs followed the **trail** of the lost boy.	**smell**	315

TRAIN

The **train** came into town empty.	**train**	174
How long did he **train** for the team?	**practice**	870

TURN

Turn the bolt with your hand.	**turn**	587
When is it my **turn** to watch?	**next-turn**	114
They **turned** all the animals loose.	**release**	790
They **turned** the defeat into a victory.	**change**	1038
He **turned** a quick profit and left the country.	**made**	319

UGLY

He is in an **ugly** mood.	**awful**	316
Why is your dog so **ugly**?	**ugly**	318
That is an **ugly** thing to say.	**bad** or **awful**	61 316

USE

Let me **use** your new sewing machine.	**use** or **borrow**	657 1231
We are **used** to going to work early.	**habit**	1169
I **used** to play football in college.	**past**	216

VANISH

He just **vanished** from sight.	**disappear**	722
Don't worry, by morning the ice will have **vanished**.	**melt**	934

VISION

My grandmother's **vision** is improving.	**sight**	2
Last night she had a **vision**.	**dream**	876

WAIT

She didn't like **waiting** tables all day.	**serve**	819
Wait a minute for Dad to get here.	**minute**	237
I will **wait** until your return.	**wait**	978

WATCH

Watch your baby brother for an hour.	**supervise**	910
Watch me while I change this light.	**watch-me**	232
Watch out! That dog will bite.	**careful**	913
We can **watch** TV tonight.	**look-at**	18

WELL

After a long illness, he is now **well**.	**healthy**	1023
How **well** do you know him?	**good**	6

WHICH

Which man is she planning to marry?	**which**	203
No one was arrest, **which** was only fair.	**that**	16

WORD

What does that **word** mean?	**word**	359
Mom needs a **word** with you.	**talk**	290
We will be back after this **word** from our sponsor.	**advertisement** or **announcement**	917 810

WORK

You begin **work** next week on Monday.	**work**	76
If this doesn't **work**, I give up.	**succeed**	650
Grandfather can **work** any puzzle.	**solve**	934
My car doesn't **work** anymore.	**run**	496

always, 641
amazed, 550
America, 1279
American, 1279
American Sign
   Language, 128
amid (among), 976
amid (between), 753
amid (with), 9
among, 976
amongst, 976
amount, 443
anger, 336
angry, 336
anguish, 750
animal, 822
anniversary, 933
announce, 810
announcement, 810
annoy, 746
annual, 220
annually, 220
another, 646
answer, 871
anticipate, 388
anxious (eager), 451
anxious (excited),
   898
anxious (nervous),
   452
anxious (worried),
   453
any, 389
anyhow, 380
anyway, 380
apologize, 554
apparently, 720
appeal, 352
appear (look like),
   378
appear (seem), 720

appear (show up),
   721
appearance, 378
appears, 720
apple, 1053
applicant, 1150
apply (put on), 874
apply (reserve), 1149
apply (use), 657
apply (volunteer),
   1150
appointment, 858
appreciate, 233
apprehend, 691
approach, 682
appropriate, 161
approve (accept),
   768
approve (seal), 730
approximately, 512
area, 356
argue, 1004
arithmetic, 797
arm, 409
army, 995
around (in-the-area),
   512
around (round), 689
arrange, 724
arrest, 691
arrive, 514
art, 515
article (newspaper),
   1026
article (thing), 1025
artist, 515
artwork, 515
ashamed, 1192
ask, 357
asleep, 79
assignment, 76

assist, 156
associate
   (relationship), 985
associate (socialize),
   748
association (group),
   41
association
   (relationship), 985
assume, 247
astonished, 550
at last (success), 650
at the back, 745
athletics, 495
attempt, 906
attend, 8
attention, 1144
attitude, 1140
attorney, 1128
attractive, 759
attribute, 769
audience, 957
auditory, 366
aunt, 106
Australia, 1281
Australian, 1281
authority, 1207
authorize, 730
automobile, 169
autumn, 461
available, 928
average, 869
avoid, 745
award (give), 197
award (prize), 558
aware, 518
aware of, 817
away, 519
awful (terrible), 316
awful (ugly), 318
awkward, 1249

baby, 111
bachelor, 125
back (anatomy), 407
back (come back),
   865
back (support), 1229
background, 764
bacon, 1075
bad, 61
bake, 618
ball, 940
balmy, 151
banana, 1056
bankrupt, 654
bar (prevent), 821
bare, 928
barn, 25
barrier, 520
base (foundation),
   868
baseball, 937
basement, 1184
bashful, 1193
basic, 815
basis, 815
basketball, 938
bath, 638
bathe, 638
bathroom, 633
battle (fight), 992
battle (war), 993
be careful, 913
be quiet, 807
beach, 967
bear (animal), 846
bear (tolerate), 749
beard, 1141
beat (conquer), 1042
beat (punch), 1043
beaten, 766
beautiful, 317

because, 1191
become, 521
bed, 600
bedroom, 634
been there, 1217
beer, 499
before (in front of), 328
before (past), 216
before (prior to), 329
before long, 708
begin (start), 551
begin (take up), 544
behave, 189
behavior, 189
behind, 745
believe, 334
bell, 640
below (beneath), 374
below (less than), 375
beneath, 374
benefit, 726
beside, 923
best, 524
better, 523
between, 753
beverage, 22
bicycle, 949
big, 32
bike (bicycle), 949
bike (motorcycle), 173
biker, 173, 949
biking, 940
bill, 979
biologist, 803
biology, 803
bird, 20
birth, 872
birthday, 873
biscuit, 1082

bite, 900
bite into, 900
bitter, 1058
black, 90
blame, 980
blanket, 692
blaze, 895
blind, 322
block (prevent), 821
block (stuck), 820
blood, 525
blow up (explosion), 994
blow up (mad), 552
blue (color), 97
blue (depressed), 1153
board, 1121
board of trustees, 1122
boast, 1171
boat, 947
boating, 947
body, 405
bologna, 1073
bomb, 994
book, 698
boots, 658
bored, 354, 355
boredom, 354, 355
boring, 354, 355
born, 872
borrow, 1231
boss, 133
both, 488
bother, 746
bottle, 1243
bought, 303
boundary, 786
bowl (dish), 632
bowl (game), 944

bowler, 944
bowling, 944
box, 626
boy, 10
boyfriend, 137
bra, 679
bracelet, 670
brag, 1171
brain, 5
brassiere, 679
brave, 1023
bread, 1091
break (fracture), 719
break (intermission), 262
break (vacation), 1165
break off (disconnect), 1037
breakdown, 727
breakfast, 1110
breast, 408
breeze, 473
brew, 499
bridge, 867
brief (summary), 1254
brief (time), 756
bright (light), 395
bright (shiny), 100
bright (smart), 396
brilliant, 1266
bring, 1203
broad (wide), 705
brochure, 699
broke (fracture), 719
broke (no money), 654
broken (fractured), 719
brother, 105

brown, 91
buck, 572
budget, 574
bug (cold), 154
bug, 823
build, 814
builder, 814
building, 813
bunny, 843
bureaucrat, 714
Burger King, 1119
buried, 697
burn, 895
bury, 697
bus, 180
buss, 926
business, 528
busy, 528
but (except), 863
but (however), 1047
butt, 424
butter, 1079
butterfly, 1265
butt in, 747
buy, 303
by (follow), 775
by (near), 69
by (pass), 879
by one's self, 776

cabbage, 1103
cake, 1094
calculator, 277
calculus, 797
calendar, 222, 982
call (named), 308
call (summon), 309
call (telephone), 310
call (yell), 311
call for, 1211
call off, 487

call on, 309
calm, 807
calm down, 1255
camera, 891
camp, 757
camping, 757
can (able), 184
can (maybe), 188
can (possible), 186
Canada, 1282
Canadian, 1282
cancel, 487
can-do, 710
candy, 1101
cannot, 185
cannot be repeated, 656
can't, 185
cap, 665
captain, 133
captions, 191
capture, 691
car, 169
car accident, 901
cards (playing cards), 953
care, 386
careful, 913
careless, 1162
carry, 1204
cat, 31
catch (apprehend), 691
catch (ball), 690
catch ball, 690
cattle, 825
caught (apprehend), 691
caught (stuck), 820
cause (make), 321
cave in, 727

ceiling, 604
celebrate, 933
cell phone, 312
cellar, 1184
cemetery, 697
center, 909
cents, 575
certificate, 295
certification, 295
certified, 295
chair, 598
change, 1038
character, 1140
charge (bill), 979
charge (blame), 980
charge (responsible), 771
chart, 982
chase, 341
chat, 290
chatting, 290
check (account), 485
check (correct), 487
check (investigate), 486
check (mark), 484
check off, 484
cheek, 399
cheerful (friendly), 1139
cheerful (happy), 163
cheese, 1066
chef, 1106
chemical, 802
chemist, 802
chemistry, 802
cherish, 731
chest, 403
chicken, 20
child, 116
childish, 818

children, 117
chilly, 153
chin, 413
China, 1283
Chinese, 1283
chips, 1107
chocolate, 86
choice, 1041
choose, 1041
Christ, 596
Christian, 596
Christmas, 1273
church, 591
cigarette, 1163
cinema, 684
circle, 1159
citizens, 103
city, 344
class (group), 41
class (sophisticated), 1228
clean, 62
clean up, 63
cleaned out, 927
clear, 395
clerk, 305
clever, 396
clock, 1180
close (near), 69, 130
close (secret), 751
close (shut), 529
closed captions, 193
closet, 602
clothes, 663
clouds, 466
cloudy, 466
clumsy, 1249
coach, 133
coast, 967
coat, 680
coax, 1247

Coca Cola, 83
cochlear implant, 372
code of ethics, 1186
coffee, 85
Coke, 83
cold (aloof), 155
cold (illness), 154
cold (temperature), 153
collapse, 727
collect, 1183
collector, 1183
college, 40
collision, 901
color, 88
colorful, 88
column, 1026
combine, 1155
come, 17
come again?, 206
come back, 864, 865
come here, 864
come over (now), 864
come over (visit), 17
comes to (total), 287
come up, 721
coming, 17
command, 440
commence (open), 530
commence (start), 551
commercial, 917
committee, 1124
commode, 605
common, 989
common sense, 1151
communicate, 291
communication, 291

drip, 494

drive, 171

drizzle, 472

drop (fall down), 809

drop (give up), 545

drop (let go of), 522

drop (reduce), 851

drop off, 166

drop out (quit), 877

drove, 171

drown, 1174

drugs (illegal), 816

drugs (medicine), 1019

drunk, 1175

dry (boring), 355

dry (thirsty), 1109

duck, 830

due, 1046

dumb, 1161

duplicate (copy), 1182

during, 238

Dutch, 1289

duty (responsible), 771

duty (work), 76

dwell on, 1270

dwelling, 25

each, 381

each other, 748

eager (excited), 898

eager (motivated), 451

early, 483

earmold, 371

earn, 1183

earth, 804

east, 702

Easter, 1274

eastern, 702

easy, 718

eat, 23

eater, 23

economy, 574

educate, 149

education, 149

effort, 906

egg, 1077

Egypt, 1284

Egyptian, 1284

either, 536

eject, 1197

elaborate, 1228

elbow, 415

elderly, 458

elect, 537

election, 537

electric, 1200

electricity, 1200

elementary, 815

elephant, 835

eliminate, 283

else, 646

e-mail, 271

embarrass, 1192

emerge, 721

emotions, 435

emphasis, 1210

emphasize, 1210

employer, 133

empty, 928

encourage, 772

encyclopedia, 918

end, 343

endure (suffer), 750

endure (tolerate), 749

enemy, 643

energy, 1207

engagement (appointment), 858

engagement (marital), 857

engagement (war), 993

engine, 862

England, 1285

English, 1285

enjoy, 555

enjoyable, 555

enough, 157

enter, 64

entrance, 64

enthusiasm, 451

enthusiastic, 451

entire, 553

envious, 1225

environment, 742

envy, 1225

equal, 540

equipment, 1025

era, 1039

erase, 1160

erratic, 963

error, 168

escape, 490

establish, 1214

estimate, 247

Europe, 1286

European, 1286

evaluate, 1201

evaluation, 1201

even, 540

evening, 28

event (happening), 501

event (what's up?), 539

ever (always), 641

ever (past), 216

ever since, 245

every, 381

every day, 47

every now and then, 244

every week, 226

every year, 220

everybody, 383

everyday, 47

everyone, 383

everything (all), 382

everything (included), 880

evidence, 538

evil, 1170

exact, 788

exactly, 788

exaggerate, 916

exam, 683

examination (medical), 1009

examination (test), 683

examine, 777

example, 685

except, 863

exception, 863

exchange, 791

excite, 898

excited (eager), 898

excited (jump for joy), 448

excitement, 898

excuse me (forgive), 442

excused (dismiss), 441

exercise, 860

exhausted, 1222

expand, 705

expect, 388

expel, 258

expensive, 579

experience, 789
expert (gifted), 710
expert (skilled), 761
expertise
  (experience), 789
expertise (skilled),
  761
expire (all gone), 927
expire (die), 743
expire (license), 294
explain, 932
explosion, 994
express, 1263
expression (facial),
  717
expression (let it
  out), 1263
exterior, 585
external, 585
eye, 411
eyeglasses, 678

fable, 915
face (appearance),
  378
face (confront), 328
face (meet), 332
facial expression, 717
facility, 813
factory, 862
fail (flop), 1233
fail (lose), 766
failed to see (missed),
  774
failure, 766
fair (even), 540
fair (so-so), 1264
faith, 570
fake, 115
fall (autumn), 461
fall (fall down), 809

fall down, 809
false, 115
familiar, 518
family, 41
famous, 811
fancy, 1228
fantastic (great), 450
fantastic (wow), 1272
fantasy, 915
far, 644
farm, 779
farmer, 779
fascinated, 353
fascinating, 353
fast (hurry), 1000
fast (quick), 896
fasten, 1036
fat, 881
father, 112
fault (blame), 980
fault (responsible),
  427
favor, 37
favorite (pet), 1223
favorite (prefer), 432
fax, 272
faxed, 272
fear, 778
federal, 1127
feeble, 1219
feel, 435
feet, 401
female, 11, 144
fever, 1256
few, 323
fib, 1260
fiction, 915
field (profession),
  711
fifth, 566
fifty cents, 578

fight, 992
fighter, 992
figure (count), 852
figure (feel), 435
figure (number), 861
figure (person), 102
figure (shape), 853
figure (solve), 797
figure out (decide),
  754
figure out (solve),
  797
file, 265
fill, 556
film, 684
filthy, 899
final, 557
finally, 650
finance, 574
find (discover), 249
find (look up), 1176
find out, 249
fine (cost), 979
fine (well), 454
finger, 417
fingers, 418
fingerspell, 783
finish (complete),
  342
finish (end), 343
finish it (stop), 866
fire (blaze), 895
fire (terminate), 258
firefighter, 147
fireman, 147
fireworks, 994
first (original), 350
first week (of the
  month), 240
fish (noun), 845
fish (verb), 952

fisherman, 952
fishing, 952
fit (go together),
  1155
fix, 331
flag, 914
flame, 895
flat, 1031
flee, 490
flexible, 929
flight (airplane), 177
flight (run off), 490
flip-flops, 674
floor, 603
flop, 1233
flower, 1035
flutter, 179
fly (airplane), 178
fly (bird), 179
flyer, 699
fog, 474
folder, 265
follow (accept), 768
follow (imitate), 1181
follow (trail), 775
fond of, 37
food, 23
fool (person), 426
fool (trick), 327
foolish, 426
foot, 401
football, 939
for, 70
forbidden, 1129
force, 320
forecast, 559
forehead, 416
foreign, 733
foresee, 559
forest, 19
foretell, 559

green, 98
grievance, 386
grin, 1137
grip, 431
ground, 971
grounds, 815
group (audience), 957
group (family), 41
grow (grow up), 647
grow (plants), 648
grow up, 647
grown, 647
guard (person), 136
guard (protect), 752
guess, 247
guide, 649
guilty, 1215
gun, 651
guy, 143
gym, 860

habit, 1169
habitat, 306
habitually, 724
had, 159
hair, 398
hair dryer, 607
half-dollar, 578
halftime, 262
Halloween, 1275
halt, 387
hamburger, 1072
hand (noun), 402
hand (verb), 197
handbag, 666
handkerchief, 672
handsome, 760
happen, 501
happy, 163
hard (difficult), 325

hard (solid), 459
hard of hearing, 127
Hardee's, 1117
hare, 843
harsh, 1029
has, 159
has been, 245
hat, 664
hate, 716
have, 159
have not, 246
have to, 362
hay, 977
hazard, 1003
he, 12
head (anatomy), 402
head (boss), 133
head (guide), 649
head cold, 154
health, 405, 1023
healthy, 1023
hear, 4
hear something, 366
hearing (person), 1271
hearing aid (behind-the-ear), 369
hearing aid (in-the-ear), 370
hearing person, 1271
heart, 406
heaven, 590
heavy (thick), 883
heavy (weight), 390
height (measure), 855
height (tall), 35
helicopter, 176
help, 156
henceforth, 330
her, 12

her (possessive), 54
here, 164
hers, 54
herself, 58
hid, 248
hide, 248
high (advancement), 921
high (costly), 579
high (height), 35
high (stoned), 505
hill, 970
him, 12
himself, 58
hinder, 746
hire, 301
his, 54
historian, 799
history, 799
hit (punch), 1043
hit (success), 650
hoard, 957
hockey, 945
hog, 833
hold (grip), 431
hold (suspend), 298
hold up (suspend), 298
holiday, 1165
Holland, 1289
home, 306
honest, 886
honor, 999
hoodie, 675
hope, 388
horrible, 316
horrific, 316
horse, 827
hospital, 1017
hot (eager), 451
hot (furious), 337

hot (temperature), 152
hot dog, 1074
hotel, 345
hour, 235
house (audience), 956
house (home), 25
house (look after), 910
how, 202
how many, 205
how much, 205
however, 1047
howl, 311
huge, 32
human, 102
humid, 465
humorous, 429
hungry, 364
hunt (animals), 652
hunt (look for), 377
hunting, 652
hurricane, 475
hurry, 1000
hurry off, 1206
hurt, 1008
husband, 119
hypothesis, 915

I, 1
I agree, 984
I love you, 339
I see, 984
ice cream, 1080
idea, 583
identify, 890
if, 785
ignorant, 1161
ignore, 687
ignore me, 688

place of worship, 591, 592

plan (prepare), 725

plane, 177

plant (factory), 862

plant (grow), 648

plant (seeds), 1113

plate, 1241

play (drama), 348

play (frolic), 24

player, 24

playing cards, 953

playing with, 326

pleasant, 1139

please, 233

pleased, 1194

pleasure, 555

plenty, 157

plus, 285

pocketbook, 666

poem, 1152

point (meaning), 931

point (there), 12

police, 136

policeman, 136

policy, 690

polite, 1227

politics, 1127

pond, 966

pony, 827

poor (broke), 1048

poor (pity), 1268

poorly, 1048

pop (father), 112

pop (soda), 81

pop up, 721

popcorn, 1081

pork, 833

portion, 256

position, 356

positive, 285

possess, 159

possible, 186

postage stamp, 734

poster, 781

postpone, 1208

pot, 997

potato, 1067

potato chips, 1108

pound (weight), 707

power, 1207

practice, 870

pray, 589

prayers, 589

preach, 588

preacher, 588

precious, 731

precise, 788

predict, 559

prefer (choose), 1041

prefer (favorite), 432

preference, 432

pregnant, 1022

prepare (plan), 725

prepared (ready), 723

present (gift), 740

present (here), 164

present (introduce), 739

present (now), 7

present (offer), 738

preserve, 784

preserves (jelly), 1085

president, 1126

pressure, 1157

pretend, 915

pretty, 317

prevent, 821

previous, 239

previous to, 329

price, 979

pride, 793

principal, 1187

principle, 690

print, 983

prints (foot), 853

prior to, 329

prison, 961

prisoner, 961

private, 751

privilege, 160

prize, 558

probably, 188

probation, 889

problem, 325

procedure (progress), 922

procedure (system), 744

procedure (way), 696

proceed, 681

process, 922

proclaim, 810

produce, 319

product, 1025

profession, 711

professor, 149

proficient, 761

profit, 726

program, 1005

progress (advance), 922

progress (improve), 314

project, 1006

promise, 959

promote (advance), 921

promote (advertise), 917

promotion, 921

proof, 538

proper, 161

prophesy, 559

propose, 738

protect (defend), 752

protest, 386

proud, 793

prying (nosy), 456

psychiatrist, 1014

psychiatry, 1014

psychologist, 800

psychology, 800

public, 1271

public address system, 546

publicize, 917

publish, 983

pull, 653

pull for, 1229

pull out, 935

pumpkin, 1060

punch (hit), 1043

punish, 1196

purchase, 303

purple, 96

purpose, 1188

purse, 666

push, 885

push away, 885

put, 196

put a stop to, 786

put aside (keep), 784

put away (keep), 784

put down (insult), 531

put down (record), 394

put off, 1208

put on (apply), 874

put to use, 1149

put together, 1036

put up (notice), 781

than, 508

thank, 234

thank you, 234

thanks, 234

Thanksgiving, 836, 1277

that (definite), 12

that (indefinite), 16

that's enough, 866

that's it, 984

theater, 348

their, 55

theirs, 55

them, 13

theme, 893

themselves, 60

then, 507

theory, 1148

there (point), 12

thermometer, 1256

these, 52

they, 13

thick (dense), 1142

thick (heavy), 883

thick (width), 884

thigh, 422

thin, 882

thing, 1025

think, 5

think about (dwell on), 1270

think about (wonder), 385

think for yourself, 755

think over, 385

think the same, 231

thinker, 5

third, 564

third week (of the month), 242

thirsty, 1109

this (definite), 12

this (indefinite), 51

this (present), 7

thorny, 1267

those, 13

threat, 1003

through (completed), 342

through (passage), 349

throw, 955

throw away, 562

throw out, 1197

thumb, 423

thunder, 477

Thursday, 211

ticket, 509

tie (even), 540

tie (knot), 569

time (o'clock), 26

time (period), 1039

timid, 1193

tiny, 34

tired, 1222

tissue, 264, 672

title, 893

to, 65

to the left, 165

to the right, 162

toast, 1086

today, 49

together, 489

toilet, 605

told, 526

told me, 527

tolerate, 749

tomato, 1062

tomorrow, 230

tonight, 48

too, 988

toothbrush, 608

toothpaste, 609

topic, 893

tornado, 479

tortoise, 840

total (all), 553

total (complete), 556

total (sum), 287

touch, 1217

tour, 808

toward, 682

towel, 355

town, 344

trade (exchange), 791

trade (profession), 711

tradition, 1169

traffic, 181

tragic, 338

trail (follow), 775

trail (path), 696

trailer, 172

train (locomotive), 174

train (practice), 870

trait, 769

transformation, 974

translate, 974

transliterate, 974

transport, 1204

trash, 758

travel, 808

treasure, 731

tree, 19

trees, 19

trick, 327

trip (fall), 809

trip (travel), 808

triumph, 767

trophy, 558

trouble, 453

truck, 180

true, 1259

trust, 570

truth, 1259

truthful, 886

try, 906

Tuesday, 209

turkey, 836

turn (change), 1038

turn (next), 114

turn down, 437

turn loose, 790

turn off, 586

turn on, 587

turtle, 840

tutor, 149

TV, 625

twenty-five cents, 576

twilight, 481

twin, 125

two of us, 139

type (keyboard), 275

type (kind), 920

ugly (awful), 316

ugly (not pretty), 318

unable, 185

unbelievable, 1272

uncle, 107

unclear, 695

under (beneath), 374

under (less than), 375

understand, 158

underwear, 673

unfair, 510

unfasten, 1037

unfortunate (pity), 1268

unfortunate (sorry), 554

unhappy, 338
unite, 1036
universe, 805
university, 40
unkind, 1029
unknown, 517
unlock, 530
unsuccessful, 766, 1233
unsure, 335
until, 549
untruth, 1260
up, 627
up and down, 963
up to now, 245
upon, 67
upset, 1024
upstairs, 628
urge, 1247
us, 14
USA, 1301
use, 657
used to (custom), 1169
used to (past), 216
usual, 1221
utilize, 657

vacant, 928
vacation, 1165
vaccination, 83
vague, 695
Valentine's Day, 1276
valuable, 894
value (important), 894
value (worth), 905
vanilla, 87
vanish, 722
variety, 1218
various, 1218

vegetables, 1063
very, 548
vicinity, 512
victimize, 1185
victory (celebrate), 933
victory (win), 767
video relay, 281
Vietnam, 1302
Vietnamese, 1302
view (idea), 583
village, 344
vinegar, 1100
virus, 154
vision (dream), 876
vision (see), 2
visit, 313
visitor, 313
visually, 367
visually impaired, 322
vocabulary, 360
voice, 410
volleyball, 941
volunteer, 1150
vote (election), 537
vow, 959
vulgar, 958

wages, 1183
wait (pass the time), 978
wait (serve), 819
wait a minute, 237
wait on (serve), 819
waiter, 819
walk, 502
walkout, 535
wall, 520
Walmart, 1115
want, 77

war, 993
warehouse, 305
warm, 151
warn, 889
wash, 622
wash face, 614
wash hands, 615
waste (squander), 562
waste (trash), 758
waste time, 916
watch (look at), 18
watch (supervise), 910
watch me, 232
watch out (careful), 913
water, 80
watermelon, 1061
way (path), 696
way (procedure), 696
way to go, 438
we, 14, 139
weak, 1219
weakness, 1219
wealth, 956
wealthy, 956
wear, 657
weather, 470
wed, 140
wedding, 140
Wednesday, 210
week, 225
weekend, 50
weekly, 226
weep, 506
weigh, 707
weight, 707
wiener, 1074
weird, 848
welcome (invite), 301

welcome (thanks), 234
welfare, 1172
well (fine), 454
well (good), 6
well (healthy), 1023
well known, 811
Wendy's, 1116
went, 8
west, 701
western, 701
wet, 465
whale, 829
what (itemize), 207
what (pardon me?), 206
what's going on?, 539
what's up?, 539
when?, 200
where (place), 356
where (question), 204
which (comparison), 203
which (indefinite), 16
while, 238
whiskey, 542
white, 94
who, 199
whole, 553
whom, 199
whose, 199
why, 201
wicked, 1170
wide (broad), 705
width (broad), 705
width (thick), 884
wife, 118
will, 183
willing, 503
win, 767

Lightning Source UK Ltd.
Milton Keynes UK
UKHW03f2057011018

329824UK00005B/15/P